Kari

To your greats su

[signature]

:)

6/20/2010

The Quest
for Software
Requirements

MAVEN
MARK
BOOKS

The Quest for Software Requirements

Roxanne E. Miller

Probing questions to bring
nonfunctional requirements into focus;
proven techniques to get the right
stakeholder involvement.

Published by MavenMark Books, LLC
For information about special discounts for bulk purchases,
please visit www.MavenMarkBooks.com

Software Requirements Questions, an electronic version of the elicitation questions contained in this book, is available at www.RequirementsQuest.com

ISBN: 978-1-59598-067-0

Publisher's Cataloging-In-Publication Data
(Prepared by The Donohue Group, Inc.)

> Miller, Roxanne E.
>   The quest for software requirements : probing questions to bring nonfunctional requirements into focus; proven techniques to get the right stakeholder involvement / Roxanne E. Miller.
>   p. ; cm.
>   Includes bibliographical references.
>   ISBN: 978-1-59598-067-0
>   1. Computer software--Development. 2. Requirements engineering. I. Title.
>   QA76.76.D47 M55 2009
>   005.1

Project Editor: Kira Henschel
Book Cover Design: Timpano Group

Bound and printed in the United States of America.

TABLE OF CONTENTS

5.1 ACS
5.2 AVL
5.3 EFC
5.4 INT
5.5 REL
5.6 SRV
5.7 USE
6.1 FLX
6.2 MNT
6.3 SCL
6.4 VER
7.1 IOP
7.2 POR
7.3 REU

To my sunshines, Leanne and Tara

To my mother, Barbara

In loving memory:

Lawrence L. Brostowitz, Sr.

ACKNOWLEDGMENTS

This book started as a dream and became a reality thanks to family and friends. A loving thanks to my daughters, Leanne and Tara, whose unconditional love supported me through all the trials and tribulations. Their patience, understanding, and sacrifice of quality time with me have made this and so many other dreams come true. Thanks to my mother, Barbara, for her guidance, faith, and inspiration. She is the person I admire most as a role model for her "survivability," spiritual strength, relentless persistence, and professional dedication to the education of others. And, thanks to my five sisters and five brothers for the life experiences and "stories" we share.

I am so grateful for the support from Suzanne Ebert and Polly Ann Thomas. They are always there, believing in and encouraging—sometimes even pushing—me to do my best. A sincere thanks to Bruce Opsal, who provided invaluable assistance with research and multiple iterations of, "What do you think of this?" A special thanks to Jim Dawkins and Diane Brussow, who contributed greatly during the early growth stages of Requirements Quest®.

My thanks for the encouragement received from several mentors with whom I have worked or who were willing to coach me over the years. James Minehan remains a true and devoted friend, and recognized the diamond in the rough when presented an "opportunity." Leilani Allen at times seemed to be merciless, but her vision and tutelage have been the foundation of my career. Steven Davis gave me my first book on requirements and advised me to read it cover to cover, which I actually did. *Software Requirements*, by Karl Wiegers, now in its second edition, remains to be one of my most referenced and recommended books. Karl Wiegers reviewed the first rough draft of my book—four years ago. Karl is a fabulous role model and continues to assist me in opening new doors of opportunity. My friend Stephen Withall, a wicked reviewer with a wonderful sense of humor, gave me an opportunity to experience a slice of the publishing process, and unknowingly gave me the nudge and confidence I needed to complete this effort.

I have a deep respect for the professional talents and devotion of my reviewers and colleagues in the industry: John Argentiero, Carla Baumgartner, Terri Brouillard, Ginny Cashbaugh, Michael Connor, David DeBruine, Conrad Dennis, Steve Doty, Michael Enstrom, Bahri Gungor, Mai Fei Kinney, Karl Kleifgen, Dennis Kohlmeier, Frank Kowalkowski, Marj Krause, Deanna Mount, Kara Price, Susan Rose-Adametz, Gary Rush, and Wendy Vysoky. Moreover, Deb McCormick was an exceptional, fearless, unrelenting editor. And, I am most appreciative and indebted to Joseph Chapman for his contributions in countless ways.

A special thanks to those with the expertise to pull the book together. Thank you, Kira Henschel, for your wisdom, guidance, and patience throughout the publishing process. Thank you, Melanie Schmidt, for your positive moral support, and your creativity and marketing insight. And, thank you, Jared Gehling, for your expedient, quality service and assistance in converting figures, as well as numerous miscellaneous requests.

It amazes me that, in reality, often the person who teaches learns more than those who are taught. While training on software requirements practices, I have benefited from the experiences, knowledge, and questions of thousands of students, and I thank you all. Moreover, I appreciate my clients for whom I constantly strive to find better ways of doing things to make each individual requirements producer, supplier or receiver, and his or her organization more successful. My techniques have been sharpened through our shared work experiences. It has been my privilege to collaborate with each and every one of you.

PREFACE

PURPOSE AND SCOPE

This book answers a question that is critical to the success of any system development project, "How can the system's nonfunctional requirements best be defined?"

Simply defined, while functional requirements describe *what the system must do*, the nonfunctional requirements define *how well it must do it.*

Nonfunctional requirements embody important elements of quality for software systems. A thorough specification of nonfunctional requirements creates systems (whether developed or purchased) that:

- Have fewer errors.

- Have more realistic time and cost estimates.

- Result in greater user satisfaction.

- Are more comprehensive.

- Better fit business needs.

The Quest for Software Requirements applies a user-focused classification for various categories of nonfunctional requirements. The intent of this book is to bring greater consistency, clarity, and understanding to the term "nonfunctional." The nonfunctional classification comprises three software user needs:

- OPERATION REQUIREMENTS.
  How well does the system perform for daily use?

- REVISION REQUIREMENTS.
  How easy is it to correct errors and add functions?

- TRANSITION REQUIREMENTS.
  How easy is it to adapt to changes in the technical environment?

These three requirement groups are further subdivided into 14 common nonfunctional categories. Cumulatively, this book provides over **2,000 suggested questions** to help you elicit nonfunctional requirements. In addition, this book offers step-by-step guidance on how to:

- Build a stakeholder profile and get the right people engaged.

- Prepare for and conduct a successful requirements-gathering interview.

WHO SHOULD REFERENCE THIS BOOK

This book can help you perform one or more requirements roles, which are introduced here and defined in Chapter 2, "Involve the Right Stakeholders."

A *requirements producer* is an individual who elicits, analyzes, represents, and validates requirements for desired changes made to business policies, business processes, and supporting systems. The requirements producer is a liaison between the business area with a business need ("What needs to be done?") and the solution delivery team ("How will the solution be implemented?").

Those fulfilling the requirements producer role are known by a variety of job titles such as business analyst, business systems analyst, systems analyst, and requirements engineer. Moreover, some people perform more than one role in an organization. Thus, a project manager, lead developer, or software engineer might perform the requirements producer role in defining requirements.

This book can help the requirements producer avoid errors caused by missed requirements. It can help the requirements producer improve the quality and the quantity of gathered requirements by asking more questions to better understand what the business needs.

A *requirements supplier* is any individual with responsibility for defining the business needs. Some individuals (such as business sponsor, product manager, and executive leader) provide the strategy and direction of the system, while others (such as business lead, customer representative, and subject matter expert) provide details that define the necessary system functions. Requirements suppliers may reside in a particular business area or within the technology department. *The Quest for Software Requirements* can help the requirements supplier validate the accuracy, completeness, and quality of the requirements.

A *requirements receiver* is any individual who uses the specified requirements to implement a solution. A requirements receiver might be an individual who is responsible for designing and developing the solution, testing the requirements, training users, writing user procedure manuals, or managing the project. This book can help the requirements receiver to review the requirements, contribute to requirements-related issue resolution, and identify inaccurate or omitted requirements.

BENEFITS OF USING THIS BOOK

This book provides practical solutions that will help you:

- Understand the vital nature and complexity of nonfunctional requirements.
- Elicit nonfunctional requirements of the system environment of any enterprise more accurately.
- Get the right stakeholders involved during a requirements management process.
- Better prepare for, and conduct, requirements-gathering interviews.

Along with your improved skills, you and your organization will be positioned to experience the following benefits:

- Greater predictability for project success through reduced requirements errors.
- Increased opportunity of finding and resolving requirements-related anomalies during the requirements definition phase, and thereby reducing rework in subsequent, more costly phases of the project.
- Increased customer/client satisfaction because the resulting system will better reflect the user needs and concerns.
- Better communication between the requirements producer and the requirements suppliers and receivers because the requirements are easier to understand and interpret consistently.

SKILLS AND EXPERIENCE NEEDED BY THE READER

This book can be used by requirements producers, suppliers and receivers regardless of your skills and experience with software requirements activities (such as elicitation, analysis, representation, and validation, which are explained in Chapter 1, "Requirements in Context"). *The Quest for Software Requirements* intentionally tries to stay clear of acronyms, jargon, technology, tools, and methodologies. This book is written in plain language that can be read and absorbed easily by anyone seeking to increase his or her understanding of software requirements.

Reference this book whenever you encounter a software system where one or more of the nonfunctional requirement categories presented might be relevant.

A list of suggested reading is provided in each chapter of this book. You are encouraged to invest time to read one or more of the books. Readers who have read at least one of these recommended books or who are already experienced with software requirements are likely to find this book very beneficial.

HOW THIS BOOK IS ORGANIZED

As the "**Book At A Glance**" diagram inside the front cover illustrates, there are two parts to this book:

PART ONE: RIGHT PROCESS, RIGHT PEOPLE, RIGHT TOOLS

The three chapters in Part One are intended to get you started on the *right* path with software requirements.

> **Chapter 1, Requirements in Context**, launches your requirements understanding with a brief overview of software requirements terminology and explains levels of requirements. The chapter also describes nonfunctional requirements in context with software development process models.

Chapter 2, Involve the Right Stakeholders, guides you through the steps to build a stakeholder profile, a technique that helps to identify the knowledge expertise of individual stakeholders. This chapter also helps to uncover business areas and topics that lack expert representation. Essentially, stakeholder profiling will help you get the right stakeholders engaged.

Chapter 3, Interviewing Tips and Tools, offers you several tips and suggested techniques for preparing and conducting a requirements-gathering interview. Ordinary requirements producers, extraordinary interviews!

PART TWO: RIGHT APPROACH, RIGHT QUESTIONS

Part Two answers the most frequent question that requirements producers ask about eliciting requirements, "What should I ask?" The four chapters in Part Two are the heart of this book.

Chapter 4, Understanding Nonfunctional Requirements, helps you define nonfunctional requirements, and provides a user-focused classification scheme of 14 common nonfunctional categories.

Chapter 5, Operation Requirements, explains seven operation categories that describe the user need for a software system that performs well for daily use.

Chapter 6, Revision Requirements, defines four revision categories that relate to the user concerns for ease of correcting errors and adding new functions to the software system.

Chapter 7, Transition Requirements, describes three transition categories that define the user need for a software system that adapts easily to its changing technical environment.

WHAT THIS BOOK IS NOT

This is not a book about the process and activities for requirements development or requirements management. While it does include elicitation techniques, this book does not include techniques for analyzing, representing, and validating software requirements. These topics and techniques are sufficiently covered in other good books.

This book does not address any particular business industry. Nor does this book advocate any particular development model, methodology, or requirements management tool. Instead, this book explains a vital part of defining the software systems of any enterprise.

COLLABORATION BEYOND THIS BOOK

"Practice makes perfect," it is said. Of course, no one has lived long enough to discover whether this is true of software requirements definitions. Through trial and error, you will develop a set of questions that become natural or comfortable for your personal style. You'll discover for yourself which questions trigger the desired responses that ultimately bring about the highest quality requirements.

Success comes to all of us through collaboration. If you have questions that you find work really well in eliciting nonfunctional requirements, or if you have examples of nonfunctional requirements, you are encouraged to share them with others. Your suggested questions and requirement examples may be sent to Questions@RequirementsQuest.com. Additional questions might be posted on the Internet. Individuals will be recognized for their contributions and might be included with acknowledgment in future editions of *The Quest for Software Requirements*. The suggested elicitation questions contained in this book are available electronically via Microsoft Excel® file entitled *Software Requirements Questions*. To learn more, please visit http://www.RequirementsQuest.com.

Cheers to your greater success!

rem

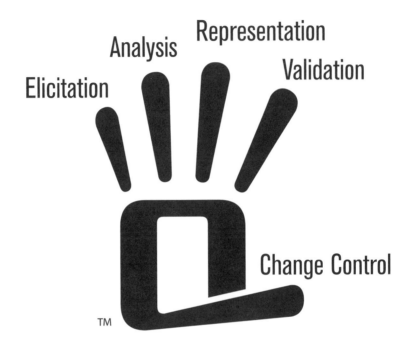

This Requirements Quest® logo ("the hand"), developed by author and expert Roxanne E. Miller, symbolizes the organization's five-stage Requirements Management Process and emphasizes the importance of user involvement, both internal and external, as a critical factor for project success. The five stages of the process are symbolized by the five fingers on "the hand." The first four fingers represent the iterative activities of requirements development: Elicitation, Analysis, Representation, and Validation. Upon successful refinement, detailing, and approval, the requirements are baselined in the Change Control stage (represented by the thumb), where requests for change are monitored to maintain scope.

PART ONE: RIGHT PROCESS, RIGHT PEOPLE, RIGHT TOOLS

While Part Two is the heart of this book and loaded with suggested questions, the three chapters in Part One tell you all you need to know to use the suggested questions with confidence. That confidence comes from knowing the requirements process, the appropriate people you should interview, and how to be effective in your interviews.

Chapter 1, "Requirements in Context," describes the relationship of nonfunctional requirements with the requirements hierarchy (three levels of requirements), the requirements management process, software development models, and a requirements framework. It also identifies what should *not* be included in requirements specifications.

Chapter 2, "Involve the Right Stakeholders," delivers step-by-step instructions for building a stakeholder profile, which will help you identify your stakeholders and why each stakeholder should be engaged on your project. The stakeholder profile is a tangible tool that will help you secure and manage the resources you need, not just the ones you're told you can use. This chapter answers another question that requirements producers frequently ask, "Who should I ask?"

Chapter 3, "Interviewing Tips and Tools," provides tips for mastering the most frequently used elicitation techniques. Based on real-life experience, I promise they work. Successful interviews aren't just for journalists anymore!

The goal of
requirements management
is to obtain one, and only one,
consistent interpretation
of the requirements from all
stakeholders.

REQUIREMENTS IN CONTEXT

Whether you are building a new in-house system, using commercial off-the-shelf software packages, or making enhancements to existing software, you will apply techniques to discover, illustrate and communicate the requirements. I based this book on a premise that a requirements process—regardless of structure or formality—is used to define the requirements. This process for gathering and specifying requirements can be applied to large and small systems. Additionally, you can apply it whether your system development environment is waterfall, iterative, or agile.

This chapter provides you with an overview of software requirements terminology. It provides a high-level view of requirements and where they fit in software development models and a requirements framework. I'll start by providing a commonly used definition for the term *software requirement*.

1.1 WHAT IS A SOFTWARE REQUIREMENT?

The *Oxford American Dictionary* defines the noun "requirement" simply as "a need." In the software development industry, we use the term *requirement* in a broader and in-depth context. In order to identify a complete set of requirements, we must ask questions in six requirements focus areas, as illustrated in Figure 1-1.

The *need* is just a starting place for identifying *what* information is used. From there, we must understand *who* (or what) uses the information and *why* they need it (what business purpose or function they are trying to perform). We also have to understand *when* the information will be used, *where* it will be used, and *how* (process and procedures) it will be used.

Figure 1-1 Requirements Focus Areas

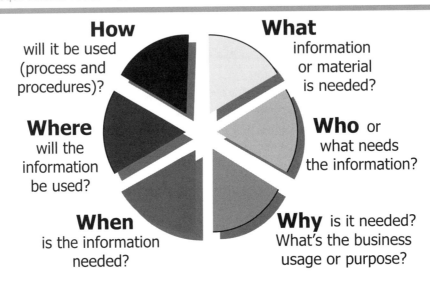

By asking questions in all six focus areas, you minimize the risk of omitting requirements. Due to their importance, the suggested elicitation questions contained in this book are organized by focus area. This requirements framework, as I call it, is explained later in this chapter.

As you'll read in Chapter 4, "Understanding Nonfunctional Requirements," the software industry lacks common definitions for the terms we use to describe our requirements activities. Among the numerous definitions of software requirements you might find, I prefer to use the version given by the Institute of Electronic and Electrical Engineers (IEEE):

> "*A software requirement is:*
> 1) *A condition or capability needed by a user to solve a problem or achieve an objective.*
> 2) *A condition or capability that must be met or possessed by a system or system component to satisfy a contract, standard, specification, or other formally imposed document.*
> 3) *A documented representation of a condition or capability as in (1) or (2)."*
> [IEEE, 1990]

This definition is written from the user's and the developer's view of the requirements. That is, the user is concerned with the external behavior of the system. On the other hand, the developer is more concerned with the internal workings of the system. The term *user* in element (1) of this definition should perhaps be generalized to the term *stakeholder,* as not all stakeholders are users. Simply defined, a *stakeholder* is anyone who is interested in or impacted by the outcome of the system (or product) under development. For example, the manufacturer of dog food refers to the dog as the user because the dog will be consuming the product. However, the dog's owner is considered a stakeholder (and is not a user) in the manufacturing process in order to understand the needs (requirements) and concerns of the customer buying the product.

I think of requirements as a set of graphical and textual representations that describe the functions and attributes of a system environment that provides value to a stakeholder. The perspective of all stakeholder viewpoints must be considered during the development of software requirements.

> The goal of requirements management
> is to obtain one, and only one,
> consistent interpretation
> of the requirements from all stakeholders.

A stakeholder profiling technique is presented in Chapter 2, "Involve the Right Stakeholders." The technique helps you identify stakeholder roles (various viewpoints) and get the right stakeholders involved in requirements development.

1.2 LEVELS OF REQUIREMENTS

This section provides definitions for fundamental terms that are used in the software requirements discipline. Software requirements are often grouped into three distinct levels of requirements, or a requirements hierarchy, as shown in Figure 1-2.

Figure 1-2 A Requirements Hierarchy (Levels)

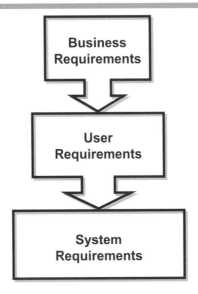

Business-level requirements represent the high-level objectives of the organization, customer or client who requests the system. These requirements typically come from several stakeholders, including but certainly not limited to, the funding sponsor for a project, the acquiring customer, the manager of the users, the marketing department, and a product visionary. The business requirements describe why the organization is implementing the system (why the project is being done), and the objectives the organization hopes to achieve (measurable business benefits that align with the organization's vision).

User-level requirements bridge the needs of the business (business-level requirements) and the requirements of the solution to be developed (system-level requirements). User requirements describe user goals or tasks that the users must be able to perform with the product. User requirements identify what the user will be able to do with the system.

Gause and Weinberg [Gause, 1989] broadly define the term **user** as anyone who affects or is affected by the product. This definition includes people and things (machines, computers, and external systems) that interact with the business process under development, as well as other people and things that receive by-products (information and materials) from the business process or system. To elicit user requirements thoroughly, you may need to include stakeholders other than direct end-users.

System-level requirements describe the top-level requirements for a system that contains multiple subsystems. According to the Institute of Electronic and Electrical Engineers (IEEE), *system* is defined as:

> *"An interdependent group of people, objects, and procedures constituted to achieve defined objectives or some operational role by performing specified functions. A complete system includes all of the associated equipment, facilities, material, computer programs, firmware, technical documentation, services, and personnel required for operations and support to the degree necessary for self-sufficient use in its intended environment."* [IEEE, 1998]

Therefore, a "system" can be a computer, a software application, a subsystem, a whole business enterprise, or a manual process performed by a human.

System-level requirements describe what functions the business process (whether manual or automated) must enable the users to perform (functional requirements), and the attributes and constraints of the environment that affect how well the users perform those functions (nonfunctional requirements).

> Provided the product meets its required amount of functionality,
> the non-functional properties—how usable, convenient, inviting
> and secure it is—may be the difference between an accepted,
> well-liked product, and an unused one.
> —Suzanne and James Robertson, authors of
> *Mastering the Requirements Process* [Robertson, 2006]

Within the system level requirements, there are two viewpoints: system function/feature and system environment. The *functional requirements* (system function/feature view) describe functionality that must be built into the business process to enable the users to perform their business goals or tasks. A "feature" is a set of logically related functional requirements that provides a capability to the user and enables the accomplishment of the user's business goal.

On the other hand, *nonfunctional requirements* describe the system environment view or characteristics of the system. They describe the constraints imposed on the design and construction of the system, as well as quality attributes related to the user need for operation, revision, and ability to handle change or growth.

Some definitions of functional and nonfunctional requirements are explored in Chapter 4, "Understanding Nonfunctional Requirements." Let's move on to understand the relationship of the levels of requirements and a requirements management process.

1.3 A REQUIREMENTS MANAGEMENT PROCESS

In simple words, *software requirements management* is the process of studying user needs to arrive at a definition of the software requirements. A *software requirements specification* generally is used to refer to the document that contains the clear and precise requirements.

Yet again, inconsistencies in industry terminology exist with regard to what to call the requirements discipline. Some authors refer to the discipline as requirements engineering, while other authors refer to it as requirements management.

Requirements management, as defined by Leffingwell and Widrig, is:

> *"a systematic approach to eliciting, organizing, and documenting the requirements of the system, and a process that establishes and maintains agreement between the customer and the project team on the changing requirements of the system."* [Leffingwell, 2003]

I prefer the term *requirements management* and subdivide the following activities into five components, as shown in Figure 1-3. The first four components are collectively referred to as *requirements development*.

Figure 1-3 A Five-Stage Requirements Management Process Model (based on [Wiegers, 2003])

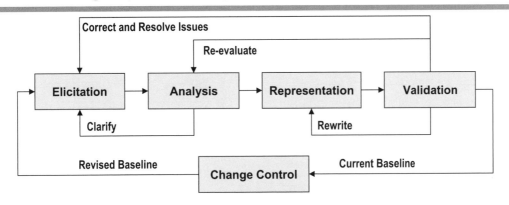

The five components of the requirements management process are described as follows:

- REQUIREMENTS ELICITATION is the process of identifying stakeholder classes, defining the project scope, identifying requirement sources, and applying techniques to gather the information.

- REQUIREMENTS ANALYSIS is the process of analyzing the information elicited, resolving conflicts, documenting assumptions, constraints, and dependencies, and working with the stakeholders to establish priorities.

- REQUIREMENTS REPRESENTATION (also known as specification) is the process of specifying the business needs using a combination of graphical models and textual documents.

- REQUIREMENTS VALIDATION is the process of reviewing the represented information with the stakeholders for quality characteristics such as completeness, correctness, and feasibility.

- CHANGE CONTROL is the process of maintaining a set of approved or baselined requirements throughout the lifecycle of the development project.

Note in Figure 1-3 that requirements management is an iterative process. The lines connecting the four development stages are not simply linear. At any time in the process, a previous stage can be revisited. For example, during the analysis of information gathered in elicitation, it is discovered that two different stakeholders provided seemingly different responses to the same elicitation question. Revisiting each stakeholder and asking further questions is done to "clarify" the information gathered.

Furthermore, the iterative process is performed at each level in the requirements hierarchy (business, user, and system) as shown in Figure 1-4. As you move from the high-level business requirements to the detailed system requirements, you involve different stakeholders. Thus, within each level, you will elicit, analyze, represent, and validate information provided by the various stakeholders.

Figure 1-4 Requirements Management and the Levels of Requirements

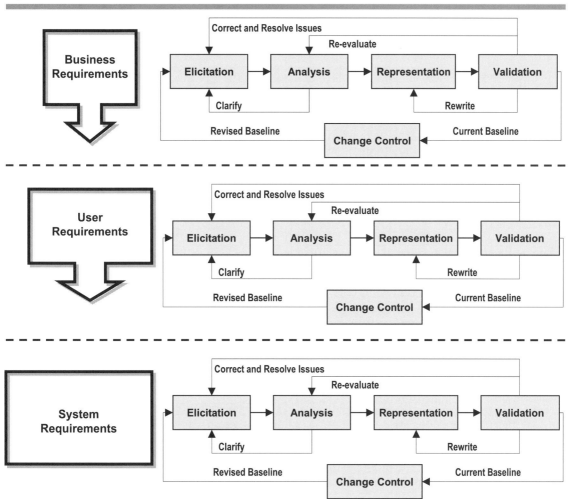

Many organizations and individuals have discovered the benefits of applying a requirements management process such as those described in Table 1-1.

1.4 REQUIREMENTS AND THE SOFTWARE DEVELOPMENT LIFECYCLE

A *software development lifecycle* defines the steps required to develop software systems. That is, the purpose of a software development lifecycle is to establish the order of stages or phases of work activities involved in software development, as well as to determine the entry and exit criteria for transitioning or progressing from one stage to the next. Thus, a software process model addresses two software implementation project questions:

(1) What should we do next?

(2) How long should we continue doing it, or when are we done?

Many software project teams experience frustration as a result of performing development tasks in the wrong order. Software process models are important because they provide guidance on the order (stages or phases) in which the project team should perform its major tasks. The names of these stages or phases vary, but the concepts of each are as follows:

- ♦ PLAN: The view of the business enterprise as a whole. What is the overall strategy for the system development effort? What is the scope? What are the priorities?

- ♦ REQUIREMENTS: The detailed analysis of the business areas impacted. What business functions are performed? What data are required by who, when, where, and why? Who performs each function and how?

- ♦ DESIGN: The investigation and application of technology components to meet business needs. In this stage, for example, functions become program specifications or data structures become database designs. At this point, human interfaces are also factored into the proposed solution.

Table 1-1 Benefits of Requirements Management

Business Objective	Benefits of a Requirements Management Process
Satisfy customer needs	+ Promotes complete, clear, and correct definition of the business requirements. + Enables the project team to fully understand and meet the needs of customers the FIRST time. + Enables early identification of missing requirements and requirements deficiencies, ambiguities, and errors.
Meet project deadlines	+ Provides the method for controlling and prioritizing requirements, which form the basis for creating an accurate project schedule. + Allows identification of requirements changes that may affect the schedule. + Reduces scope creep by communicating any changes, and obtaining agreement on project schedule.
Lower project cost	+ Manages cost by reducing extraneous features. + Reduces rework by involving business owners and development team members in a formal validation of the requirements early in the project lifecycle. + Provides the means to more accurately estimate timeframes and work estimates.
Promote communication	+ Provides a common understanding of where and how requirements documents are to be managed, which promotes and supports reuse. + Promotes full definition, including the use of supporting information. + Offers a formal process for proposing and managing changes to requirements. + Promotes discussing and investigating the impact of changes prior to making them. + Improves communication between team members and business owners or customers through a formal requirements review process, which helps to ensure customer needs can be met the first time.
Maintain a practical project scope	+ Promotes tracking relationships between requirements to aid in impact analysis on proposed changes. Keeps project team focused on the goals of the project.
Comply with certification standards (e.g., Capability Maturity Model Integration, or CMMI)	+ Provides guidelines for documenting requirements in a consistent manner. + Allows analysis of requirements and requirement relationships. + Drives the use of requirements as a basis for solid application development and testing.

- ◆ CODING: The actual building of the solution system in the coding or construction stage.

- ◆ TESTING: The validation and verification activities to demonstrate that the solution system meets the business requirements.

- ◆ IMPLEMENTATION: The transition or integration of the system into the new infrastructure of the enterprise. This stage includes activities such as training, definition of new roles and processes, and conversion of existing data.

- ◆ OPERATION: The ongoing monitoring and maintenance of the production environment.

With regard to software development lifecycles, the scope of this book concentrates on the requirements phase.

The following are some of the well-known software development lifecycles:

- ◆ Waterfall Model

- ◆ Spiral Model

- ◆ Iterative Approach

- ◆ Extreme Programming (Agile)

The waterfall model and iterative approach are briefly described in this book to give you an understanding of requirements within the broader development lifecycle. There are books and many papers that are solely devoted to describing these models and others in more detail. I encourage you to read some of these to understand software development models more comprehensively.

1.4.1 Waterfall Model

As early as the 1950s, the software industry recognized value in developing software in successive stages. Also recognizing that there are increased costs when software defects are revealed late in the development cycle, the industry adopted a logical, step-by-step process model that transitions from a requirements phase, to a design phase, to a coding phase, to a testing phase, and so on.

Under the influential work of Winston Royce in the 1970s, the waterfall model, depicted in Figure 1-5, provided two major enhancements:

(1) Feedback loops between stages, thereby recognizing that work done in the design phase impacts the requirements, that work done in the coding phase will cause design to be revisited, and so on.

(2) Prototypes developed in parallel with requirements analysis and design activities.

Figure 1-5 Waterfall Model of Software Development (based on [Royce, 1970])

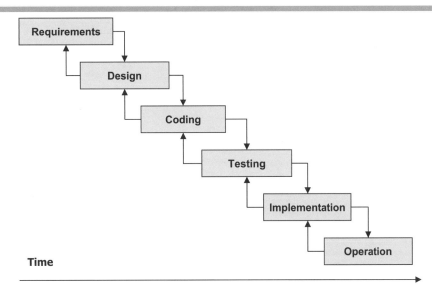

1.4.2 Iterative Approach

Many development teams have migrated to the *Iterative Approach* introduced by Philippe Kruchten [Kruchten, 1999]. It is an approach that is viewed by some to be a combination of the best aspects of the *Waterfall Model* and *Spiral Model* (developed by Barry Boehm [Boehm, 1988]). This view will not be debated or challenged in this book.

In the Waterfall Model, time moves forward through a series of sequential stages or phases. For example, the requirements activities precede design, and design activities precede coding, and so on. Conversely, the lifecycle phases in the Iterative Approach are decoupled from the logical order of activities that occur in each phase, which enables the team to revisit various activities such as requirements, coding, and testing during various iterations of the project. In addition, each successive iteration is intended to mitigate whatever risks are known at that particular iteration.

The Iterative Approach is comprised of four phases (as shown in Figure 1-6): inception, elaboration, construction, and transition. In the inception phase, the scope and feasibility of the project are identified. In the elaboration phase, the requirements are refined and an early feasibility prototype is demonstrated. The focus is on implementation in the construction phase, whereby the coding is typically done, and the system architecture and design are fully developed. In the transition phase, the testing and user training is performed, and the system is deployed to the user community.

Figure 1-6 Phases in an Iterative Approach

Inception	Elaboration	Construction	Transition

Time →

Within each phase, the project typically executes multiple iterations. For example, you can see there are more than two iterations in the construction phase pictured in Figure 1-7. An *iteration* is defined as *a sequence of tasks with an established plan and evaluation criteria that results in some type of executable*. Each iteration builds on the work products produced in the prior iteration. Therefore, the project is released in an "iterative and incremental" manner.

The tasks within an iteration are organized into a set of disciplines (shown in Figure 1-8), such as Requirements, Analysis and Design, Implementation, and so on. Each discipline is made up of a logically related set of tasks, and each defines how the tasks must be sequenced in order to produce a work product or artifact.

During a specific iteration, the team devotes as much time as appropriate in each discipline. The isolated iteration would look very similar to a mini-waterfall. The size of the "hump" shows the relative amount of effort invested in a discipline. For example, Figure 1-8 indicates that a significant amount of time is spent refining the requirements during the three iterations in the elaboration phase.

Figure 1-7 Phase Iterations (resulting in variable releases)

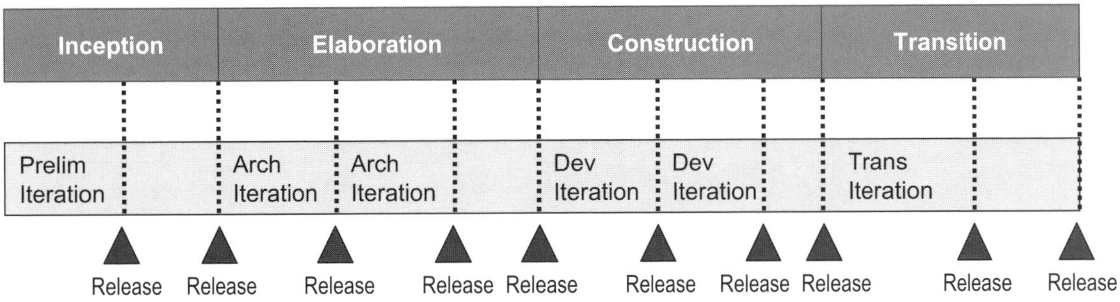

The diagram presented in Figure 1-8 was adopted with permission from the Rational Unified Process [IBM, 2009]. The Rational Unified Process, often referred to as RUP, is an iterative software development process framework created by Rational Software Corporation, a division of IBM since February 2003.

Figure 1-8 Disciplines of the Iterative Approach [IBM, 2009]

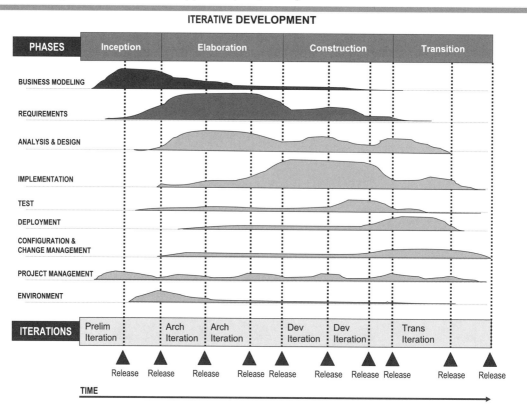

1.5 A REQUIREMENTS FRAMEWORK

While a *software development lifecycle* defines the stages or phases required to develop a system, a *requirements framework* defines the perspectives of the roles in the development lifecycle, and the view that each role has in the development and implementation of requirements throughout the lifecycle stages.

In 1987, John Zachman published his *Framework for an Information Systems Architecture* [Zachman, 1987]. He makes two significant observations about the software development lifecycle:

(1) It is important to recognize that systems are developed by distinct groups (consisting of multiple roles) with different viewpoints in parallel with the movement from one development stage or phase to another.

(2) At each stage in the development lifecycle, one must consider each different perspective or point of view related to data, function, network, people, time, and motivation.

Zachman's framework is typically depicted as a tabular matrix of six rows and six columns. The rows of the matrix represent the different perspectives and the columns represent the areas of interest that are viewed from each perspective. The most recent version of Zachman's diagram and definitions can be viewed online [Zachman, 2009].

While agreeing in general with the meaning behind Zachman's framework, for the sake of simplicity, I respectfully modified the matrix to coincide with the application of its meaning as used in the context of this book. Figure 1-9 shows the translation of Zachman's framework (rows and columns) to my modified version. Succeeding this translation, Table 1-2 on page 22 illustrates the resulting modified version, and will henceforth be referred to here simply as the REQUIREMENTS FRAMEWORK. None of my modifications to terminology or organization in any way changes the fundamental structure of Zachman's Framework. The definitions of the modified matrix are presented in the following sub-sections.

Figure 1-9 Zachman Framework Modification Translation

Modified Rows (Perspectives)

Zachman	Modified Version
Scope Strategists	Scope Requirements Supplier
Business Executive Leaders	Business Model Requirements Supplier
System Architects	System Model Requirements Receiver
Technology Engineers	Design Requirements Receiver
Components Technicians	Construction Requirements Receiver
Operations Workers	Operations Requirements Supplier

Modified Columns (Areas of Interest)

Zachman	Inventory (what)	Process (how)	Network (where)	Organization (who)	Timing (when)	Motivation (why)
Modified Version	Data (what)	Process (how)	Logistics (where)	Roles (who)	Timing (when)	Purpose (why)

1.5.1 Requirements Framework Perspectives (Rows)

In the context of this book, the rows of the requirements framework represent the perspectives or viewpoints of the roles in a requirements management process (explained in Chapter 2, "Involve the Right Stakeholders"). As the following explains, the six perspectives in Zachman's Framework are condensed into two views:

(1) REQUIREMENTS SUPPLIER'S VIEW: *Requirements suppliers* are individuals who are responsible for defining the business needs to be satisfied. This includes supplying all the detail from the initial idea or inception through each incremental iteration of the system development. The *requirements supplier's view* includes scope, business models, and operations. Scope defines the vision and mission of the enterprise. Business models convey the conceptual nature of the business (structure, processes, organization, and so on). Operations define what the new system is going to be.

(2) REQUIREMENTS RECEIVER'S VIEW: *Requirements receivers* are individuals who receive and use the requirements specifications as the input to develop their work products relating to implementing the requirements. They assist in the requirements process by validating individual requirements, primarily for feasibility, completeness, and conflicts. They can assist in validating additional quality characteristics such as necessity, priority, and traceability. The *requirements receiver's* view includes system, technology, and components aspects of development. System models are used to explore optional solutions. Technology and construction components are used to demonstrate feasibility of the system under development.

1.5.2 Requirements Framework Areas of Interest (Columns)

All six columns in Zachman's Framework are used in the context of this book. The columns are re-ordered (from left to right), but retain essentially the same meaning and are described as follows:

♦ **DATA (what)**: This column relates to the information used by the enterprise. Functional requirements describe the data while the nonfunctional requirements are about the data.

♦ **ROLES (who)**: This column comprises the people and organizations or other systems that are involved or interact with the business enterprise. The functional requirements address the interaction between the role and the business process while the nonfunctional requirements are about taking care of the roles.

Table 1-2 Requirements Framework

	DATA (what)	ROLES (who)	PURPOSE (why)	TIMING (when)	LOGISTICS (where)	PROCESS (how)
Scope, Business Model, Operations *Requirements Supplier's View*	Identify and define the data used by the business enterprise	Identify and define who performs a role in the business processes	Identify and define the business goals and strategies	Identify and define the events and triggers of business processing	Identify and define the enterprise locations and network	Identify and define processes and procedures of the business
System Model, Design, Construction *Requirements Receiver's View*	Design, construct, and test data entities	Design, construct, and test interfaces and system work	Design, construct, and test system to enforce business rules	Design, construct, and test system cycles	Design, construct, and test system locations and network	Design, construct, and test system processing

- **PURPOSE (why)**: The motivation behind what the business does is described in this column. The functional requirements describe the ends and means while the nonfunctional requirements describe the environment to support accomplishment of the ends and means.

- **TIMING (when)**: This column identifies the effects of time on the business enterprise. Functional requirements describe the processing of events while nonfunctional requirements describe the timing of the events.

- **LOGISTICS (where)**: Logistics is concerned with the geographical distribution of the data and functions of the enterprise. Functional requirements describe locations while nonfunctional requirements support the locations.

- **PROCESS (how)**: This column incorporates the processes and procedures the enterprise executes. Functional requirements describe the processes while nonfunctional requirements support the processes.

1.5.3 Requirements Framework Applied

The modified Requirements Framework depicted in Table 1-2 is used as the foundation for organizing the lists of suggested elicitation questions contained in Part Two, Chapters 5 through 7. Each nonfunctional category presented in this book includes numerous possible elicitation questions. The questions are first grouped under the six areas of interest (columns) and further separated by perspective (rows).

Applying this Requirements Framework, the "Requirements" phase of a project might be defined as the process of translating the executive leader or business owner's views of the business enterprise into the development team's view. This presumes, of course, that this is for a particular project whereby the scope was defined during the "Planning" phase.

1.6 WHAT REQUIREMENTS ARE NOT

Stephen Withall presents one of the most detailed explanations of the contents of a requirements specification that I have yet to encounter—and I do mean detailed. Comparing Withall's recommended structure, as shown in Figure 1-10, with others of equal reputation, you could conclude that there are definitely elements that are NOT identified as content for a requirements specification. Let's take a look at some of the elements that don't belong—despite the fact that they often appear in them.

1.6.1 "Why" and "What" (Requirements)—Not "How" (Design)

Notice that each of the three requirements levels explored previously in Section 1.2 focuses on "why" or "what." The "why's" and "what's" keep focus on the business process and the flow of information and materials in to and out of the business process.

- Business Level: "Why" is the project being done?

- User Level: "What" does the user need?

- System Level: "What" does the system have to do to support the user?
  (Functional Requirements) and "What" attributes, constraints, or standards must
  be applied to the design and construction of the system in order to support the
  user? (Nonfunctional Requirements).

"How's" typically describe the design elements or the way in which the system will be constructed. How will the information or material be presented to the user? How will the system receive, store, and retrieve the information that is desired? The "how's" are the solutions to providing "what" is needed.

For example, during requirements-gathering interviews, I often hear sponsors say that they want a new screen or a new report. The screen or report is the "how," or the means by which the desired information is presented to the user. The information displayed on the screen or printed on the report is "what" the users really need to perform their role or achieve their goal.

Figure 1-10 Suggested Structure of a Requirements Specification [Withall, 2007]

1. Introduction

    1.1 The Purpose of the *<System Name>* System

    1.2 The Purpose of this Document

    1.3 The Format of Requirement Definitions

    1.4 Glossary

    1.5 References

    1.6 Document History

2. Content

    2.1 Scope

    2.2 Major Assumptions

    2.3 Major Exclusions

    2.4 Key Business Entities

    2.5 Infrastructure

3. *<Functional Area A Name>*

4. *<Functional Area B Name>*

5. *<Functional Area C Name>*

6. Major Nonfunctional Capabilities

Certainly, legitimate solution constraints may dictate that the solution be delivered via a screen or a report. Still, the screen and report are "how," not "what." It is absolutely essential that the solution team first correctly identify what is needed before a solution is designed and constructed.

1.6.2 Exclude Project-related Information

Project-related information (such as budgets, schedules, implementation plans, project plans, configuration management plans, verification plans, project task lists, and risk management plans) is frequently packaged with the requirements documentation. This is often done for the convenience of any number of project team members in an attempt to centralize information. In general, this must be strictly avoided since changes in the project-related information increase the volatility and foster the tendency for "the requirements" to be out of date. This compromises the integrity of the requirements as they become less trustworthy and more likely to be ignored.

Moreover, the inevitable debates that occur regarding the project-related information should be separated from discussions on what the system is supposed to do. There are different stakeholders who must contribute and participate in the discussions, and the purpose of each discussion is significantly different.

Essentially, if the information doesn't focus on describing the functionality or behavior of the system or the quality attributes or constraints of the system environment, then the information doesn't belong in the requirements specification.

1.6.3 Business Rules are Not Requirements

Defined loosely, business rules are the decisions made regarding policies and procedures for how a business will operate day to day. The Business Rules Group's definition is as follows:

> A **business rule** is a statement that defines or constrains some aspect of the business. It is intended to assert business structure or to control or influence the behavior of the business. [BRG, 2000]

Almost every business in the world has business rules, but the degree to which the rules are documented and accessible vary greatly. The following are commonly applied business rules:

♦ An employee is entitled to four weeks of paid vacation following their fifth consecutive year anniversary of full-time employment.

♦ An employee with at least one month of employment is entitled to company paid holidays.

♦ Employees are paid bi-monthly with 24 pay periods in a calendar year.

> While business rules represent the management decisions and policies relating to the operations of the business, requirements relate to a specific application or system that is being considered or developed, which usually automates the business processes.

Requirements are documented at a specific point in time to define what changes are necessary in the specific application or system to enforce any changes in the business rules. Therefore, you will generally derive functional and nonfunctional requirements from business rules in order to enforce the rules or support the regulations and standards that govern the operation of the business.

Let's say, for example, that an organization currently has an automated system to process payroll. The current system, whether a purchased software package or an in-house developed application, is processing according to business rules that dictate 24 payroll periods. That is, employees are paid bi-monthly on the 1st and 16th day of the month (with additional rules to handle non-business processing days throughout the year such as holidays and weekends).

Continuing the example, executive leadership of the organization makes a decision to purchase a new payroll system. A two-year "Payroll Project" is planned and launched to convert from the current system to the new system. Executive leadership has also decided to change the number of payroll periods from 24 to 26. The new business rule is to process payroll on a bi-weekly basis every other Friday (again, taking non-business days into account). The new business rule will take effect upon installation (the go-live date) of the new system.

The requirements specifications created for the Payroll Project will detail all the changes necessary to convert payroll processing from 24 to 26 periods. These detailed requirements will describe the necessary changes to processes, sub-processes, procedures, calculations, event triggers, error and exception handling, and so on. The requirements describe what the new payroll system must do (functional) and how well it will do it (nonfunctional).

1.6.4 Standards are Business Rules (which are NOT Requirements)

Standards are the written or unwritten business rules, regulations, and/or contracts that dictate the business operations. Standards are typically set by upper management to guide the day-to-day business decisions.

Standards are the required level of quality that the product or system must measure against or comply with. Standards are often imposed on a business by external government or regulatory agencies. In these instances, the imposed standards must be adopted by the business as business rules (whether they like it or not). If the business does not operate within compliance of these forced business rules, the business risks going out or being put out of business.

Sources for standards, however, are not to be overlooked when identifying requirements stakeholders. Examples of sources for standards are included in Chapter 2, "Involve the Right Stakeholders."

1.7 CHAPTER SUMMARY

♦ Software requirements are grouped into three distinct levels: business (why is this project being done), user (what information and materials are needed to conduct business), and system (what should the system do—functional, and how well should it do it—nonfunctional).

♦ A requirements management process involves the iterative activities for eliciting, analyzing, specifying, validating, and managing changes to requirements. This iterative process is applied beginning at the high-level business requirements, through the user requirements level, and on to the detailed system level requirements.

♦ A number of software development models exist and help a project team order the phases of work. The requirements management discipline is one of the various work phases. Thus, the requirements management process is performed regardless of which specific development model is used (unless, of course, the requirements phase is ignored). The timing and formalities in specifying the requirements may differ from model to model, but the requirements process is still applied.

♦ While a development lifecycle focuses on the stages or phases of a project effort, the architecture framework asserts that it is necessary to recognize the varied perspectives or views of the roles that perform the development process. Applying the architecture framework not only helps to identify project stakeholders, but also provides guidance for the line of questions that relate to the various views held by the stakeholders.

♦ In order to better understand requirements, it is necessary to explore what are not requirements such as project-related information, design, business rules and standards.

1.8 SUGGESTED READING

A Guide to the Business Analysis Body of Knowledge, Version 2.0, International Institute of Business Analysis, [IIBA, 2009]. The BABOK® is an excellent source of *requirements activities and defined terms*.

CMMI®: Guidelines for Process Integration and Product Improvement, 2nd Edition, by Mary Beth Chrissis, Mike Konrad, and Sandy Shrum, [Chrissis, 2007]. *Requirements Management* is an engineering process area at maturity level 2, and *Requirements Development* is an engineering process area at maturity level 3.

Managing Software Requirements: A Use Case Approach, 2nd Edition, by Dean Leffingwell and Don Widrig, [Leffingwell, 2003]. This book provides a nice *A-to-Z overview of software requirements*.

Mastering the Requirements Process, 2nd Edition, by Suzanne Robertson and James Robertson, [Robertson, 2006]. This book presents an effective *overview of the requirements management process*, although focusing mostly on specifying requirements using their Volere approach.

Software Requirement Patterns, by Stephen Withall, [Withall, 2007]. This book is an *excellent source for real-life requirement examples*. Withall reports that as much as 65 percent of requirements crop up over and over across systems. This book presents the templates for 37 requirement patterns grouped into eight domains to help you *write better requirements*.

Software Requirements, 2nd Edition, by Karl Wiegers, [Wiegers, 2003]. Chapter 4 provides a generous explanation of the industry *role of the requirements analyst*. Overall, the book provides a *good end-to-end understanding of requirements engineering*, requirements development and requirements management.

2 INVOLVE THE RIGHT STAKEHOLDERS

Lack of user input, incomplete requirements,
and changing requirements are the major reasons why
information technology projects do not deliver all of their
planned functionality on schedule and within budget.
—The Standish Group International [Standish, 1995]

Far too often, development teams make the mistake of leaving an essential person out of the requirements process. Before describing ways to identify and involve the right people in the requirements definition process, I want to emphasize that people are not the only source for requirements.

2.1 UTILIZE THE RIGHT SOURCES

Requirements can be identified through several sources. However, keep in mind that it is unlikely you would use all of them on a particular project effort. You might consider using the following sources:

- ENTERPRISE ANALYSIS to gain an understanding of the current state of the business process. This is usually done by creating a variety of models that help people "see" their business.

- REQUIREMENTS DOCUMENTS for current systems. Searching requirements specifications from previous projects can uncover potentially reusable material, thus saving time and duplication of effort.

- PROBLEM REPORTS AND ENHANCEMENT REQUESTS for a current application.

- FORM ANALYSIS to understand the communication channels in the organization. A form is simply a way to structure data entry and retrieval.

- BUSINESS ARTIFACTS such as training manuals, end-user documentation, and procedure guides.

- MARKETING SURVEYS AND USER QUESTIONNAIRES. These are great techniques to use when there is a very broad audience of stakeholders with little or no opportunity (usually due to time and cost) to elicit from all of them.

- OBSERVING USERS AT WORK. Observation may be performed in an active-visible manner (the observer is actively interjecting questions while the user is working) or a passive-invisible manner (the observer is silent and non-intrusive).

- EXPERIENCING LIFE AS A USER. Figuratively, walk in the user's shoes for a day. This is only possible when the work is not too complex or dangerous to be taken on by a novice. Working with users can help you understand the problems they encounter.

♦ SCENARIO ANALYSIS of user tasks. In the most general sense, a scenario is a step-by-step account of what an end-user does to achieve a desired goal. A set of logically-related scenarios (associated to the same user goal) can help the development team see the big picture of the work performed.

♦ INTERVIEWS and discussions with end-users and stakeholders. This is the most direct way to find out what the users need—ask them. While there are many elicitation techniques to choose from, I've included a thorough explanation of interviewing in Chapter 3, "Interviewing Tips and Tools."

♦ WORKSHOPS with a group of stakeholders bring the right collection of people together, and enable them to correct and improve on their own requirements (increasing buy-in). The workshop approach is a cycle, in which all participants contribute in building the requirements deliverable.

Whether requirements are gathered from one or all of the above sources depends on what defines the critical success of the project, the resources available (monetary, personnel, software and hardware, old documents), and any schedule constraints under which the product or service must be delivered. Based on the risks of developing the software system, the team must select the appropriate combination of resources to tap into.

2.2 ENGAGE THE RIGHT PEOPLE

The key to a successful project is involving all the right people. Certainly this includes individuals who are part of the project team itself. Additionally, there will be individuals who are invited to participate that are external to a particular business department or to the organization.

2.2.1 Stakeholders: Client vs. Customer vs. End-User

The terms client, customer, and end-user (informally called user) are often used differently from one organization to another or from one industry to another. Therefore, I feel it is necessary to establish their meanings as used in the context of this book. It might be important for you to establish consensus on these terms within your organization and certainly within your project team.

I use the term *client* to define the person or organization (indeed, some clients are external) which is invoiced or paying the bill for the actual development and/or implementation costs of the system. The client is the department whose budget will carry the cost of the project effort. In many organizations, the client is referred to as the project sponsor.

The *customer*, on the other hand, is the person who buys a system or service that is sold for public use. The customer may be synonymous with user if the customer is ultimately the person who uses the system.

In software development models, an *end-user* is any person who is affected by or has an affect on the system being built, or is any system that needs to interface with the system under development.

It is critical to involve a variety of stakeholders, consisting of individuals who might be a client (sponsor), a customer, and an end-user, to define a set of requirements that are complete.

A *stakeholder* is any person who has:

♦ A vested interest and/or decision-making authority in the development of the system.

♦ An expert understanding of the current process.

♦ The vision of what the future process should be.

♦ A role in the development process.

♦ A vested interest as a direct or indirect end-user of the system.

Industry research and reports tell us year after year of the importance of user involvement as a project success factor. This chapter is devoted to helping you achieve project success by getting the right people involved.

2.2.2 Potential Stakeholders

There is a saying, "two heads are better than one." It is the collaborative efforts of all the stakeholders that dramatically increase the accuracy of the requirements gathered, and significantly reduce the likelihood that requirements are missed. Involving the end-users and other key stakeholders early in the requirements-gathering process, as well as throughout the development and implementation lifecycle, increases their commitment or buy-in into the requirements. This typically results in fewer changes to the requirements during the later development phases when the cost to change requirements is significantly higher.

I use a simple classification of requirements management roles as shown in Figure 2-1. I recommend using a classification such as the one here to organize and identify potential stakeholders at the start of a project and throughout the development and implementation phases.

Figure 2-1 Requirements Management Roles

Requirements Producer	Requirements Supplier
Requirements Supporter	Requirements Receiver

This grouping of stakeholder roles serves as a checklist or tickler of those who should be involved in the requirements development process. I suggest that the stakeholders who are involved in the early planning phase of the project (which typically includes the project sponsor, project manager, and business analyst) conduct a brainstorming session to identify a starter list of stakeholders. The following list identifies potential stakeholders by the role(s) they may play in the development of the system:

(1) REQUIREMENTS PRODUCER. This is any individual who is responsible for capturing the requirements (eliciting, analyzing, representing, and coordinating the validating and approval of the requirements). "Producers" are also responsible for managing the requirements to ensure compliance and integration throughout the development or installation of the system. *Business Analysis* is a term commonly used to encompass the activities performed by the requirements producer. Examples of requirements producers in the area of requirements management include the following:

- ◆ Requirements Architect
- ◆ Requirements Engineer
- ◆ Business Analyst
- ◆ Data Analyst
- ◆ Network Engineer
- ◆ System Analyst/Engineer
- ◆ Software Analyst/Engineer

(2) REQUIREMENTS SUPPLIER. The supplier is any individual who is responsible for defining the business needs to be satisfied. This includes supplying all the detail from the initial idea or inception through each incremental iteration of the system development and implementation. Examples of requirements suppliers are as follows:

- ◆ Business Owner or Business Initiator
- ◆ Business Model Analyst
- ◆ Project Sponsor or Champion
- ◆ Product Manager

- Functional Manager

- Key Executive Participants

- Business Coordinator

- Business Team Member

- Business Subject Matter Expert (SME) or Business Area Knowledge Expert

- Technical Subject Matter Expert (SME) or Application Expert

- Customer Representative

(3) REQUIREMENTS RECEIVER. A receiver is any individual who receives and uses the requirements specifications as the input to develop their work products relating to implementing the requirements. "Receivers" assist in the requirements process by validating individual requirements, primarily for feasibility, completeness, and conflicts. Receivers can assist in validating additional quality characteristics such as necessity, priority, and traceability. Following are examples of requirements receivers:

- Project Manager

- Data Warehouse Specialist

- Database Administrator

- Developer (Programmer)

- Usability Engineer

- Network Planner

- Operations Analyst

- System Designer

- Technical Architect
- Test Analyst/ Quality Control/ Tester
- End-user Trainer
- Writer or Editor

(4) REQUIREMENTS SUPPORTER. The requirements supporter is any individual responsible for supporting the requirements management process and project effort. "Supporters" may be involved in looking at both the completed requirements specifications and the requirements processes that are followed to judge their effectiveness for future projects. "Supporters" provide support in the capacity of managing, controlling, or sponsoring the effort. They assist the individuals who are responsible for eliciting, analyzing, representing, validating, or managing the requirements set for the project. Examples of requirements supporters are as follows:

- Project Manager
- Program Manager
- Project Director
- Facilitator
- Process Owner
- Quality Assurance
- Practice Leader

2.2.3 Institutionalized Stakeholder List

I recommend that each organization create a defined list of stakeholders that are appropriate for their specific business. For example, Table 2-1 provides simple examples of stakeholder roles in three different industries. Undoubtedly, these roles would vary considerably when applied to systems in different departments across the organization.

Each organization should name the roles that are meaningful to the business, and then provide a definition for each role so that the terms are used consistently. Figure 2-2 on the following page lists a starter set of examples to consider in creating a stakeholder roles checklist.

Table 2-1 Stakeholder Role Examples by Industry

Banking Roles	Insurance Roles	Higher Education Roles
Teller	Agent	Student
Personal Banker	Policyholder	Professor
Examiner	Claim Adjuster	Chancellor
Borrower	Insured	Dean
Lender	Beneficiary	Alumni
Loan Officer	Claimant	Undergraduate
Account Holder	Attorney	Advisor
Co-signer	Physician	Scholarship Donor
Trustee	Witness	Resident Assistant

Figure 2-2 Stakeholder Roles Checklist

Requirements Suppliers:

- ❏ Sponsor/Champion/Client
- ❏ End-User/Customer
- ❏ Business Subject Matter Expert (SME)
- ❏ Business Process Area Experts
- ❏ Technical Subject Matter Expert (SME)
- ❏ Government Authority
- ❏ Regulatory or Compliance Authority
- ❏ Industry Standards Authority
- ❏ Special Interest Groups
- ❏ Cultural Interest Groups
- ❏ Public Opinion Representatives
- ❏ Professional Organizations
- ❏ Market Analysts
- ❏ System End-users
- ❏ System Buyers
- ❏ Recycling and Waste Managers
- ❏ Usability and Efficiency Experts
- ❏ Business Support Departments
  - ▪ Audit
  - ▪ Sales
  - ▪ Marketing
  - ▪ Accounting
  - ▪ Legal
  - ▪ Human Resources
  - ▪ Mail Room
- ❏ Test Market Representatives
- ❏ Inspectors
- ❏ Business Architect
- ❏ Business Strategist

Requirements Receivers:

- ❏ User Acceptance Test Group
- ❏ Development Team Members
  - ▪ System Architect
  - ▪ Quality Assurance
  - ▪ System Analyst
  - ▪ Designer
  - ▪ Developer (Programmer)
  - ▪ Database Administrator (DBA)
  - ▪ Data Warehouse Specialist
  - ▪ Tester
  - ▪ Release Coordinator
  - ▪ Technical Writer
- ❏ Production Support Personnel
- ❏ End-user Trainer or Training Personnel
- ❏ Network Planner
- ❏ Usability Engineer
- ❏ Business Operations Support Personnel
- ❏ Technical Operations Support Personnel
- ❏ Implementation Architect
- ❏ Configuration Management
- ❏ Product Disposers

Requirements Supporters:

- ❏ Project Sponsor
- ❏ Business Process Owner
- ❏ Project Manager
- ❏ Requirements Management Process Owner
- ❏ Project Team Members
- ❏ Implementation Support Team
- ❏ Project Investors
- ❏ Maintenance and Service Staff

The stakeholder roles identified for your specific organization must also be defined. This will help people to use the terms consistently and avoid potential confusion or requirement errors on projects.

Furthermore, each organization should maintain a list of government, regulatory, and industry standards sources (including individuals/departments to contact and contact information) that are specifically applicable to the organization's products and services. Representatives from these industry standard agencies are usually involved as requirements suppliers. You will probably recognize some of the following examples of industry standard sources:

♦   ANSI—American National Standards Institute

♦   IEEE—Institute of Electrical and Electronic Engineers

♦   ISO—International Standards Organization

2.3 BUILD A STAKEHOLDER PROFILE

Stakeholder profiling is a very effective, yet simple to use, technique for identifying stakeholders. A *stakeholder profile* helps to get the appropriate representation of all interested and affected areas. The stakeholder profile might be used to identify the appropriate individuals to involve on the project team itself, and to identify the appropriate individuals as resources for requirements. The key to a successful stakeholder profile is not only to identify an individual by name and the area that they represent, but also to define the role and responsibilities that the individual will fulfill on the project. The following are step-by-step procedures to help you engage the right stakeholders (perhaps what the National Aeronautics and Space Administration, NASA, terms the *right stuff*).

2.3.1 Step 1: Identify Stakeholder Roles

The stakeholder profile begins by identifying a list of potential stakeholders using a three-column tabular format such as Table 2-2, which provides a simple example of a Potential Stakeholder List. Reading from left to right, the columns are as follows:

♦ STAKEHOLDER NAME. This column is used to identify each potential stakeholder.

♦ TOPIC OF EXPERTISE. The middle column is used to identify the area or organizational department the stakeholder represents, as well as the specific business expertise or knowledge needed for the scope of the project.

Table 2-2 Potential Stakeholder List

Stakeholder Name	Topic of Expertise	Stakeholder Role
Michael	Workers compensation line of business management	Sponsor
Joseph	Claim assignment business rules	Subject Matter Expert
Anthony	Reserving procedures	Subject Matter Expert
Sayid	Subrogation procedures	Subject Matter Expert
Elizabeth	Reinsurance procedures	Subject Matter Expert
Jinlee	Monthly state reporting	Accounting
Lucas, Maria	Policy pricing based on loss experience	Actuarial
Anthony	Claim investigation and resolution	Claim Adjuster

◆ STAKEHOLDER ROLE. This column is used to describe the stakeholder roles in the requirements management process and their specific interest in the development of the system or product.

The route taken to complete the deliverable is of no real concern to the audience who benefits from the finished product. As is the case with so many templates used to create a deliverable, the sequence taken to build it is not the same sequence in which the deliverable is read. The potential stakeholder list is completed by working backwards—filling in the columns from right to left. Thus, completing the "Stakeholder Role" column is the first step in the procedures to build the stakeholder profile.

Start with your institutionalized Stakeholder Roles Checklist (Figure 2-2 on page 40) and select the roles appropriate for the scope of the project as typically not all roles will apply. As shown in Table 2-2, note that some stakeholder roles might apply more than once depending on the scope of topics for the particular project (e.g., Subject Matter Expert).

2.3.2 Step 2: Brainstorm Topics of Expertise

This is the most critical of the six steps to building the stakeholder profile. Identifying *why* a stakeholder might participate significantly decreases the likelihood of leaving out a key contributor. Forgetting a key contributor altogether or bringing them in late in the development lifecycle almost inevitably results in costly rework.

I recommend that the requirements producer meet with an initial subset of stakeholders such as the sponsor, project manager, functional manager, a lead business subject matter expert, and a technical lead to discuss the project scope. Current-state business models and workflow diagrams are reviewed for impacted business areas. The outcome of the meeting is a list of business areas impacted and the specific topics of business and technical knowledge that must be represented by the stakeholders selected to participate. Use the resulting list of topics to complete the column headed "Topic of Expertise" as shown in Table 2-2.

> ### Tip 2-1: Use visual aids to communicate
>
> Most people communicate more effectively when presented with a visual aid or picture. Using simple requirements models such as relationship maps, process maps and event-response tables will significantly increase the communication effectiveness of the stakeholders. Similarly, scope models such as context diagrams and use case diagrams will also help the stakeholders see what business processes and sub-processes are affected.

2.3.3 Step 3: List the Names of Potential Stakeholders

The "Stakeholder Name" column is completed by identifying one or more individuals believed to be knowledgeable in each topic of expertise. In Table 2-2, for example, both Lucas and Maria are named as potential stakeholders with knowledge of "policy pricing based on loss experience." Furthermore, one individual stakeholder (e.g., Anthony) might be named as knowledgeable in more than one business topic.

In this step, it is important to avoid pre-screening out potential stakeholders due to assumed unavailability. Try to approach this step as if it were a perfect world, and anyone you choose will be freed up to work on the project. Keep focused on the purpose of this step, which is simply identifying *potential* stakeholders. The last three steps of the six-step procedure will confirm which stakeholders participate.

2.3.4 Step 4: Survey Each Potential Stakeholder

While the first three steps of the procedures to build the stakeholder profile result in a collective list of several individuals representing various areas and roles, the stakeholder survey relates to a single stakeholder or stakeholder group representative. The stakeholder survey is used to identify the depth of knowledge that a potential stakeholder has in each of the topics of expertise needed for a particular project.

Tip 2-2: Create a "pecking order" of stakeholders

Try using the following list as a "pecking order" to identify potential stakeholders:

1. Start with the individuals assigned to the project team.
2. Next, look for individuals from within the project sponsor's business area or process.
3. Next, look within the sponsor's "partner" support business or technical areas.
4. Then, turn to others inside the company.
5. Finally, reach out to others outside the company.

This order implies that resources are decreasing in availability while increasing in possible costs associated with availability.

The template for the stakeholder survey, shown in Table 2-3 on page 47, is created by replicating the "Topic of Expertise" column from Step 2.

Each potential stakeholder is asked to complete the stakeholder survey and indicate his or her level of expertise in each topic of expertise listed for the project. Four degrees of experience might be used as follows:

(1) Little = very limited or no experience.

(2) Some = apprentice level or enough to be dangerous.

(3) Proficient = familiar with topic and good understanding of the day-to-day tasks.

(4) Expert = solid knowledge; person everyone goes to for help on the topic. (It doesn't necessarily mean the person knows it all.)

> ## Tip 2-3: Build rapport
>
> I prefer to spend about 20 minutes with the potential stakeholder in an interview setting and ask him or her to complete the stakeholder survey. It is an opportunity to build rapport and explain what the technique is and how it will be used, as well as what it is not (for example, it is not going to be used to evaluate the person's performance). If the stakeholder is not available for a face-to-face interview, call the person on the phone. Don't just send the survey in an email—make personal contact first.

After the survey has been completed, ask for other potential stakeholders. For example, if my interviewee indicates having little, no, or some experience, in any of the topics, I will ask, "Is there anyone else you would go to with questions on these topics?" Any named individuals will be added to the Potential Stakeholder List and will also be asked to complete the stakeholder survey.

Finally, ask each potential stakeholder to review the list of topics and ask, "Based on your understanding of the scope of this project, what other topics of expertise should be added? Removed?"

The key to this step is having each potential stakeholder fill out the survey for his or her expertise. The survey is not filled out by the requirements producer, project manager, project sponsor, or any other role involved in the project. If stakeholders inflate their experience level in any given topic area, you'll become aware of it during the interviews and meetings on the specific topic. On the other hand, if stakeholders deflate their expertise (say, in an attempt to avoid participating in meetings), other stakeholders will name that individual as an expert so you'll probably end up inviting them anyway.

Table 2-3 Stakeholder Survey Example

Stakeholder Name: Anthony (claim adjuster)

Topic of Expertise	Little	Some	Proficient	Expert
Workers compensation line of business management	✓			
Claim assignment business rules	✓			
Reserving procedures				✓
Subrogation procedures			✓	
Reinsurance procedures		✓		
Monthly state reporting		✓		
Policy pricing based on loss experience	✓			
Claim investigation and resolution			✓	

2.3.5 Step 5: Analyze the Stakeholder Surveys

The stakeholder surveys are compiled in a tabular format such as Table 2-4. This table uses the first letter of each degree of experience. For example, where the stakeholder indicated little or no experience, an "L" was inserted accordingly.

Table 2-4 Stakeholder Profile Assessment

Topic of Expertise	Anthony	Elizabeth	Jinlee	Lucas	Michael	Sayid	Joseph	Maria
Workers compensation line of business management	L	L	L	L	E	L	L	L
Claim assignment business rules	L	L	L	L	P	L	E	S
Reserving procedures	E	S	L	P	E	S	S	P
Subrogation procedures	P	L	L	L	L	E	S	L
Reinsurance procedures	S	E	L	S	S	L	S	L
Monthly state reporting	S	L	E	L	S	L	L	S
Policy pricing based on loss experience	L	L	L	E	L	L	L	P
Claim investigation and resolution	E	L	L	L	E	S	S	S

Key: L = Little or no experience   S = Some experience   P = Proficient   E = Expert

Alternatively, you might use a number to correspond to each degree of experience as shown in Table 2-5. For example, the number 1 signifies little or no experience, while the number 4 equates to the expert level.

Table 2-5 Stakeholder Profile Assessment (Alternative)

Topic of Expertise	Anthony	Elizabeth	Jinlee	Lucas	Michael	Sayid	Joseph	Maria
Workers compensation line of business management	1	1	1	1	4	1	1	1
Claim assignment business rules	1	1	1	1	3	1	4	2
Reserving procedures	4	2	1	3	4	2	2	3
Subrogation procedures	3	1	1	1	1	4	2	1
Reinsurance procedures	2	4	1	2	2	1	2	1
Monthly state reporting	2	1	4	1	2	1	1	2
Policy pricing based on loss experience	1	1	1	4	1	1	1	3
Claim investigation and resolution	4	1	1	1	4	2	2	2

Key: 1 = Little or no experience   2 = Some experience   3 = Proficient   4 = Expert

The stakeholder profile assessment is analyzed to make sure that all business topic areas for the scope of the project are adequately represented. Each row (relating to a specific topic area) is reviewed for adequate coverage. Ideally, you want to have at least two stakeholders in each topic that are either proficient or expert. This assumes that the saying, "two heads are better than one," holds true. Finding at least two stakeholders in each topic also helps alleviate some of the inflated egos identified in Step 4. Scanning Table 2-4, you should see that I might want to pick up a few more stakeholders in at least three of the topic areas: workers compensation line of business management, reinsurance procedures, and monthly date reporting.

The stakeholder profile assessment can be utilized as a tool for requirements producers to organize their elicitation activities, as well as to schedule meetings that work in conjunction with the availability of the stakeholders. It also optimizes the utilization of project resources by decreasing the need to have all stakeholders present for all meetings. For example, in Table 2-4, only Anthony, Lucas, Maria, and Michael might be invited to a discussion of the project requirements related to "reserving procedures." Furthermore, if I want to decrease involvement of an over-utilized stakeholder, I could leave Michael off the invite list for discussions on "reserving procedures."

Tip 2-4: Create a reusable repository of profiles

I recommend compiling stakeholder profiles for every business area. A centralized repository of profiles is reusable and will save time at the start of each project. Management might also use the profiles to cross train staff. There is some maintenance, however, to keep the profiles accurate and up to date (at least every six months). If they become outdated, then people won't trust them and will discontinue applying the stakeholder profile technique to get the right stakeholders involved. Make sure the date on which the profiles were created (and updated) is recorded.

2.3.6 Step 6: Secure Stakeholder Resources

Secure the needed stakeholders by meeting with the project manager, project sponsor, and/or a stakeholder's supervisor. Confirm the availability of stakeholders for the project timeline.

It is conceivable for no one to have a great deal of expertise on some topics. Unavailable or nonexistent resources may pose a significant project risk. This was certainly the case on one project I worked on—for a system intended to include brand-new technology, and no internal stakeholders had experience with the new technology.

Tip 2-5: Secure management support

You may need to educate the sponsor of the project on the benefits of applying the stakeholder profile technique. At the start of the project, sponsors are sometimes guilty of telling you what resources to which you can have access. Quite often when the resource to which you're directed does not have sufficient subject matter expertise to supply requirements, the resource becomes a middle man and must go to the real expert with questions. It is this true expert with whom you want to be talking directly.

Rather than telling you what resources to use, sponsors should encourage you to complete the stakeholder profile. The sponsor should work with you to identify the best approach to filling the resource needs based on the specific topics within the project scope.

One of the benefits of the stakeholder profile is the ability to utilize resources more effectively. Not all stakeholders need to be invited to all discussions. The sponsor will find it more challenging to ignore requests for specific resources when presented with a tangible model that demonstrates the lack of expertise of "assigned" resources.

2.4 CHAPTER SUMMARY

♦ Stakeholders (such as requirements suppliers and receivers) are the most common source for eliciting requirements. Creating an institutionalized list of stakeholder roles provides consistency across projects and provides requirements producers with a reusable, time-saving checklist.

♦ User involvement is a critical project success factor. The stakeholder profile technique is proven to help get the right people engaged so that fewer requirements are missed.

2.5 SUGGESTED READING

A Requirements Pattern: Succeeding in the Internet Economy, by Patricia Ferdinandi, [Ferdinandi, 2002]. This book does a good job of describing **roles and responsibilities** of the development team in Chapter 8.

Exploring Requirements: Quality Before Design, by Donald Gause and Gerald Weinberg, [Gause, 1989]. Chapter 7 explores "**getting the right people involved**."

Requirements Engineering, 2nd Edition, by Elizabeth Hull, Ken Jackson, and Jeremy Dick, [Hull, 2005]. Chapter 5 of this book includes a discussion on Requirements Engineering in the Problem Domain including the **identification of stakeholders**.

Requirements Engineering: A Good Practice Guide, by Ian Sommerville and Pete Sawyer, [Sommerville, 1977]. This book devotes Chapter 13 to **viewpoints**, which is a term that is broadly synonymous with a perspective on a system. Similar to stakeholder profiling, viewpoints are designed to reduce the risk of overlooking stakeholders and their requirements. They may also help to manage and analyze the requirements once they have been elicited.

Software Engineering, Edited by Merlin Dorfman and Richard Thayer, Institute of Electrical and Electronic Engineers (IEEE), [Dorfman, 2000]. This is an impressive compilation of software engineering papers that includes a list of software engineering **standards sources**.

Software Requirements, 2nd Edition, by Karl Wiegers, [Wiegers, 2003]. Chapter 6 describes challenges in finding the **voice of the customer,** such as identifying different classes of users and finding the sources of user requirements.

Writing Better Requirements, by Ian F. Alexander and Richard Stevens, [Alexander, 2002]. Chapter 2 provides a practical approach to **identifying stakeholders**.

PREPARATION
is the link
between
ORDINARY people
and
EXTRAORDINARY
interviews.

3 INTERVIEWING TIPS AND TOOLS

Interviewing is much more effective if it uses a structured technique or process; it is not merely asking questions. Interviewing requires the development of basic social skills, the ability to listen, and knowledge of a variety of interviewing tactics. This chapter presents suggestions in three areas of the interview techniques for gathering requirements.

3.1 PREPARING FOR THE INTERVIEW

Aside from conducting the interview itself, the real success lies in the preparations done prior to the interview. If I were asked to identify the single most important tip for a successful interview, I'd say, "never walk into an interview empty-handed." I mean that figuratively and literally! Read the following six guidelines on preparing for the interview to find out why.

3.1.1 Guideline 1: Schedule the Interview

Assuming you've used the stakeholder profile technique presented in Chapter 2, "Involve the Right Stakeholders," the next step is to schedule the interview with each identified stakeholder. For the context of this chapter, I'll use the term interviewee instead of stakeholder. Additionally, the content of this chapter is presented with the intent that you are interviewing one interviewee at a time.

The goal of the interview is *quality* requirements as well as quantity. For example, responses to your prepared list of questions might give you the level of detail you are seeking, while other responses prompt you to ask additional probing or follow-up questions. You want to make the most of the allotted time with the interviewee, and gather as much useful information from them as you can. Schedule the date, time, and place of the interview that is the most convenient for the interviewee.

Where you conduct the interview—in a neutral setting or in the interviewee's normal work environment—depends on the interviewee and the purpose or level of desired detail. A neutral setting helps to reduce outside distractions such as the interviewee's phone, computer, other audio disruptions, and perhaps other co-workers that might interrupt. Neutral settings help when the nature of your questions involve getting the interviewee's opinions or vision.

Conducting the interview in the interviewee's normal work environment can offer the benefit of having colleagues nearby to provide additional information. The interviewee may want to share examples from an existing system, or access reference manuals, documents, forms, and other tools used as work aids. It usually is very helpful for you to experience an interviewee's work setting.

Tip 3-1: Deal diplomatically with cell phones

Here's a way to politely ask interviewees to turn off their cell phones. You might say, "We can really optimize the limited time we have by shutting out distractions. Would you mind turning off your cell phone while we talk?"

Select a convenient date and time for the interview. Take into consideration the interviewee's normal working hours. Does the person arrive early or late? Does the person leave early or late? Does the person work flexible hours in which he or she is unavailable on certain days of the week or leaves earlier on a particular day of the week? What is the person's usual lunch period? Are there any times of the day when the person is particularly busy? Remember, the goal is to select a time and place that maximizes the focus or attention of interviewees. As a general rule, do not schedule an interview:

- **Between two other appointments on an interviewee's calendar.** You want to be certain you have adequate time to complete the interview.

- **During the first hour or the last hour of the work day.** Some people are either too distracted or too tired. Of course, for other people, these are the most effective times to catch them. Be alert and don't over-generalize.

- **The day prior to or the day following a vacation or holiday.**

It's also true that you might extract different useful information from the same person at different times, or in different environments. If you talk to interviewees when they're relaxing at the end of the day, they might be a lot more forthcoming about ideas, or much more prepared to speculate. They just might tell you stories or embarrassing information that would otherwise remain hidden! Just like an experienced private investigator, there might be things you can only find out after interviewees think the interview is over, and you've put your pen and paper away.

3.1.2 Guideline 2: Prepare an Agenda

The interview is really just a form of a meeting. You want to follow good meeting etiquette. Having an agenda for the interview is essential to keeping the interview on track. The agenda sets the tone for specifically what will and will not be discussed as appropriate. Depending on the interviewee and the anticipated level of detail you are seeking, allow time to ask probing and follow-up questions to your prepared questions. At times, deviating from the agenda can also be

---

Tip 3-2: Use your agenda as a visual aid

The agenda is your visual aid (tool) for keeping the interview on track. Most adults communicate more effectively in a visual mode. You can take advantage of the visual nature of the interview using a printed copy of the agenda. Although you send the agenda prior to the interview, I recommend that you print a hardcopy and take it to the interview. Make a comment such as, "I took the liberty of printing a copy of the agenda for you," as you hand the interviewee the agenda. Now that the agenda is in front of the interviewee, you can use it as needed to visually capture the interviewee's attention.

If the interviewee is getting a bit off track, you can literally point to the next discussion topic or question on the agenda as you say, "Thank you, [*interviewee name*], let's go on to the next question." The closer you move in, and the longer you point to the item, the more you draw in the interviewee's attention. As soon as you have the interviewee focused, move the interview in the direction you want to go. You're back in control.

Of course, the effectiveness of this tip is dependent on the time you spend preparing your questions and your agenda. And, with some interviewees, the interview might go better if they are unaware of the agenda.

---

effective, depending on what you learn as you go along. Essentially, be flexible. Here is a summary of what to include in the agenda:

- ◆ PURPOSE. Clearly state the purpose of the interview and the specific topics of discussion. You may even consider providing an example question.

- ◆ SCHEDULE CONFIRMATION. Communicate the interview logistics—date, time, and place.

- PARTICIPANTS. Identify all participants including a note taker if one is used (highly recommended as it typically increases the quantity of information gathered; however, I understand that resources are often unavailable). See Section 3.1.4 for more information on this.

- FORMAT. Explain how the interview will be conducted. This is helpful when it is necessary to educate the interviewee on the interview process. What topics will be discussed? Are you allotting a specific length of time to cover each topic? Are you asking the interviewee a list of questions he or she was given at the start of the interview? Have you sent the interviewee a list of questions prior to the interview that you'll be reviewing? Are you going to ask prepared questions that only you have a copy of?

   Additionally, you might provide an opportunity for the interviewee to add topics you did not include but that directly relate to the subject for which you are gathering information. There may be hidden knowledge or processes of which you and others are not aware.

- PREPARATION ACTION ITEMS. Communicate to the interviewee any expectations about materials that he or she is to review prior to the interview, or work products that should be brought along to the interview. Also let the interviewee know if there are work products or documents that you will be bringing to the interview. Action items should specify who is responsible, what is to be done, and by when.

- FOLLOW-UP ACTIONS. Explain what the interviewee can expect after the interview. Note, this is a great opportunity to educate the interviewee on the requirements-gathering process you're using (refer to the requirements process overview presented in Chapter 1, "Requirements in Context"). The actions of who, what, and when should be agreed upon at the close of the interview.

A suggested format of an interview agenda is presented in Tool 3-1 on the next page.

Tool 3-1 Suggested Interview Agenda Format

This simple agenda format might be used to communicate the logistics of the interview.

Purpose:

Date: _____   Time: _____ to _____   Duration: _____

Place: Building _____   Room _____

Participants:

Topics (or questions) for discussion:

Preparation action items:

Post-interview action items:

Attachments:

3.1.3 Guideline 3: Distribute the Interview Materials

As a general rule of thumb, it is better to start with a draft of something to review than to start with a blank canvas, provided you do not unnecessarily constrain the interviewee or interject your own bias. Depending on where you are in the requirements-gathering process, or what iteration or phase in the project, there usually is something to review. If you're at the very beginning, there generally is something such as an e-mail (electronic mail), a problem report, or an enhancement request that triggered the project. If you use a project development life cycle methodology, there may be project deliverables such as a project overview, project definition, or

---

Tip 3-3: Provide questions prior to the interview if appropriate

"To send or not to send?" That is the question you must answer regarding whether or not you provide the interviewee with a list of questions prior to the interview.

Sending a list of prepared questions to interviewees in advance allows the interviewee adequate time to research and prepare. This is very beneficial when you are seeking a lot of factual information and actual statistical or historical data. You should validate (through the stakeholder profiling technique presented in Chapter 2, "Involve the Right Stakeholder") that you have the right subject matter expert(s) so you feel confident that you have accurate facts. Be aware of interviewees who supply you with the responses to your questions and then declare that the interview is no longer necessary.

Conversely, providing the list of questions to the interviewee at the start of the meeting, or not at all, also has advantages. The person will not have had time to ponder the questions in advance so responses are candid and not rehearsed. This is a good approach when eliciting opinions and estimates, and works well when asking for the interviewee's vision.

---

business case. At a minimum, the interview agenda should be distributed prior to the interview. Again, use good meeting etiquette, and send all materials out in a timeframe that is adequate relative to the amount of material the interviewee is expected to review.

3.1.4 Guideline 4: Recruit a Note-taker

A lot of us like to think that we are able to multi-task. However, the interview is not the time to do so. It is a talented individual indeed who is able to "actively" listen and record notes at the same time. Recruiting someone who can take notes makes it easier for you to actively listen. It also increases the quantity of requirements you are able to elicit, as you don't have to slow down the interview process by note-taking. I am not suggesting that you take no notes at all; in fact, I find it necessary to jot down key words or phrases in order to help me remember and paraphrase what I just heard. Jotting down a few key words can also help you to remember to go back and ask additional probing questions.

I know that it is difficult to find an available (or even willing) note-taker. I suggest pairing up with a buddy to take notes. You might take notes for the buddy's interviews and he or she will take notes for yours. Whenever possible, try to use the same note-taker. This person will get used to your interview style and approach, and will also learn your preferences about the level of detail for notes. Make sure it's someone with at least a modicum of understanding of what's going on. Otherwise the note-taker may miss important points, or write something down incorrectly.

You might consider tape recording or videotaping the session when a note-taker is not an option or available. However, most interviewees don't like being recorded.

A note-taker is particularly recommended when you are conducting an interview with someone whose time is considered extremely valuable (or expensive), whose time is not easily granted, and with whom you are unlikely to get an opportunity for a follow-up interview.

Tip 3-4: Ask permission to bring a note-taker

When interviewing only one person, ask permission to bring a note-taker or to record the interview before the agenda is delivered. Do not ask at the start of the interview and risk offending the interviewee. Bringing someone into the room unexpectedly may make the interviewee feel uneasy. Avoid giving the "two-against-one" impression—the interrogation.

3.1.5 Guideline 5: Prepare a List of Questions

Yes, I said prepare. Say it with me, "Prepare!" In addition to the agenda, a list of prepared questions is essential to keeping the interview on track. Having a prepared list of questions does not mean you have to literally read off each question—although in some cases, reading the questions exactly as they are written is very helpful. Some questions are intended to be follow-up questions based on the interviewee's response. For example, based on the interviewee's response, you might skip a question or two, or skip an entire section of questions. Or you might add extra follow-up questions on the spur of the moment. Consider the following suggestions in preparing your list of questions:

- **Arrange the list of questions in a logical order,** and grouped by relevant issue. For example, group your questions by the type of requirement (user, functional, and nonfunctional) you are eliciting.

- **Determine how much time to spend** on each issue, topic, or logical group of questions.

Tip 3-5: Apply a business requirement statement format

For interviews at the business requirements level, write the following statement format on a white board and ask the interviewee to help fill in the blanks:

The **PURPOSE** of the _____ [*insert project name*]

IS TO _____
[*describe what the project team is expected to implement or deliver*]

SO THAT _____
[*describe measurable business benefits*]

♦ **Understand the types of questions used and the expected answers.** You should give some thought to what answers you might get in response to your questions. This will help you know whether or not the interviewee actually answered your question. It will also help you know the direction you'll take in asking additional probing questions.

♦ **Use the questions to maintain the direction of the interview.** Just as there is a logical hierarchy or relationship among the requirement types (refer to Chapter 1, "Requirements in Context"), there is a logical progression to the interview questions. You would not, for example, want to start your interview by asking questions to elicit functional requirements (system level) if you have not already identified the user requirements (user level).

3.1.6 Guideline 6: Identify the Success Criteria

How will you know whether or not the interview was a success? Was the purpose to identify top-level business requirements? If so, did you capture all of the specific measurable business benefits? From the interview notes, are you able to produce a deliverable that represents the business requirements? Was the purpose of the interview to validate all of the users and focus on gathering user requirements? Using your agenda, were you able to keep the interview on track? Did you successfully discuss all the topics identified in your agenda? Did you run out of time? Did you schedule too much time? If you achieve everything before the end of the allotted time, close the interview. Don't pad it out unnecessarily.

The checklist presented in Tool 3-2 will help you to organize and plan your session. The success criteria for your interview will be based on the level of the requirements, which equates to the level of detail that you seek. Refer back to Chapter 1, "Requirements in Context," for an explanation of requirement levels.

Tool 3-2 Interview Preparations Checklist

❑ 1. Interviewee is contacted and request for interview granted.

❑ 2. Convenient date/time/place is confirmed with interviewee.
- Date: _____
- Time: _____
- Place: _____

❑ 3. Place/location reservations are confirmed.
- Confirmation number: _____
- Conference call information: _____
- Building/room number: _____
- Address: _____
- Create a map and instructions to the site if the location is offsite or unfamiliar to the interviewee.

❑ 4. Necessary equipment is accessible or reservations confirmed.
- Video camera, screen, projector
- Audio recording device
- Conference telephone
- White board, markers, eraser
- Flip chart, markers, easel
- Note pads, writing instruments
- Personal computer or laptop
- Internet connectivity
- Power source (electrical, battery, other)

❑ 5. Facility environment is verified.
- Lighting
- Temperature (climate) controls
- Table, chairs, other
- Food and beverages

❑ 6. Agenda is prepared.

❑ 7. Pre-interview review materials are identified.

❑ 8. Agenda and pre-interview review materials are distributed to interviewee.

❑ 9. If a note-taker is involved:
- Prior permission granted by interviewee to have a note-taker or recording device present.
- Note-taker is briefed on interview process or format, as well as any other special instructions.

❑ 10. Interview list of questions is prepared.

❑ 11. The interview success criteria are

_____

_____

3.2 ASKING THE RIGHT QUESTIONS

Asking the right question is as much how you ask it, as it is what you ask. Altering the way a question is phrased can make all the difference in the response it invokes. For example, if I ask you, "Are your lights on?", your response will most likely be a simple "yes" or "no." However, if I alter the question by adding just a single word and ask, "Why are your lights on?", I should expect you to respond with one or more reasons for your lights being on. What questions you ask will depend on the following two key components: why you ask, and what you expect. Both should be given considerable attention when deciding what types of questions you ask.

3.2.1 Why Do You Ask?

You must know why you are asking each question. In other words, you must know the purpose or goal for asking each question. Are you seeking facts? Are you seeking an opinion from the interviewee? Are you intending to change the direction of the discussion? Do you need to get the interviewee to elaborate on a particular topic? Are you asking the interviewee to explain something? Your answers to these questions will change the types of questions you will use in the interview. I'll give you examples of types of questions to ask depending on what your purpose or goal is in Section 3.2.3.

Tip 3-6: Ask "why?"

Asking "why" is a powerful way of discovering requirements. The question "why?" used by itself might seem threatening so be careful not to overuse it. "Why" questions can be stated in an unaggressive manner such as:

- "What is the underlying reason for that?"
- "What is the rationale behind that?"
- "Would you explain why you need it to do that?"
- "What is the purpose of doing that?"
- "Help me to understand why it is done that way."
- "How does that happen? Can you explain why it matters?"

3.2.2 What Do You Expect?

Knowing what you expect relates to the expected response from the interviewee. Once you've asked your question, what is the expected response? By this, I mean what kind of response are you expecting to hear? Giving some thought to what you expect the interviewee to respond with will help you with the following:

(1) **Knowing whether or not the interviewee answered your question.** If the question was not answered, it will be necessary for you to interpret why not. Perhaps the interviewee did not understand the question, in which case you will need to rephrase the question and ask it again. Or, perhaps the interviewee does not want to admit he or she doesn't know the answer, in which case you may want to move on to another topic.

(2) **Deciding which direction to take regarding follow-up questions or your next line of questioning.** For example, say you have already elicited the business, user, and some functional requirements, and you are now interviewing for more detail on the functional and nonfunctional requirements. You may ask a question related to interoperability (an indication of how easily the system can exchange data or services with other systems) such as, "What other systems or processes does the current system need to exchange data or services with?" If the interviewee's response is "none," then you will want to skip your prepared questions related to interoperability. However, if the response indicates that there are other systems to

---

Tip 3-7: Deal tactfully with "information hoarders"

Some interviewees are very protective of the knowledge they hold and do not want you to interview someone else. Other interviewees might not be the subject matter expert and are too embarrassed or shy to acknowledge this. A question such as, "Is there anyone else I should talk to about this?" might not be well received. To avoid offending someone, the following question generally works quite well, "In the event you're out of the office for any reason, who is your backup?"

---

interface with, then you will want to proceed with your prepared questions related to interoperability.

(3) **Assessing the appropriate level of detail for the particular purpose of the interview.** For example, you may ask the project sponsor, "Why is this project being done?" This question is typically asked early in the requirements-gathering process in order to identify the business requirements. The sponsor might respond by telling you that three new management reports are needed, and proceeds to give you some details about these reports. While this information or level of detail is important, it is probably too detailed for the intent of the current interview. Before describing the information desired on a report, you should identify which users are interacting with the business. You will want to better understand the work the users perform. Once you understand the purpose of the work, you can then fill in the details about the information needed.

3.2.3 The Right Types of Questions

CONTEXT-FREE QUESTIONS are high-level questions posed early in the project to obtain information about the project goals, objectives, and scope. These questions are most useful in identifying the business requirements in an interview with the project sponsor. Context-free questions are appropriate for any project regardless of business or process, and are independent of any specific design or technology. Table 3-1 contains a sampling of context-free questions based on Gause and Weinberg [Gause, 1989].

OPEN-ENDED QUESTIONS are questions that allow the interviewee to answer freely. The interviewee will provide facts, give an opinion, or explain something. "Is dinner ready?" is an example of a closed-ended question, typically characterized by a "yes" or "no" response. On second thought, perhaps this question isn't such a good example! I've heard of situations when this question invites very colorful elaboration! In other words, don't try this one at home.

Open-ended questions are good for a tester to consider when determining if a requirement or condition passed or failed. However, closed-ended questions are generally not as useful in

Table 3-1 Example Context-Free Questions

C1	Who is the customer? (Who is paying?)
C2	What problems would this product or system solve? For whom?
C3	What related problems are not being addressed by this project? Why?
C4	What problems could this product or system create?
C5	Who else do you think should be involved in this project and why?
C6	Why is this project visible to upper management? Who is upper management?
C7	What is the business reason for wanting to solve this problem?
C8	What obstacles or roadblocks are there to the success of this project?
C9	How long has this concept or product been considered? What were its previous innovations?

Tip 3-8: Convert to open-ended questions

As a rule of thumb, you can turn most close-ended questions into open-ended ones by adding the word "what" or "why" to the beginning of the question.

eliciting details. And, of course, a question that is too open could cause the interviewee to go off topic.

If you ask a closed-ended question, you usually end up asking a follow-up question in order to get at the information you were seeking initially. If the purpose of the interview is to maximize the quantity of information gathered in the allotted time, the interview will be more effective if the right questions are asked to begin with. This allows more time to ask additional worthy questions, rather than follow-up questions that are attempting to get at the very same information.

For example, let's say you ask a business manager, "Do you have any employees?" Because it was a closed-ended question, the business manager responds simply by saying,

"Yes." Then you have to ask a follow-up question such as, "What is the maximum number of employees who will need security access?" Now, this simple dialog exchange might not seem like a big deal, but expand this type of dialog over a one-hour interview, and then see how much time is wasted. You need to make your questions open-ended in order to get right to the point.

DIRECT QUESTIONS are used to obtain factual and objective responses. Generally speaking, direct questions are led by one of the following: *who, what, where, when, why* or *how*. Here are some examples of direct questions that result in factual responses—although be aware that the responses might not be complete or even accurate.

- Who uses this billing information?
- What information is needed for that task?
- Where is the report being distributed?
- When does the user need the information?
- Why is it done in that sequence?
- How many regions are there currently?

ELABORATION QUESTIONS or phrases are used to elicit subjective responses or opinions. Subjective responses and opinions are helpful in gaining insight to potential alternative solutions to the current problem—though it is not your responsibility to pursue solutions. Often the users of a system have ideas about how to improve the system. The following phrases and questions are used to prompt the interviewee to elaborate on the topic or to give his or her opinion:

- Tell me more about that.
- Explain what you mean by that.
- Describe what happens next.
- What do you think about this?

- How do you feel about it?

- Where could the workflow be improved?

- What concerns do you have?

Tip 3-9: Don't "lead the witness"

Avoid questions that provide or anticipate the response. For example, instead of asking, "Should it be done daily or weekly?" ask, "How often should it be done?"

You might want to first demonstrate some level of understanding on the subject. Don't hide everything you know, in case it makes you look inexperienced!

LADDERING QUESTIONS are used to raise or lower the level of information gathered. They usually begin with "how," "what," or "why," and are used to prompt the interviewee to respond with a different level of detail. For example, ask "why" questions to raise the level of the discussion (move up the ladder). If the interviewee is giving too much detail about how a process is done, ask, "Why is the user (role) doing this?"

On the other hand, use "how" questions or elaboration questions, as described in the previous section, to lower the level of detail (move down the ladder). If the interviewee is not giving enough detail about the work that is done, ask, "How does the user do that?"

Laddering questions are particularly useful when the interviewee has a tendency to talk about how to design the system, instead of giving the requirements for the system. Let's examine the following interview dialogue to see how laddering questions can help raise the level of the conversation.

Interviewer: "What does the clerk do next in the order process?"
Interviewee: "The clerk clicks on the check order button on the New Order Screen."
Interviewer: "Why does the clerk click the check order button?"

Tip 3-10: Differentiate fact from opinion

Be aware of the difference between facts and opinions. Whenever possible, facts should be validated by another source to confirm the accuracy. With opinions, you should investigate whether other people hold different opinions. Opinions are liable to vary more than perceptions or facts do.

Unfortunately, knowing the difference between facts and opinions isn't easy. You might want to ask a follow-up question such as, "Is that your opinion or a fact? If it is a fact, do you have something to substantiate it?"

Interviewee: "She does this to find out if all the items ordered are in stock."

Interviewer: "Why does the clerk need to know if all the items ordered are in stock?"

Interviewee: "Because if any items ordered are not in stock, the clerk has to submit a backorder request along with the order."

Interviewer: "So the next step in the order process is to fill out a backorder request for each item that is not in stock. Is that right?"

Interviewee: "Yes, that's right."

In the above example, the interviewer used the "why" questions to raise the level of detail. Clicking the button on the screen is a step in "how" (design) the clerk performs the next step in the order process. The actual next step in the process is to complete the backorder request.

Before getting into the details of the process or the information needed, it is important to understand the purpose for doing the process. You must first clearly identify the user goals that the system is supporting. That is, what business functions do the users need to perform?

Tip 3-11: Don't confuse "how" with design

Don't confuse "why" and "how" questions with the "whys and whats" of requirements and the "hows" of design.

Furthermore, the interview is not an "interrogation." Be careful not to offend interviewees or make them feel that you are questioning their skills or authority.

METAQUESTIONS are questions about questions. Metaquestions are helpful in assessing the progression of the interview. These questions are intended to be a litmus test of the interview process itself and are typically closed-ended type questions. Table 3-2 lists some examples of metaquestions.

Table 3-2 Example Metaquestions

M1	Am I asking too many questions?
M2	Do my questions seem relevant?
M3	Are you the right person to answer these questions? Are your answers definitive?
M4	To be sure that we understand each other, I've found it helps me to have things in writing so I can analyze them later. May I write down your responses? Is it OK for a note-taker to capture our discussion?
M5	(*Use this if your communication thus far has only been in writing.*) The written material has been helpful, but I find that I understand some things better if I can discuss them face to face. Can we get together at some point to discuss the material further?
M6	Is there anything else I should be asking you?
M7	Are there important topics I haven't mentioned?
M8	Is there anything you would like to ask me?
M9	May I return or call you with more questions later, in case I don't cover everything in our allotted time?

Tool 3-3 Suggested Questions (Part Two: "Right Approach, Right Questions")

Over 2,000 suggested questions for eliciting nonfunctional requirements are included in Part Two, "Right Approach, Right Questions." These questions can help you prepare for your requirements-gathering interview and feel confident that you're asking the right questions. After reading Chapter 2, "Involve the Right Stakeholders," and a good part of Chapter 3, "Interviewing Tips and Tools," you might realize that there's a little bit of work involved in developing "good" requirements.

3.3 CONDUCTING A STAR INTERVIEW

Interviewing can be a very exhausting activity. Interviewing is mentally and physically draining due to the level of concentration and focus that is required by the interviewer in order to get the most out of the interview, both in terms of time allowed and the quality and quantity of information elicited.

This section provides guidance for conducting your interview, but not just any interview—a **STAR** interview:

♦ **S**tart with style.

♦ **T**QLR (apply the active listening strategy: Tune in, Question, Listen, and Review).

♦ **A**sk questions.

♦ **R**ecap and wrap-up.

3.3.1 *STAR—Start with Style*

Starting the interview with style means following the Golden Rule. That is, treat others as you would want to be treated. The interview should be conducted in a professional manner, and with the utmost courtesy toward the interviewee. It is important to show respect for the interviewee's expertise or area of authority, and to express genuine appreciation for the time the person invested in the interview. In the following paragraphs, I give you a structure to follow when opening the interview, as well as some general guidelines for conducting the interview with style.

3.3.1.1 OPEN THE INTERVIEW

(1) **Start with introductions**. The introduction step is intended to establish good rapport with the interviewee. Begin the interview by thanking the interviewee for his or her time. If you have not met the person face to face before, continue the interview with proper introductions. Also, don't forget to introduce the note-taker and briefly explain that role.

(2) **Review the purpose and goals**. This step is intended to set the ground rules or review the expectations for the interview. Use the interview agenda to discuss the interview purpose and goals with the interviewee.

- ◆ **Explain the topics that will be discussed** and, as appropriate, which topics will not be covered. Explain how the information elicited during the interview will be used.

- ◆ **Confirm that the interviewee is still available** for the scheduled duration of the interview. This is particularly important when interviewing executive management or individuals who have heavy demands on their time. You might ask, "This interview is scheduled for 45 minutes. Is this workable for you?" The note-taker might be the timekeeper and makes sure the interview keeps within the allotted time.

- ◆ **Review the format of the interview** as needed. Briefly describe how you are going to conduct the interview. This may also include a time allocation per issue. To explain the format, you might say something like, "I'm going to use a list of questions that I've prepared beforehand to guide our discussion. Then we'll recap the discussion, and identify the next steps or any follow-up action items. Is this an agreeable format to you?"

♦ **Follow up on any materials that were distributed** prior to the interview. You want to confirm that the interviewee has adequately reviewed all the materials. If the materials are important to the interview and the interviewee has not read the materials, it may be necessary to stop and reschedule the interview.

3.3.1.2 INTERVIEW GUIDELINES

(1) **Take notes or record the interview**. Even if you have a note-taker present, most interviewers find they need to take a few notes of their own. If the note-taker focuses on capturing, as closely as possible, what the interviewee stated, then your notes may just be phrases to help you keep the interview moving, or one or two words to jog your memory about a follow-up question to the interviewee's current response. Try to avoid writing word for word what the interviewee is saying. A good listener should be intent on listening, and not writing feverishly while the person is talking.

Tip 3-12: Explain your interview style

Assuming you do not have a note-taker and are not recording the interview, you might explain your style, "I'm not very good at multi-tasking; that is, I'm not listening effectively if I'm writing. What you have to share with me is important so I'm letting you know that I'll ask a question or two, listen to your response, and then I'll need to pause to take notes."

This is a positive way to say that you prefer to devote your whole attention to what the interviewee is saying. It makes the interviewee feel more important!

---

(2) **Stay on track**. Your primary goal in the interview is to maximize the quality and quantity of information in the allotted time. Use your agenda as a visual aid, as well as your prepared list of questions to maintain control of the discussion. This can be quite a balancing act as you ask "elaboration" type questions, and allow the interviewee to answer fully. If you have an interviewee who tends to stray from the questions or "builds a clock" when asked for the time, you'll want to remain courteous and cajole the interviewee back on track.

Here are some example phrases or questions you might use to keep the interview moving. Notice that these are "close-ended" questions, as they are intended to be a checkpoint in the discussion, and won't encourage the interviewee to continue to elaborate.

♦ "In order for us to keep within our allotted time, may I move on to the next question?"

♦ "Is this a topic that is more important than the others, or should we continue to the next topic?"

♦ "Did we capture the key points on this topic? May we go forward?"

♦ "We've spent about 10 minutes on this topic. Should we continue discussing this topic or continue to the next topic?"

Tip 3-13: Make phone interviews "visual"

The face-to-face interview is always preferred. You cannot maintain eye contact or observe body language while conducting a telephone interview.

However, when face-to-face interviews are not feasible, sharp listening skills and your list of prepared questions will still enable you to conduct a highly effective interview. Keep the interviewee visually engaged by referencing the agenda, "Looking at our agenda, let's move on to Question 3."

♦ "May we go to the next question, and come back to this topic if we have time at the end?"

(3) **Pay attention**. I recommend using the following guidelines for maintaining good rapport throughout the interview, and to monitor the interview process.

♦ **Use the person's name**. People want to be recognized, and there's no better way to do it than to use their names. And, occasionally, in between questions, you can thank the interviewee for his or her answers. For example, "Thank you, James, my next question is…"

♦ **Maintain good eye contact** with the interviewee. This increases active listening, which we'll discuss in more detail in the next section.

♦ **Use one-word responses or short phrases** to indicate that you are listening. You might say something like, "Yes," "I see," "Go on," "Okay," or "Great." Take care not to overdo it, especially if you think the interviewee might begin to feel this is a deliberate tactic on your part. You don't want to become repetitive or annoying.

♦ **Observe the interviewee's body language**. Look for signs of fatigue, distraction, indifference, irritation, agitation, or discomfort. Look for any kind of unhappiness, really. Also use the metaquestion approach to help gauge how the interview is proceeding. End the interview and reschedule, if necessary.

♦ **Respect the interviewee's personal space**. Ideally you want to sit approximately four feet or less from the interviewee. Sitting across a table is good for note taking; just be sure that the table doesn't put too much space between you. Personally, I prefer sitting "a corner" away: if the interviewee sits on one side, I'll tend to sit at one end. Then the table doesn't appear to be a barrier. We're not on opposing sides!

◆ **Maintain good posture.** Be aware of your own body language. You should sit facing your interviewee. Your arms and legs should be uncrossed to give an "open" and receptive expression. A simple gesture, such as a nod, can also indicate to the interviewee that you are listening. Sitting in your seat with a straight posture or a slight lean forward also indicates you are interested in what the interviewee is saying.

Tip 3-14: Maintain an active listening posture

To open your body language, try sitting forward on the chair seat so that your back is not against the seat back. Adjust the seat height so that your hips are slightly lower than your knees. Sit with both feet flat on the floor. This will help you maintain your balance and your posture. Your upper torso will naturally lean forward to also maintain your balance. This open body language gives interviewees the impression that you are truly interested in what they have to say, which, of course, you are. Right? I repeat, right?

3.3.2 *STAR—TQLR, An Active Listening Strategy*

One of the biggest mistakes you can make as an interviewer is to "reload," that is, formulate the next question or response in your mind, instead of truly listening to what the interviewee is saying. I recommend using the **TQLR**—Tune in, Question, Listen, and Review—strategy for active listening. The **TQLR** strategy has been around for many years, but its origin is uncertain. (Perhaps no one was taking adequate notes in the meeting at which it was devised!)

(1) TUNE IN. This means getting ready to listen, and giving the interviewee your full attention. During your preparations for the interview, you selected a time and place that minimized distractions for both the interviewee and yourself. You must also get mentally psyched up to listen to your interviewee—but don't take deep breaths as if warming up for a boxing match.

(2) QUESTION. Ask yourself questions while you are listening. This is not you thinking about what your next question will be because you have already prepared your list of questions. Rather, your job as a good listener is to identify the main ideas or points that the interviewee is making. In other words, question your comprehension of what is being presented to you. Here are some good questions to ask yourself while you are listening:

- ♦ What is the purpose of what I am listening to? (To give me directions? To give me information? To give me examples?)

- ♦ What is new in what I am hearing? Is it important? Do I need to remember it? Do I need to ask follow-up questions to get more information?

(3) LISTEN. Listen to get answers to your questions. Listen for clues or phrases that help you predict what is coming. Here are some example phrases:

- ♦ "There are three reasons why …" (Expect to hear three items).

- ♦ "First … Second … Third …" (There they are).

- ♦ "And most important …" (Here comes a main point).

- ♦ "Also …" (Here comes something similar).

- ♦ "Remember that …" (This is probably important).

- ♦ "Et cetera." Or "And so on." There is more that the interviewee is not telling you. Be alert and perk up whenever you hear "et cetera" or equivalents, because it might mean the interviewee should have given you an exhaustive list, but didn't.

(4) REVIEW. This is your ability to recall what was said. When you hear something important, repeat it to yourself immediately. Say it in your own words. Write it down in short form so you can relay what you understood. Rephrase your understanding back to the interviewee for confirmation of accuracy. For example:

You ask, "What are the four steps to process a payment?"
"Well," the interviewee says as he or she begins the response, "the first thing I do is ..."
And, then continues with, "Next I do this ... Then this ... Then this ... Next this ... And finally this ..."

Applying the **Q** (Question) and the **L** (Listen) from the **TQLR** listening strategy, what the interviewee is telling you sounds as if there are more than four steps. You need to confirm what you understood; this is not the same as simply repeating what you heard.

You ask for confirmation by saying, "Let me summarize what I understood to be the four steps to processing a payment. First, you do ..."
"Yes, that is correct," the interviewee affirms.

Restate each step and wait for the interviewee to affirm the accuracy.

3.3.3 *STAR—Ask Questions*

Use your list of prepared questions to navigate your interviewee through the interview. Remember that your prepared list is a guide and typically will not be used verbatim during the interview. Based on some of the answers the interviewee gives, you may want to skip some questions on your prepared list, or you may want to ask an additional set of questions. In addition, you will need to ask follow-up questions to probe further, or ask clarifying questions to reduce communication errors.

3.3.3.1 FOLLOW-UP QUESTIONS

Earlier in this chapter, I described various types of questions to ask such as open-ended, elaboration, and laddering. Follow-up questions are the questions you ask as a result of a response to a previously asked question. The intent of the follow-up question is to probe for additional information, or to raise or lower the level of detailed information in the response.

Tip 3-15: Schedule the interview at the right time

Due to the level of concentration that is required to actively listen, don't schedule more than three or four interviews in a normal 8-hour work day. Try not to exceed 60 minutes per interview.

If you have several interviews to conduct in a short period, I recommend staggering the days you interview. For example, schedule three interviews per day on Tuesday and Thursday. Schedule no interviews on Wednesday and Friday so that you have time to review and analyze your notes within 24 hours of the interview. The sooner you review the notes and write down your thoughts regarding any follow-up questions you may need to ask, the better. (Mondays are reserved for last-minute preparations for Tuesday's and Thursday's interviews.)

Apply the **TQLR** strategy described in the previous section, and "listen" for clues or phrases that indicate that you should ask follow-up questions. Here are some good clues to listen for and corresponding follow-up questions to ask:

- **Response**: "I don't know." Or "I'm not sure."
  Follow-up: "Who else should I ask about this? Is this outside your area of responsibility?"

- **Response**: "Yes" or "No," or vague answers.
  Follow-up: Ask open-ended questions and/or elaboration questions.

- **Response**: Technology-oriented terminology is used. It may be an indication that the interviewee is telling you "how" to design the product.
  Follow-up: "Why does the user need that screen?" "Is this a solution constraint? What is it based on?"

- **Response**: Ambiguous answers or unfamiliar terminology.
  Follow-up: "What do you mean by that? Could you please define that term?" Or

you could ask for a source where specialist terminology is defined—especially if you're encountering more than a few new terms. You don't want to exhaust all of your interview time asking for definitions. Furthermore, a written source is likely to give you better formal definitions than an interviewee.

> ## Tip 3-16: Ask follow-up questions
>
> Don't be afraid to ask follow-up questions or clarifying questions in order to better understand the interviewee. Your responsibility is to elicit accurate and complete information. Believe me, when the wrong product is delivered, the client or project sponsor won't mind asking questions!

3.3.3.2 CLARIFYING QUESTIONS

You must be sensitive to communication errors, and be listening for errors throughout the interview. Here are some common communication errors to listen for:

♦ **Observational.** People perceive things differently.

♦ **Recall.** Memory is fallible—and usually self-serving.

♦ **Interpretation or ambiguity.** Listen for words such as "small," "special," and "normal." Do you have the same understanding of what the words mean? How will you know unless you ask?

♦ **Contradictions.** The information given contradicts with previously provided information, either from the current interviewee or by a previous interviewee.

♦ **Facts.** You'll want to validate any facts that the interviewee gives. Generally, this is accomplished by talking to another subject matter expert about the same topic area or asking the same series of questions. Use the relative importance or significance of the information as a guideline for validating facts. The higher the importance, the more you need to validate the facts as true.

Tip 3-17: Save time—don't type up interview notes

Save yourself the time and hassle of typing up the notes taken during the interview, and sending the notes to the interviewee for confirmation of the accuracy. That is, more often than not, I find that typing up the notes and trying to get the interviewee to read them and respond, to be a waste of time.

My experience has shown that if you do a good job reviewing (refer to the TQLR explanation in Section 3.3.2), then the accuracy of the information gathered is confirmed before you leave the interview. As much as 50 percent of the information gathered in an interview never translates to requirements.

As described in Chapter 1, "Requirements in Context," requirements development is the process of eliciting, analyzing, representing, and validating the information. The interview is an elicitation activity. During requirements analysis the information is combined with other gathered information, and conflicts are identified and resolved. Therefore, the accuracy of the "requirements" derived from an interview should be confirmed during the requirements validation activity.

Moreover, I have seen design and coding begin based on information presented in interview notes (prior to validation and approval). And, you can guess what happened. That's right—rework!

3.3.4 STAR—Recap and Wrap-up

The interview generally comes to a close when all the questions have been asked and answered, or when the allotted time has passed. However, that isn't the end just yet. As they say, "It's not over, well, until it's over!" As you bring the interview to a close, it is important to leave the interviewee informed of what will happen next. These wrap-up activities can take as much as ten minutes (or more). Plan for adequate time at the end of the interview, and set a realistic length of time to conduct the interview including the activities to open and close the interview.

I use the following general steps to bring closure to the interview:

Step 1: Summarize the information that was elicited. This helps to confirm to the interviewee that you understood what he or she told you.

Step 2: Discuss and assign any unanswered questions that arose during the interview. The purpose here is not to discuss how to resolve the issues, but to make sure that you've accurately identified the issues. Once you have identified the issues, assign each one for resolution. Agree on the individual who will take responsibility for researching or resolving the issue, and set a target resolution date (be specific and realistic). If necessary, discuss any potential obstacles to meeting the target resolution date.

Step 3: Solicit and answer the interviewee's questions about the interview.

Step 4: Discuss the next steps (allot about three to five minutes for this). This is your chance to educate your business expert, sponsor, or user on the requirements process. The interview is a technique used in the elicitation stage, and is just the beginning of the iterative requirements management process. You'll want to analyze the information gathered in the interview, and integrate the new information with information that was previously received. The information then has to be documented and validated by the stakeholders.

Step 5: Evaluate the interview process. Identify ways in which you may improve it.

Step 6: Thank the interviewee!

Tip 3-18: Say "thank you!"

"Thank you" goes a long way in building rapport with stakeholders. Besides, it just makes people feel better.

On a side note, I usually receive better service in a restaurant by thanking the server. For example, I might say, "Please, when you have a moment, I'd like another napkin, thank you." If you use the server's name, the service usually is even better. Try it!

3.4 CHAPTER SUMMARY

♦ Interviewing stakeholders is certainly not the only source for requirements; it just happens to be a commonly used elicitation technique.

♦ I know there are people, and you might just know some of them, who do not believe in taking the time to prepare for any sort of interview (even a job interview). I challenge them to compare the time it takes to prepare well for a requirements-gathering interview, as opposed to the time spent fixing problems with the system due to missed or poorly defined requirements. Get my point? As Nike® says, "Just do it."

♦ Interviewing is very much a social skill that requires practice to master. Good listening skills are an essential element to being really effective.

3.5 SUGGESTED READING

Exploring Requirements: Quality Before Design, by Donald Gause and Gerald Weinberg, [Gause, 1989]. **Context-free questions** are explored in Chapter 6, while "the tried but untrue use of **direct questions**" is described in Chapter 4.

Requirements by Collaboration: Workshops for Defining Needs, by Ellen Gottesdiener, [Gottesdiener, 2002]. This book dives into the **facilitated workshop** elicitation technique. It is a wonderful alternative to the one-on-one interview, as it is known to significantly reduce the requirements-gathering time.

Writing Better Requirements, by Ian F. Alexander and Richard Stevens, [Alexander, 2002]. Chapter 3 describes techniques for gathering requirements from stakeholders such as **interviews**, workshops, experiencing life as a user, observing users at work, acting out what needs to happen and prototypes. Additionally, Chapter 4 identifies **other sources of requirements**.

It is better to ask *a few* well-thought-out questions, than *a lot* of questions without thinking.

PART TWO

PART TWO: RIGHT APPROACH, RIGHT QUESTIONS

Part One establishes a foundation of software requirements terminology and context. It also provides step-by-step guidelines for building a stakeholder profile (Chapter 2, "Involve the Right Stakeholders") and conducting an outstanding requirements-gathering interview (Chapter 3, "Interviewing Tips and Tools"). This foundation sets you up for success in applying what you're about to learn here in Part Two.

Part Two is comprised of four chapters that define nonfunctional requirements and offer over **2,000 suggested elicitation questions**.

Chapter 4, "Understanding Nonfunctional Requirements," provides an in-depth definition of nonfunctional requirements, and explains why these critical requirements are so difficult. It provides a user-focused classification for 14 common nonfunctional requirement categories, which are comprised in three groups.

Chapters 5 through 7 provide definitions, example requirements, suggested elicitation questions, and suggested reading for each nonfunctional category shown in Table II-A.

Table II-A A User-focused Classification of Nonfunctional Requirements

User Needs	User Concerns	Nonfunctional Categories
Chapter 5 Operation Requirements	How well is it guarded against unauthorized access?	Access Security (ACS)
	How dependable is it during normal operating times?	Availability (AVL)
	How fast, how many, and how well does it respond?	Efficiency (EFC)
	How accurate and authentic are the data?	Integrity (INT)
	How immune is the system to failure?	Reliability (REL)
	How resilient is the system from failure?	Survivability (SRV)
	How easy is it to learn and operate the system?	Usability (USE)
Chapter 6 Revision Requirements	How easy is it to modify to work in different environments?	Flexibility (FLX)
	How easy is it to upkeep and repair?	Maintainability (MNT)
	How easy is it to expand or upgrade its capabilities?	Scalability (SCL)
	How easy is it to show it performs its functions?	Verifiability (VER)
Chapter 7 Transition Requirements	How easy is it to interface with another system?	Interoperability (IOP)
	How easy is it to transport?	Portability (POR)
	How easy is it to convert for use in another system?	Reusability (REU)

THE ANATOMY OF A NONFUNCTIONAL REQUIREMENT CATEGORY

This section describes the presentation layout of each nonfunctional category included in chapters 5 through 7. As shown below and in Figure II-B, each nonfunctional category consists of the following components:

(a) **Nonfunctional Category Name.** Each category is named.

(b) **User Concern Short Description.** A brief question is used to identify a general concern that users have regarding the software system.

(c) **Related Categories.** What is the relationship of this particular nonfunctional category to other categories? What other categories might influence this category? If changes are made to this requirement category, what other categories might be affected?

(d) **Category Definition.** Each nonfunctional category is defined.

(e) **Category Discussion.** The nature of the nonfunctional category is described along with further information to clarify the category.

(f) **Category Examples.** Real-world requirement statements are provided to illustrate requirements derived from the requirements-gathering activities.

(g) **Category Suggested Questions.** A list of suggested questions is divided by a requirement framework (refer to Chapter 1, "Requirements in Context") or interest areas as follows:

- ♦ DATA—**What** information is used within the system?

- ♦ ROLES—**Who** (user roles) provides and/or receives information in performing these business functions?

- ♦ PURPOSE—**Why** is the information necessary? What is the business rationale or strategy?

- ♦ TIMING—**When** is the information used?

- ◆ LOGISTICS—**Where** is the information used?

- ◆ PROCESS—**How** is the information used?
  Is there a process or procedure that drives usage?

Within each requirement interest area, the questions are further subdivided by perspective or view. That is, who are you asking—requirements supplier or requirements receiver?

Additionally, each question is numbered with a unique identifier for ease of reference. Each category is assigned a three-character abbreviation, for example, **EFC** is assigned to Efficiency. Questions intended for requirements suppliers have an **S** following the question ID, for example **EFC28S**. Questions intended for requirements receivers have an **R** following the question ID, for example **EFC35R**. If a question might be used for requirements suppliers and receivers, the question ID is followed with a **B** (both), for example **EFC37B**.

Finally, each individual question is followed by an explanation of the target or intent of the question for further understanding of the question and why it might be asked. These are placed along the right-hand margin under the label **Ask this to:**.

This book describes common categories of nonfunctional requirements that apply to software systems. Your organization might determine that additional categories are necessary based on the particular products and services offered. The components of the above "anatomy of a nonfunctional category" might serve as a pattern for developing and defining additional nonfunctional categories (a comprehensive list of nonfunctional types is included in Chapter 4, "Understanding Nonfunctional Requirements").

Figure II-B Example: Anatomy of a Nonfunctional Category

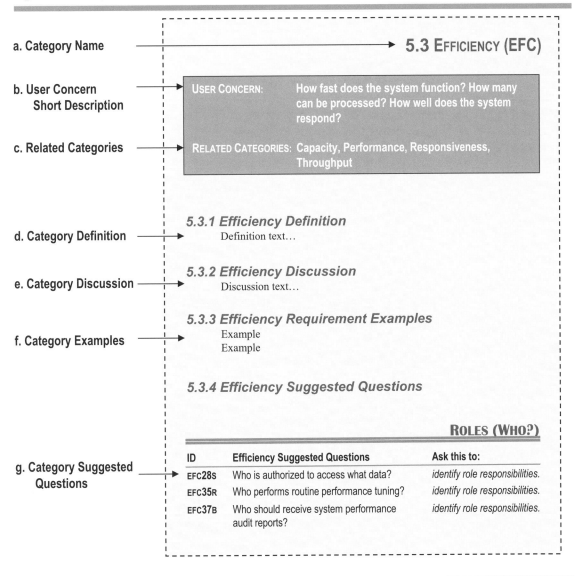

a. Category Name → 5.3 EFFICIENCY (EFC)

b. User Concern Short Description → USER CONCERN: How fast does the system function? How many can be processed? How well does the system respond?

c. Related Categories → RELATED CATEGORIES: Capacity, Performance, Responsiveness, Throughput

d. Category Definition → **5.3.1 Efficiency Definition**
Definition text…

e. Category Discussion → **5.3.2 Efficiency Discussion**
Discussion text…

f. Category Examples → **5.3.3 Efficiency Requirement Examples**
Example
Example

5.3.4 Efficiency Suggested Questions

ROLES (WHO?)

g. Category Suggested Questions →

ID	Efficiency Suggested Questions	Ask this to:
EFC28S	Who is authorized to access what data?	*identify role responsibilities.*
EFC35R	Who performs routine performance tuning?	*identify role responsibilities.*
EFC37B	Who should receive system performance audit reports?	*identify role responsibilities.*

HOW TO USE THE SUGGESTED QUESTIONS

This book offers questions that might be asked. The collective set of questions is certainly not an exhaustive or all-inclusive list. The following steps are intended to provide guidance for helping you organize the questions you choose to ask.

Step 1: Where are you in the process?

Questions should be chosen based on the iterative process of eliciting requirements and the level of detailed information already known (business, user, or system), as well as the level of detail being sought. Nonfunctional requirements are generally explored in the development of system level requirements as described in Chapter 1, "Requirements in Context." It is important to note that in many of the possible questions, the term system is used interchangeably to reference a business process or sub-process that is automated by a software system or software application, or to a product that relies on a software component to operate.

Step 2: Who are your stakeholders?

You must consider the requirements role (supplier or receiver) when deciding which questions to ask. You'll find that some questions are repeated from one stakeholder to another. Although it is possible to find one person who can effectively answer all the questions, don't count on it—besides, two heads are better than one. Get to know the stakeholders. Chapter 2, "Involve the Right Stakeholders," guides you through a technique that helps to identify the knowledge expertise of individual stakeholders, as well as uncover business areas and topics that need stakeholder representation. The stakeholder profiling technique explained in Chapter 2 will help you get the right stakeholders engaged.

Step 3: What nonfunctional categories are relevant to your project?

Chapter 4, "Understanding Nonfunctional Requirements," introduces the 14 common categories of nonfunctional requirements, while chapters 5 through 7 provide definitions, examples, and suggested questions.

Step 4: What are your success criteria?

It is highly unlikely that you will ask all of the questions in this book for a given project effort. Each individual question is followed by a brief explanation of the target or intent of the question. Review these explanations to help you select questions based on what you're trying to accomplish. Furthermore, some questions are very similar, and depending on the perspective of the stakeholder and the requirements focus, you might choose one question over another. However, you might intentionally ask similar questions because you anticipate a varied response. Chapter 3, "Interviewing Tips and Tools," explains that slight changes in the wording of a question can significantly alter the interpretation of the question.

Step 5: Prepare your list of questions.

You are encouraged to rewrite the questions and put them in your own words. Chapter 3, "Interviewing Tips and Tools," guides you through effective preparation activities and describes how to conduct a successful interview.

Step 6: Follow your game plan.

Ask your list of prepared questions (explained in Chapter 3).

Step 7: Anticipate follow-up questions.

Apply an active listening strategy (explained in Chapter 3), and ask questions to probe further into the response to your original question. Rephrase the response and ask questions to both clarify and confirm that you understand the response you get.

A nonfunctional requirement
is a specification of how well
a software system
must function.

4 UNDERSTANDING NONFUNCTIONAL REQUIREMENTS

This chapter is intended to help you understand the challenges of hard-to-identify nonfunctional requirements. We'll take a look at problems with definitions of the term *nonfunctional*, as well as factors that contribute to difficulties in understanding these requirements. Additionally, we'll examine various industry efforts to classify nonfunctional requirements. Finally, we'll define the user-focused classification scheme chosen for this book.

Over years of mentoring and coaching on business analysis and requirements management practices, I have repeatedly found that people struggled in formulating nonfunctional requirements. When asked to review a requirements specification (please refer to Figure 1-10 in Chapter 1), I found the functional requirements section to be quite lengthy (not necessarily a metric of quality, mind you), while the nonfunctional requirements section was, far too often, empty.

This book is my personal quest to help people understand these overlooked nonfunctional requirements. My experience has shown that an increased knowledge leads to people asking more questions that elicit nonfunctional requirements. This generally results in a significant reduction in missed requirements. The goal is to define *better requirements* (helping project teams identify requirements that they otherwise wouldn't have), which contribute to *better systems*.

Get the Users "IN" the Doghouse and Keep Yourself "OUT."

The Quest for Software Requirements

4.1 ARE THE DEFINITIONS DYSFUNCTIONAL?

The complexity of software systems is due partly to its functionality, and partly to its nonfunctionality. For the time being, let's simply define functionality as what the system must do and nonfunctionality as how well the system must do it.

We know that functional requirements are important. Try leaving out necessary functions and see how long it takes for users and others to complain. There are many good books that adequately explain functional requirements including definitions, examples, and guidance on how to elicit, analyze, represent, and validate them. In other words, a fair amount of coverage in literature has been given to system functionality. Therefore, I only briefly incorporated functional requirements in this book because of their integrated relationship to nonfunctional requirements.

Let's begin with reference to a variety of definitions for functional and nonfunctional requirements from well-known and respected sources for comparison purposes. Although functional definitions are included, the focus of this book is on defining nonfunctional requirements. Additionally, keep in mind that all of the referenced definitions are within the terminology and scope of software requirements (refer to Chapter 1, "Requirements in Context," for an overview of software requirements terminology).

4.1.1 A Variety of Definitions

Only five definition sources were selected, shown in Table 4-1 on the next page, and used in my comparative analysis to derive the definition I use henceforth in the context of this book. Some sources were left out, frankly because I didn't agree with them. I struggle with so-called definitions that don't actually define the term but just provide examples.

I won't even provide the source for my least favorite definition: "A nonfunctional requirement is anything that is not functional." Are you kidding me? How do you take a source seriously with a definition like that?

Table 4-1 Definitions for Functional and Nonfunctional Requirements

"*Functional requirement*—A system/software requirement that specifies a function that a system/software system or system/software component must be capable of performing. These are software requirements that define behavior of the system, that is, the fundamental process or transformation that software and hardware components of the system perform on inputs to produce outputs." [Thayer, 2000]	"*Nonfunctional requirement*—in software system engineering, a software requirement that describes not what the software will do, but how the software will do it, for example, software performance requirements, software external interface requirements, software design constraints, and software quality attributes. Nonfunctional requirements are difficult to test; therefore, they are usually evaluated subjectively." [Thayer, 2000]
"*Functional requirements*—These are statements of services the system should provide, how the system should react to particular inputs and how the system should behave in particular situations. In some cases, the functional requirements may also explicitly state what the system should not do." [Sommerville, 2007]	"*Non-functional requirements*—These are constraints on the services or functions offered by the system. They include timing constraints, constraints on the development process and standards. Non-functional requirements often apply to the system as a whole. They do not usually just apply to individual system features or services." [Sommerville, 2007]
"*Functional requirement*—Something that the product must do. Functional requirements are part of the fundamental processes of the product." [Robertson, 1999]	"*Non-functional requirement*—A property, or quality, that the product must have, such as an appearance, or a speed or accuracy property." [Robertson, 1999]
"*Functional requirement*—A statement of a piece of required functionality or a behavior that a system will exhibit under specific conditions." [Wiegers, 2003]	"*Nonfunctional requirement*—A description of a property or characteristic that a software system must exhibit or a constraint that it must respect, other than an observable system behavior." [Wiegers, 2003]
"*Behavioral requirements*—Those requirements that specify the inputs (stimuli) to the system, the outputs (responses) from the system, and behavioral relationships between them; also called functional or operational requirements." [Davis, 1993]	"*Nonbehavioral requirements*—Requirements that describe the required overall attributes of the system, including portability, reliability, efficiency, human engineering, testability, understandability, and modifiability." [Davis, 1993]

At any rate, my comparison analysis of the definitions is explained in Section 4.1.3, "A Simplified Definition." Before jumping ahead, I challenge you to spend a few minutes analyzing these definitions yourself.

For the sake of avoiding an argument, let's assume that there are some good definitions. However, as the example definition illustrates, there are some not-so-good ones. Let's consider the latter in the next section. (Besides, the scenic route heightens the suspense of revealing my "simplified definition.")

4.1.2 A Wrong Definition?

In a conversation with Stephen Withall, author of *Software Requirement Patterns* [Withall, 2007], Withall pointed out that it seems we insist on separating the system-level requirements into two buckets as pictured in Figure 4-1 (system-level requirements are explained in Chapter 1, "Requirements in Context"). Based on quantity, there are typically many more functional requirements than nonfunctional, which is why the functional bucket is larger.

Figure 4-1 System-Level Requirement Buckets

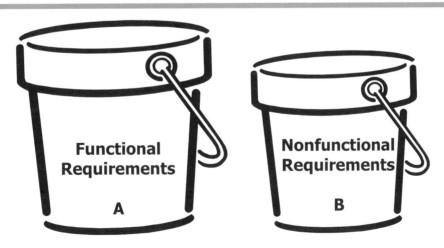

Withall further hypothesized that if we define functional requirements (Bucket A) as *what the system must do*, then one logical definition for nonfunctional requirements (Bucket B) could be *what the system should not do*. Thus, the term "nonfunctional" makes perfect sense, right? Wrong!

It is important to identify that nonfunctional requirements are NOT:

- **The opposite of functional requirements** (un-functional). This line of thinking didn't work so well in the soft drink industry for 7UP® as the "Un-cola."

- **The definition of a system that fails to function,** which ironically is the meaning of the word *dysfunctional*. I don't think this is the direction intended.

- **The end-all, catch-all of whatever doesn't fit the definition of functional requirements.** That is, if it doesn't belong in Bucket A, then it automatically defaults into Bucket B. Thus before long, Bucket B becomes the scary, elusive, black hole! With an image like this one, it is no wonder that project teams fail to adequately include these important aspects of the software system.

Theoretically (in reality?), let's say there are *only* two buckets. Everything defined as "functional" naturally falls into the first bucket (Bucket A). Some would argue that the only clean, pure, and infallible definition of "nonfunctional" is *everything that's not in the functional bucket*. The very fact that the name of the second bucket is "nonfunctional" is a strong indication that *all things that aren't functional requirements* are, indeed, what the bucket contains. This might explain why we see many definitions for nonfunctional requirements resorting to mentioning the name of the first bucket—as if that's their way of making sure there's nothing left over.

Now suppose the second bucket was wrongly labeled or horribly misnamed. (Gasp!) Did you know that for a long, long time, people believed that our planet was flat? What if there are really more than two buckets at the system requirements level? Is it possible that we could prove the theory of "nonfunctional" requirements to be false? Maybe, just maybe mind you, we discover there are at least four requirement buckets: functional, operation, revision, and transition. We'll explore these possibilities in sections 4.4, "Classification Efforts," and 4.5, "A User-Focused Approach."

Let's face the reality of current nonfunctional definitions. This next section unveils my simplified definition.

4.1.3 A Simplified Definition

Let's start by analyzing the nonfunctional definitions included in Table 4-1 on page 100. First, we'll remove the following elements (with the remaining text shown in Table 4-2 on the following page):

- "Nonfunctional requirement" (or other similar reference) from the beginning of each definition simply to cut down on the words.

- "Examples" of nonfunctional requirements.

- "Descriptive" information about nonfunctional requirements that don't add to the definition.

- Inclusion or reference to "functional requirements."

From the remaining text, we can extract words that are common across the definitions. This reveals three words that are used to identify the subject of the definition: *software, system*, and *product*. In reviewing the definitions behind these words, I interpret the terms as interchangeable and I prefer the term *system*.

Upon further analysis of the scaled-down versions, we can identify three additional words that are used to *describe* the subject (system): constraint, quality, and attribute. Naturally, I had to dig up definitions of these terms. Unfortunately, the definitions added little or no value. The more I dug for answers and depth of understanding, the more I felt like I was just digging a deeper and wider hole. Needless to say, I was frustrated. And, in this discouraged state, I began to ponder: if experts and industry organizations come up with definitions as confusing as these, is it any wonder that the less-expert of us write poor requirement specifications? Don't dismay; help is on the way.

Table 4-2 Scaled-down Nonfunctional Definitions

Original Definition	Scaled-down Version
"*Nonfunctional requirement*—in software system engineering, a software requirement that describes not what the software will do, but how the software will do it, for example, software performance requirements, software external interface requirements, software design constraints, and software quality attributes. Nonfunctional requirements are difficult to test; therefore, they are usually evaluated subjectively." [Thayer, 2000]	… how the **software** will do it.
"*Non-functional requirements*—These are constraints on the services or functions offered by the system. They include timing constraints, constraints on the development process and standards. Non-functional requirements often apply to the system as a whole. They do not usually just apply to individual system features or services." [Sommerville, 2007]	… **constraints** on the services or functions offered by the **system**.
"*Non-functional requirement*—A property, or quality, that the product must have, such as an appearance, or a speed or accuracy property." [Robertson, 1999]	… **property** or **quality** that the **product** must have
"*Nonfunctional requirement*—A description of a property or characteristic that a software system must exhibit or a constraint that it must respect, other than an observable system behavior." [Wiegers, 2003]	… **property** or characteristic that a **software system** must exhibit or **constraint** that it must respect
"*Nonbehavioral requirements*—Requirements that describe the required overall attributes of the system, including portability, reliability, efficiency, human engineering, testability, understandability, and modifiability." [Davis, 1993]	… required overall **attributes** of the **system**.

At the conclusion of my extensive analysis, I derived the following simplified definition for use in the context of this book:

> A nonfunctional requirement
> is a specification of how well
> a software system
> must function.

Alas! Now that we have a clear definition, all of our problems have disappeared—unfortunately, not. Moving right along … Let's look at the difficulties of eliciting nonfunctional requirements.

4.2 NONFUNCTIONAL CHALLENGES

Perhaps surprisingly, nonfunctional requirements have received far too little attention in software engineering literature. They are certainly less well understood compared to other factors in the development and selection of high quality systems. Inconsistent terminology, confusing definitions (as seen in the previous section), and the absence of a universally accepted classification scheme make understanding nonfunctional requirements a challenge.

The term "nonfunctional" has been disliked by many people in the software requirements industry—most especially by me—for a long time. This may be due in part by a misperception of the term itself. People often correlate negation—for example, words in the English language such as "no," "not," "non-," and "none"—with importance, or the lack thereof, as is often the perception with the term nonfunctional.

In addition to alternative names such as *quality attributes*, *quality requirements*, and *nonbehavioral requirements*, nonfunctional requirements also have been referred to by nicknames such as "*ilities*" and "*ities*." These nicknames are derived from descriptors that end in the suffix "-ility," such as portability, reliability, usability, and survivability. Nonfunctional requirements are commonly characterized by adjectives, while functional requirements are characterized by verbs, according to Suzanne and James Robertson [Robertson, 2006].

No doubt also stemming from inconsistent terminology and confusing definitions, we cannot agree on how to spell these important requirements. Is it "non-functional" or "nonfunctional" (with or without a hyphen)? This may be quite trivial to many, but it is still an indication of the lack of uniformity. I prefer spelling the term without the hyphen. And, for what it's worth, so does *Webster's Dictionary*! However, there are specific references throughout the book where I use the hyphenated spelling—this is only done out of respect for the other author. Within your organization, I recommend choosing one and being consistent in using it.

Without a uniform classification, a possible starting point for eliciting nonfunctional requirements might be an "overwhelmability" list of nonfunctional types, such as Table 4-3 on the following page. It is highly unlikely, however, that all of these types will apply to your particular project and your specific organization. This is due to the subjective and relative nature of nonfunctional requirements (explained in Section 4.3). Quite honestly, working from an overwhelming list such as this would not exactly make me eager to focus on nonfunctional requirements!

In conclusion, the significance of the term name and how it is spelled pale in comparison to a consistent definition of what the term means. Let's turn our attention to understanding more about the nature of nonfunctional requirements that make them difficult to identify.

4.3 VITAL, YET WHY SO DIFFICULT?

> Errors of omission or failing to properly account for
> nonfunctional requirements are generally acknowledged
> to be among the most expensive errors and the most difficult
> to correct following the implementation of a software system.

Nonfunctional requirements are vital to the success of software systems. If nonfunctional requirements are not properly addressed, undesirable results occur such as unsatisfied users, developers, and clients, and schedule and budget overruns to correct the software that was developed without the nonfunctional requirements in mind.

Table 4-3 Overwhelmability List of Nonfunctional Types (based on [Chung, 2000])

Absorbability	Confidentiality	Guidance	Planning Cost	Space Boundedness
Access Control	Configurability	Human Engineering	Planning Time	Space Performance
Accessibility	Connectivity	Impact Analyzability	Plasticity	Specificity
Accountability	Consistency	Implementability	Portability	Stability
Accuracy	Controllability	Independence	Precision	Standardizability
Adaptability	Coordination Cost	Informativeness	Predictability	Storability
Additivity	Coordination Time	Inspection Cost	Process Management Time	Structuredness
Adjustability	Correctness	Inspection Time	Productivity	Subjectivity
Affordability	Coupling	Installability	Project Stability	Supportability
Agility	Customer Evaluation Time	Integrity	Project Tracking Cost	Surety
Appealability	Customer Loyalty	Interchangeability	Promptness	Survivability
Attractiveness	Customizability	Internal Consistency	Prototyping Cost	Susceptibility
Auditability	Data Space Performance	Interoperability	Prototyping Time	Sustainability
Augmentability	Decomposability	Intuitiveness	Quality	Tankness
Authenticity	Degradation of Service	Iterativeness	Quantitativeness	Testability
Autonomy	Deliverability	Learnability	Readability	Testing Time
Availability	Dependability	Legibility	Readiness	Throughput
Buffer Space Performance	Development Cost	Leveragability	Reconfigurability	Timeliness
Capability	Development Time	Likeability	Recoverability	Toleranceness
Capacity	Disposability	Main Memory Performance	Recovery	Traceability
Changeability	Distributivity	Maintainability	Recyclability	Trainability
Clarity	Diversity	Maintenance Cost	Reengineering Cost	Transferability
Cleanability	Domain Analysis Cost	Maintenance Time	Reliability	Transitionability
Cleanliness	Domain Analysis Time	Manageability	Repeatability	Transparency
Code Space Performance	Duplicatability	Maneuverability	Replaceability	Understandability
Cohesiveness	Ease of use	Maturity	Replicability	Uniform Performance
Commonality	Efficiency	Mean Performance	Response Time	Uniformity
Communication Cost	Elasticity	Measurability	Responsiveness	Unparochialness
Communication Time	Enhanceability	Migratability	Retirement Cost	Usability
Communicativeness	Evolvability	Mobility	Reusability	User-friendliness
Comparability	Execution Cost	Modifiability	Risk Analysis Cost	Validity
Compatibility	Expandability	Modularity	Risk Analysis Time	Variability
Completeness	Expendability	Multiness	Robustness	Verifiability
Component Integration Cost	Extendibility	Naturalness	Safety	Versatility
Component Integration Time	Extensibility	Nomadicity	Scalability	Versionability
	External Consistency	Observability	Security	Visibility
Composability	Fault-Tolerance	Off-Peak-Period Perform-	Self-containedness	Volatility
Comprehensibility	Feasibility	ance	Self-descriptiveness	Wrappability
Computability	Flexibility	Operability	Sensitivity	Workability
Conceptuality	Foolproof-ability	Operating Cost	Similarity	Zero-defectness
Conciseness	Formality	Peak Period Performance	Simplicity	
	Generality	Performability	Software Cost	

There are numerous contributing factors or reasons that the nonfunctional requirements are difficult to identify. Three major factors that influence the complex nature of nonfunctional requirements are as follows:

(1) SUBJECTIVE. They can be viewed, interpreted, and evaluated differently from user to user. For instance, one user contends that a two-second response time is acceptable, while another user feels that a sub-second response time is necessary. Similarly, what is deemed "easy to learn" by one user may not be evaluated as such by another, less-experienced user.

(2) RELATIVE. The interpretation of relevance and importance might vary depending on the specific system under consideration, as well as the products and services produced by a business. For example, organizations in the financial industry such as banks and insurance companies are likely to view precision, accuracy of information, and access control (security) of the confidential information as prominent quality attributes. Manufacturing organizations that use software to help make their products typically emphasize safety as an attribute to prevent employee accidents. On a different track, a software system developed for a one-time-use project such as a data conversion will probably not emphasize the ease of repair or the maintainability quality attribute.

(3) INTEGRATED. The goals of nonfunctional requirements can conflict with one another. Nonfunctional requirements typically have a broad effect on systems. That is, nonfunctional requirements are combined to produce a whole, complete system.

For example, there is an interesting and perhaps complex relationship between flexibility requirements, which tend to influence the nature of the software, and performance (e.g., efficiency) requirements that tend to affect the hardware needed. Flexibility and efficiency are so closely intertwined that the project sponsor is often forced to make trade-off decisions between high performance/high costs and less flexibility as shown in Table 4-4. Keep in mind that this is a generalized list of examples, and as such will not always happen. Further, some trade-offs are less important now than they were previously—now that hardware is so powerful

Table 4-4 Typical Quality Factor Trade-offs [Charette, 1990]

Integrity vs. Efficiency	The additional code and processing required to control the access of the software or data usually lengthens run-time and requires additional code.
Usability vs. Efficiency	The additional code and processing requirements to ease an operator's tasks or provide more usable output usually lengthens run-time and increases storage.
Maintainability vs. Efficiency	Optimized code increases maintainer's efforts. Using components, modules, instrumentation, etc., however, will increase overhead.
Portability vs. Efficiency	The use of direct code, optimized code, or system utilities decreases the portability of the system.
Flexibility vs. Efficiency	Generally, a flexible system will increase overhead.
Interoperability vs. Efficiency	The added overhead for data conversion and interface routines decreases operating efficiency.
Flexibility vs. Integrity	Flexibility requires very general structures. Security may be harder to ensure.
Reusability vs. Integrity	As above, reusable software provides potential security problems.
Interoperability vs. Integrity	Coupled systems allow for more paths that can allow either accidental or purposeful access to data.
Reusability vs. Reliability	The generality required by reusable software makes providing for error tolerance and accuracy difficult.

and storage space is relatively inexpensive. In some instances, you can reduce the effects of the trade-offs with sophisticated software (usually associated with a sophisticated price tag).

When a trade-off (or potential conflict) between nonfunctional attributes arises, how should it be handled in the specification? At a minimum, it should point out the trade-off because there might be associated project risks.

Trade-offs or potential conflicts in nonfunctional requirements are sometimes the 800-pound gorilla in the room. Year after year on project after project, we hear the demands from project sponsors, business partners, and users for software systems that are "better, cheaper, and faster." Unfortunately, too often the feasibility and affordability measured in terms of resources (e.g., people, software, and hardware) to deliver all that is requested on time and within budget are nearly impossible to accommodate.

4.4 CLASSIFICATION EFFORTS

Although there is no formal definition of nonfunctional requirements, there has been considerable work done on characterizing and classifying them. In this section, we'll look at three examples of such prior works. Additionally, we'll compare several efforts and explain the classification chosen for this book.

If the example classifications by Boehm, Sommerville, and Withall that follow serve no other purpose, I find the 30-year span of time between them to be of interest.

4.4.1 Boehm's Software Quality Characteristics Tree

Similar to a family tree that is used to trace one's heritage, Barry Boehm's quality attribute tree (shown in Figure 4-2) implies that when a parent quality is met, so too are its offspring qualities. Boehm reported the results of a study regarding characteristics of software quality.

A key finding from Boehm's study showed that
explicit attention to characteristics of software quality
can lead to significant savings in software lifecycle costs.

Figure 4-2 Software Quality Attributes Tree [Boehm, 1976]

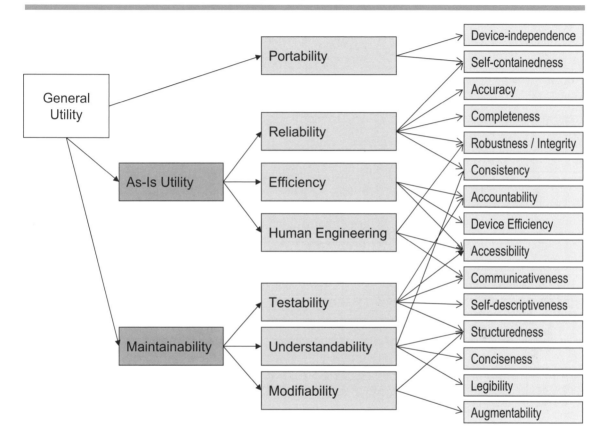

4.4.2 Sommerville's Nonfunctional Requirement Types

In this classification example, Ian Sommerville stresses that nonfunctional requirements arise because users need to achieve certain goals. These may be brought about by budget constraints, organizational policies, the need for interoperability with other software and hardware, the need for a certain development process to be followed, and external factors such as safety and security regulations. Figure 4-3 shows Sommerville's classification of nonfunctional requirements into three main requirement categories:

(1) Organizational requirements are constraints placed upon the development process of the system. They may be included because the customer for a system wishes to influence this process. Organizational requirements include requirements on development standards and methods that must be followed. For example, development will conform to International Standards Organization (ISO) 9000 standards, or the system must be developed for Microsoft Windows XP®.

(2) Product requirements specify the desired characteristics that a system or subsystem must possess. Most product requirements are concerned with specifying constraints on the behavior of the executing system. For example, the product must comply with safety regulations.

(3) External requirements may be placed upon both the product and the process, and are derived from the environment in which the system is developed. Therefore, these requirements may be based on application domain information, legal considerations, the need for the system to work with other systems, or even basic natural laws of physics.

4.4.3 Withall's Software Requirement Patterns

In this third example, Stephen Withall presents a classification based on patterns rather than functional and nonfunctional requirements. According to Withall, a **requirement pattern** is "*an approach to specifying a particular type of requirement.*"

Design patterns have been acknowledged for more than 15 years. Withall has brilliantly applied the concept of patterns to software requirements. He indicates that many types of

Figure 4-3 Nonfunctional Requirement Types [Sommerville, 1992]

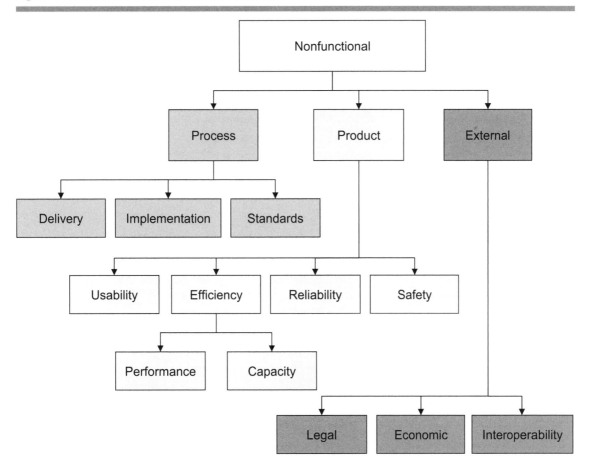

requirements crop up over and over in all kinds of systems. Requirement patterns therefore aim to let you specify better requirements more precisely with less effort. A requirement pattern applies to an individual requirement. Requirement patterns provide guidance on situations that recur in all systems such as how to tackle a requirement, what information ought to be conveyed in the requirement, as well as extra topics to consider, including development and testing.

Withall has created 37 patterns, grouped into eight domains as shown in Figure 4-4. Each domain has a theme, which all its patterns share. For readability, Figure 4-4 shows only the most significant relationships between patterns in different domains.

4.4.4 Comparing Nonfunctional Classification Efforts

In addition to the examples above from Boehm, Sommerville and Withall, there are lists provided by other authors, as well as standardization bodies. Which list should you use? The answer is simple: none of these represent the end-all perfect list. Rather, each is intended to be used as a checklist for what you might consider. You should ask yourself which nonfunctional characteristics are important to the system you encounter. Then specify the requirements related to those you identified.

I had to undergo a similar selection process in order to determine which nonfunctional categories to include in this book.

I started by studying each list independent of the others in order to understand each author's rationale behind his classification. From there I literally placed the lists side by side, as shown in Table 4-5 on page 116, and searched for similarities and differences between the lists.

Next, I noted the frequency of occurrence of any given nonfunctional category across the various lists, as shown in Table 4-6 on page 117. Generally, only those nonfunctional categories that appeared more than once were considered. For instance, *efficiency, reliability*, and *usability* are categories included in all the lists.

Unsurprisingly, I found that the terms and definitions differed. For example, *testability* found in McCall and Matsumoto's list appears to match the definition of *verifiability* found in Keller's list. Furthermore, Keller placed *verifiability* in a group called *design*, while Deutsch and

Figure 4-4 Software Requirement Patterns [Withall, 2007]

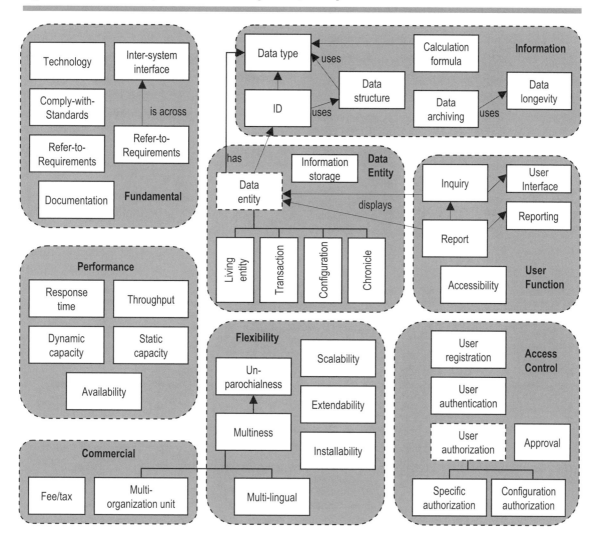

Willis placed *verifiability* in a group called *management*. As you might guess, the definitions of the groups didn't exactly match.

The nonfunctional categories included in this book are indicated in the far right column of Table 4-6, and blend the works of Keller [Keller, 1990], Deutsch and Willis [Deutsch, 1988], and McCall and Matsumoto [McCall, 1980]. The user-focused classification of these common nonfunctional categories is explained in the next section, "A User-focused Approach."

Table 4-5 A Comparison of Nonfunctional Classifications

McCall & Matsumoto 1980	Keller (RADC) 1990	Deutsch & Willis 1988	ISO/IEC 9126 1991	Sommerville 1992	Gilb 2005
Operation	Performance	Functional	Functionality	Product	Quality
Correctness	Efficiency	Integrity	Accurateness	Usability	Availability
Efficiency	Integrity	Reliability	Compliance	Efficiency	• Reliability
Integrity	Reliability	Survivability	Interoperability	• Performance	• Maintainability
Reliability	Survivability	Usability	Security	• Space	• Integrity
Usability	Usability	Performance	Suitability	Reliability	Adaptability
Revision	Design	Efficiency	Reliability	Portability	• Flexibility
Flexibility	Correctness	Correctness	Fault tolerance	Organizational	• Upgradeability
Maintainability	Maintainability	Safety	Maturity	Delivery	Usability
Testability	Verifiability	Interoperability	Recoverability	Implementation	• Entry-Level Experience
Transition	Adaptation	Change	Usability	Standards	• Training
Interoperability	Expandability	Maintainability	Learnability	External	• Handling Ability
Portability	Flexibility	Expandability	Operability	Interoperability	• Likeability
Reusability	Interoperability	Flexibility	Understandability	Ethical	• Demonstrability
	Portability	Portability	Efficiency	Legislative	Resource Saving
	Reusability	Reusability	Resource behavior	• Privacy	Financial
		Management	Time behavior	• Safety	Time
		Verifiability	Maintainability		Effort
		Manageability	Analyzability		Equipment
			Changeability		Workload/Capacity
			Stability		Throughput
			Testability		Response Time
			Portability		Storage Capacity
			Adaptability		
			Conformance		
			Installability		
			Replaceability		

Table 4-6 Common Nonfunctional Categories

	McCall 1980	Keller 1990	Deutsch 1988	ISO/IEC 9126; 1991	Sommerville 1992	Gilb 2005	This Book
Availability						X	X
Correctness	X	X	X				
Efficiency	X	X	X	X	X	X	X
Expandability (Scalability)		X	X				X
Flexibility	X	X	X			X	X
Integrity	X	X	X			X	X
Interoperability	X	X	X	X	X		X
Maintainability	X	X	X	X		X	X
Portability	X	X	X	X	X		X
Reliability	X	X	X	X	X	X	X
Reusability	X	X	X				X
Safety			X		X		
Security				X			X
Survivability		X	X				X
Testability	X			X			
Usability	X	X	X	X	X	X	X
Verifiability		X	X				X

4.5 A USER-FOCUSED APPROACH

Nonfunctional requirements can be classified based on the user's need for software quality, which I refer to as the ***user-focused approach***. Addressing a user concern will necessitate the formulation of a number of functional requirements, but the user concerns will also act to constrain other requirements that are characteristic of nonfunctional requirements. As shown in Figure 4-5, user concerns for software quality are grouped under three important aspects: its operational characteristics, its ability to undergo change, and its adaptability to new environments.

Figure 4-5 User Needs for Software Qualities [McCall, 1980]

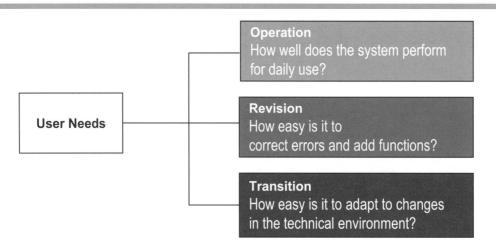

In order to apply a user-focused approach, it is necessary to understand who the user is. The software user is any person who comes in contact with the software system. User contact with the software system might occur in any of the following ways:

(a) **Using the functionality** (*operation*). The user perceives the system as an electronic tool that helps to automate what would otherwise be done manually. From this point of view, the user is concerned with how well the system operates.

(b) **Changing source code or data that drive the system** (*revision*). The user perceives the system as a set of programmed language statements. These statements are treated as a problem that must be solved. The system must be analyzed, modified, tested, and implemented as problems arise, or the business changes the way it operates.

(c) **Managing the upkeep of the software** (*transition*). From this point of view, the system carries similar characteristics as hardware. That is, the user is concerned with aspects such as packaging, transport, and compatibility with other systems.

Regardless of which form of contact the user has with the system, all users are after the same thing—software quality.

4.5.1 User Needs for Software Quality

Depending on the user's contact with the software system and the purpose and perspective for using it, user needs vary. To better understand user needs, the three aspects of software quality are further subdivided, as summarized in Table 4-7 on page 120.

The three main groups of user needs for software quality are briefly introduced here. Each group, as well as the subdivision of nonfunctional categories within each group, is explained in the subsequent chapters of Part Two.

The ***operation*** group describes the user needs for a system that performs or functions well. The operation group subdivides into the following requirement categories:

♦ **Access Security**—how well the system is safeguarded against deliberate and intrusive faults from internal and external sources.

♦ **Availability**—how dependable the system is (able to function) during "normal operating times."

Table 4-7 A User-focused Approach

User Needs	User Concerns with the Software System	Nonfunctional Categories
Operation How well does the system perform for daily use?	How well is it guarded against unauthorized access?	Access Security (ACS)
	How dependable is it during normal operating times?	Availability (AVL)
	How fast, how many, and how well does it respond?	Efficiency (EFC)
	How accurate and authentic are the data?	Integrity (INT)
	How immune is the system to failure?	Reliability (REL)
	How resilient is the system from failure?	Survivability (SRV)
	How easy is it to learn and operate the system?	Usability (USE)
Revision How easy is it to correct errors and add on functions?	How easy is it to modify to work in different environments?	Flexibility (FLX)
	How easy is it to upkeep and repair?	Maintainability (MNT)
	How easy is it to expand or upgrade its capabilities?	Scalability (SCL)
	How easy is it to show it performs its functions?	Verifiability (VER)
Transition How easy is it to adapt to changes in the technical environment?	How easy is it to interface with another system?	Interoperability (IOP)
	How easy is it to transport?	Portability (POR)
	How easy is it to convert for use in another system?	Reusability (REU)

♦ **Efficiency**—how well the software system handles capacity, throughput, and response time.

♦ **Integrity**—how well the data are maintained by the software system in terms of accuracy, authenticity, and without corruption.

♦ **Reliability**—how well the software system consistently performs the specified functions without failure.

♦ **Survivability**—how well the software system continues to function and recovers in the presence of a system failure.

♦ **Usability**—how easily the user is able to learn, operate, prepare inputs, and interpret outputs through interaction with a software system.

The *revision* group describes the user needs for a system that is easy to correct when errors occur, and is easy to add on new functions. The revision group comprises the following requirement categories:

♦ **Flexibility**—how easily the software can be modified to adapt to different environments, configurations, and user expectations.

♦ **Maintainability**—how easily faults in the software system can be found and fixed.

♦ **Scalability**—how well the software system is able to expand its processing capabilities upward and outward to support business growth.

♦ **Verifiability**—the extent to which tests, analysis, and demonstrations are needed to prove that the software system will function as intended.

The *transition* group describes the user needs for ease of adaptation to changes in the technical environment. The transition group includes the following requirement categories:

♦ **Interoperability**—how well the software system is able to couple or facilitate the interface with other systems.

♦ **Portability**—how easily the software system can be transferred from its current hardware or software environment to another environment.

♦ **Reusability**—how easily a portion of the software system can be converted for use in another system.

Before moving on to the specifics of each of these groups and their associated nonfunctional requirement categories, I'd like to share my vision for the near future of software requirements.

4.5.2 A Future Classification

I hold out hope that in the future we stop using the term "nonfunctional" and its corresponding trail of confusing definitions. Let's stop forcing everything into two "buckets" of system-level requirements: functional and nonfunctional.

Perhaps a future-state view of system-level requirements is as illustrated in Figure 4-6. Nonfunctional requirements are extinct! Rejoice!

Figure 4-6 System-Level Requirements (Future Classification)

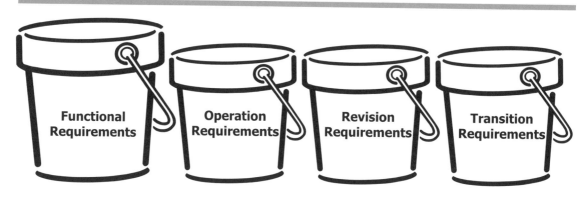

4.6 CHAPTER SUMMARY

♦ Industry challenges contribute to the difficulty of understanding nonfunctional requirements including: no agreed-upon, complete list of nonfunctional characteristics, no industry-accepted definition of the term nonfunctional, and no single, uniform classification of nonfunctional attributes.

♦ Nonfunctional requirements are vital to the success of software systems. Yet, there are three main factors that influence the nature of nonfunctional requirements and make it difficult to elicit and define them. One factor is their subjective nature. That is, they are interpreted differently by different people and organizations. Relativity is another factor, which means that organizations will emphasize those nonfunctional categories that have the most impact on their specific business processes and products. Integration is a third factor that influences the nature of nonfunctional requirements, which often results in trade-offs or compromise during development or implementation.

♦ Although there is no uniform classification of nonfunctional requirements, there are several examples of classifications presented. Furthermore, these examples were compared to identify categories that are common among classifications. These common nonfunctional categories form the foundation under which categories were chosen for inclusion in this book.

♦ The user-focused nonfunctional classification presented in this book helps an organization combat the subjective, relative, and integrated nature of these requirements. This user-focused approach is based on three needs of the software system user:

  ◊ OPERATION REQUIREMENTS. How well does the system perform for daily use?

  ◊ REVISION REQUIREMENTS. How easy is it to correct errors and add-on functions?

  ◊ TRANSITION REQUIREMENTS. How easy is it to adapt to changes in the technical environment?

4.7 SUGGESTED READING

Applications Strategies for Risk Analysis, by Robert Charette, [Charette, 1990]. Software engineering and the risks to the business are presented in Chapter 3, as well as the *interacting nature of nonfunctional requirements*.

Non-functional Requirements in Software Engineering, by Lawrence Chung, et al., [Chung, 2000]. This book presents a concentrated explanation of cataloguing methods and *non-functional requirements* (NFRs) types using an NFR Framework.

Software Quality Engineering: A Total Technical and Management Approach, by Michael Deutsch and Ronald Willis, [Deutsch, 1988]. This book presents a "Sample Software Quality Requirements Specification," including numerous examples of nonfunctional requirements that are separated by user concern. Chapter 3 describes the *classification of nonfunctional requirements by user needs and concerns*.

Software Quality Metrics Enhancements, Volume 1, by James McCall and Mike Matsumoto, [McCall, 1980]. This research report presents a *software quality framework* consisting of *quality factors*, criterion, and metrics.

Specifying Software Quality Requirements with Metrics, by Steven E. Keller, Laurence G. Kahn, and Roger B. Panara, [Keller, 1990]. This paper presents the Rome Air Development Center's *classification of software quality* consumer-oriented attributes.

5 OPERATION REQUIREMENTS

HOW WELL DOES THE SYSTEM PERFORM FOR DAILY USE?

Operation requirements define how well the software system performs for daily use. While functional requirements describe what tasks the system is to perform, the operation requirements describe how well the system performs the tasks. Generally, these requirements are of greatest concern to the user who comes into contact with the software system by using the functionality. Stated simply, the user's view of *automation* is a software system that either does the work for the user, or helps the user do the work better, faster, and cheaper.

The operation group of nonfunctional categories encompasses the concerns of the user during normal operation of the system. Operation requirements answer the user's concerns for the following software qualities:

- ACCESS SECURITY. How well is the system guarded against unauthorized access?

- AVAILABILITY. How dependable is the system during normal operating times?

- EFFICIENCY. How fast, how many, and how well does it respond?

- INTEGRITY. How accurate and authentic are the data?

- RELIABILITY. How immune is the system to failure?

- SURVIVABILITY. How resilient is the system from failure?

- USABILITY. How easy is it to learn and operate the system?

In the sequence listed above, this chapter presents the following for each operation category: definition, brief discussion, examples of requirements, and suggested elicitation questions. The introduction to Part Two explains the anatomy of a category, and provides guidance for how to use the suggested questions.

5.1 ACCESS SECURITY (ACS)

USER CONCERN:	How well is the system safeguarded against unauthorized access?
RELATED CATEGORIES:	Access Control, Authenticity, Authorization, Integrity

5.1.1 Access Security Definition

Access security is the extent to which the system is safeguarded against deliberate and intrusive faults from internal and external sources.

5.1.2 Access Security Discussion

Access security requirements protect the assets of an organization just as one would safeguard money or other forms of property. Trust is an often overlooked corporate asset; users and customers need to trust that the business will secure their private information. The business processes must provide confidentiality, privacy, and authenticity.

> It is desirable to make a system 'fool resistant.'
> It is not possible to make it 'foolproof,' since they are always improving the quality of fools.
> —David Hay, author of *Requirements Analysis: From Business Views to Architecture* [Hay, 2003]

When eliciting access security requirements, consider the following aspects:

- USER REGISTRATION—establishing new user accounts.
  - ◊ **Self-registration**. When users register themselves, anything entered must be treated as suspicious. Users can easily enter false information or enter

5.1 ACS

information about someone else (identity fraud). Identify the standard for authenticating the user-entered information.

◊ **Password format**. Setting password policies requires trade-off considerations, such as how many characters can be easily remembered by a typical user versus how easily passwords might be cracked (easily figured out by an unauthorized user).

◊ **Changing passwords**. Policies for changing passwords also require trade-off considerations. For instance, should users be forced to periodically change passwords? Should there be restrictions on what the password is changed to? Can a password used previously be reused?

◊ **De-registration of users**. If users can self-register, they are typically allowed to self-deregister. If self-registration isn't allowed, then someone must have authority and procedures to deregister users.

◊ **User data protection**. With identity theft on the rise, users are sensitive to what data they are willing to give. The data must be protected, and the system must be in compliance with federal and state privacy laws.

◊ **One-time or one-day users**. Does the organization have a need to accommodate visitors? What about special events?

♦ USER AUTHORIZATION—giving users permission to use system functions.

◊ **Delegating authority**. Some business situations are conducive to delegating authority. For instance, the user who delegates (delegator) should be able to control the level of delegated authority. For example, an executive might have an administrative assistant who needs to manage the executive's calendar and email.

◊ **Inaccessible functions**. It is common to build systems that hide or do not present functions to a specific user who does not have authority to perform such functions.

◊ **Authorization based on special events or conditions**. Some events or conditions might require extra authorization. For instance, insurance claim checks issued for more than $250,000 require a second signature from a user who is a vice-president level or above.

♦ USER AUTHENTICATION—getting proof that users are who they claim to be.

◊ **Ending user sessions**. Limiting the duration of a user session is recommended. From time to time, users must prove they are really them. For example, employees might be required to re-authenticate every 8 hours.

◊ **User forgets password**. People are human and will forget their passwords. The system must have a way for users to re-authenticate themselves, such as a "secret phrase" or the users must answer a series of security questions.

◊ **De-authentication (user logs off)**. Users must have assurance that they are completely logged out. This prevents others from sitting in their seats and performing functions as if done by the users previously signed in.

◊ **Re-authentication (user modifies user information)**. When users change the information in their profiles, it is necessary to make notification and authenticate the information.

◊ **User absence or inactivity**. It might be necessary to have users prove from time to time that it is really them. Users could walk away, leaving their session unattended. A user signed on to a web site might go to another site without logging off.

◊ **Blocking or unblocking users**. Blocking users means that they are prevented from logging in to the system, for instance, if users make several invalid attempts to enter their password. If users can be blocked, there must be a means to unblock them after adequate re-authentication.

◊ **Viewing session usage**. Storing information about user session usage can help to identify breaches in security (even if after the fact). Session information usually includes session start and stop date/time, terminal or workstation used, authentication method, and cause of session termination.

5.1 ACS

5.1.3 Access Security Requirement Examples

a) Employees shall be forced to change their password the next time they log in if they have not changed it within the length of time established as "password expiration duration."

b) Users must change the initially assigned login authentication information (password) immediately after the first successful login. The initial password may never be reused.

c) The payroll system shall ensure that the employee salary data can be accessed only by authorized users. The payroll system shall distinguish between authorized and non-authorized users.

d) Employees shall not be allowed to update their own salary information, and any such attempt shall be reported to the security administrator.

e) Only holders of current security clearance can enter the national headquarters building.

f) The access permissions for system data may only be changed by the system's data administrator.

g) Passwords shall never be viewable at the point of entry or at any other time.

h) Each unsuccessful attempt by a user to access an item of data shall be recorded on an audit trail.

i) Users shall receive notification of profile changes via preferred communication method of record when profile information is modified.

5.1.4 Access Security Suggested Questions

DATA (WHAT?)

ID	Access Security Suggested Questions	Ask this to:
ACS1S	What information must be guarded against unauthorized update or tampering?	*identify data security needs.*
ACS2S	What information must be kept confidential?	*identify data security needs.*
ACS3S	What information is considered "secret"?	*identify data security needs.*
ACS4S	What information must be guarded against unauthorized disclosure?	*identify data security needs.*
ACS5S	What would be the impact to the user/customer if data or processing were lost due to a security breach?	*identify data security needs.*
ACS6S	What would be the impact to the company if data or processing were lost due to a security breach?	*identify data security needs.*
ACS7S	What public data are accessed by the application?	*identify external sources.*
ACS8S	How secure are infrequently used data?	*identify potential gaps.*
ACS9S	How secure are infrequently used hardware/software?	*identify potential gaps.*
ACS10S	What conditions are associated with authorization?	*identify relationships between events and access.*
ACS11S	What delegation rights exist to cover periods of absence by managers or administrators of security?	*identify role responsibilities.*
ACS12S	What user actions require approval?	*identify security events and conditions.*
ACS13S	Describe the different security levels used.	*identify security events and conditions.*
ACS14S	What are the conditions to deny user/customer access?	*identify security events and conditions.*
ACS15S	What criteria must authentication (for example, password) satisfy to be acceptable?	*identify security information.*
ACS16S	What user session information should be stored?	*identify security information.*
ACS17S	What are the sources of external data used by the application?	*identify types of authentication and verification.*

DATA (WHAT?) (continued)

ID	Access Security Suggested Questions	Ask this to:
ACS18R	What safeguards must be put in place for operational (production or run-time operation) information?	*identify procedures.*
ACS19R	What safeguards must be put in place for developmental (development stages) information?	*identify security events and conditions.*
ACS20R	What safeguards must be put in place for information that resides internally?	*identify security events and conditions.*
ACS21R	What user session information is stored currently?	*identify security information.*
ACS22R	What supplemental authentication information is needed?	*identify security information.*
ACS23R	What is expected of the database system when the application is no longer in control of the data?	*identify security processes and procedures.*
ACS24B	What else should I be asking about access security "data"?	*uncover additional requirements.*

ROLES (WHO?)

ID	Access Security Suggested Questions	Ask this to:
ACS25S	What access privileges are permitted?	*clarify authorization levels.*
ACS26S	What level of access is made available without user/customer authorization and authentication?	*clarify authorization levels.*
ACS27S	Who/what provides inputs to the system?	*differentiate the user classes.*
ACS28S	What is the unique identifier for each user class?	*differentiate the user classes.*
ACS29S	What makes the user classes different?	*differentiate the user classes.*
ACS30S	Who will write security procedures and documentation?	*identify additional stakeholders.*
ACS31S	What internal users interface with the system?	*identify additional user classes.*
ACS32S	What external users interface with the system?	*identify additional user classes.*
ACS33S	How many members of each user class are estimated to use the system each month of the first year the system is operational?	*identify approximate size of the user population.*
ACS34S	Who/what receives outputs from this system?	*identify role responsibilities.*

ROLES (WHO?) (continued)

ID	Access Security Suggested Questions	Ask this to:
ACS35s	Who will want to monitor usage?	*identify role responsibilities.*
ACS36s	Who gives authorization and under what circumstances?	*identify role responsibilities.*
ACS37s	Who has the authority to grant access to the system function?	*identify role responsibilities.*
ACS38s	Who is ultimately responsible for each system function?	*identify role responsibilities.*
ACS39s	Who should be notified when unauthorized access is recognized?	*identify role responsibilities.*
ACS40s	How many levels of user/customer access are necessary?	*identify security events and conditions.*
ACS41s	What security concerns do the customers have that must be addressed?	*identify security events and conditions.*
ACS42s	How could a user collaborate with another authorized user to gain access?	*identify security events and conditions.*
ACS43s	What levels of security apply to inactive users?	*identify security needs.*
ACS44s	What level of security is expected for access to data from outside the application?	*identify user classes.*
ACS45s	How should actions requiring levels of approval be managed?	*identify user classes.*
ACS46s	How are user classes determined?	*identify user classes.*
ACS47s	What kinds of user classes are impacted by security?	*identify user classes.*
ACS48s	Who/what should not be interacting with the system?	*identify user classes.*
ACS49s	What functions does each user class need to access?	*identify user classes.*
ACS50R	What security clearance level is required of the individuals who are constructing, enhancing, or installing the system?	*differentiate the user classes.*
ACS51R	How is access authorized?	*identify additional user classes.*
ACS52R	Who needs access to perform non-routine maintenance or emergency fixes?	*identify additional user classes.*
ACS53R	Who needs access to perform routine maintenance?	*identify additional user classes.*
ACS54B	What else should I be asking about access security "roles"?	*uncover additional requirements.*

PURPOSE (WHY?)

5.1 ACS

ID	Access Security Suggested Questions	Ask this to:
ACS55s	What business policies are in place with regard to access security?	*correlate business rules and access security needs.*
ACS56s	What business policies pertain to access security?	*correlate business rules and access security needs.*
ACS57s	What business rules apply to access security?	*correlate business rules and access security needs.*
ACS58s	What business rules exist for privacy of information?	*correlate business rules and access security needs.*
ACS59s	What privacy policy has the company declared with regard to the data and its use?	*correlate business rules and access security needs.*
ACS60s	What privacy laws are applicable with regard to the data?	*correlate business rules and access security needs.*
ACS61s	What local, state, federal, and international laws affect access security?	*correlate business rules and access security needs.*
ACS62s	What happens when access expires?	*correlate business rules and access security needs.*
ACS63s	What security audits are required to monitor application security?	*identify audit needs.*
ACS64s	How often are audits conducted by internal staff? External?	*identify audit needs.*
ACS65s	What data protection laws affect access security?	*identify compliance with regulations.*
ACS66s	What expectations do the customers have about information privacy?	*identify customer expectations.*
ACS67s	What promises and assurances have been made to the customers about access security?	*identify customer expectations.*
ACS68s	What promises and assurances have been made to the customers about information privacy?	*identify customer expectations.*
ACS69s	What measures for managing hardcopy security are necessary?	*identify procedural controls.*
ACS70s	What security measures must be extended beyond basic company security?	*identify security events and conditions.*
ACS71s	What keeps the users awake at night with regard to access security?	*identify security events and conditions.*

ID	Access Security Suggested Questions	Ask this to:
ACS72S	What access security issues do the users have?	*identify security events and conditions.*
ACS73S	What will provide the users with the required level of confidence in security?	*identify security events and conditions.*
ACS74S	What are the access security concerns of the customers?	*identify security events and conditions.*
ACS75S	What expectations do the customers have about security?	*identify security events and conditions.*
ACS76S	What must be done to demonstrate sound security to the customers?	*identify security events and conditions.*
ACS77S	What system failures could cause significant economic damage to the business?	*identify security events and conditions.*
ACS78S	When do users/customers get blocked from access?	*identify security events and conditions.*
ACS79S	What other security issues should be addressed?	*identify security events and conditions.*
ACS80S	What security issues were experienced in the past?	*identify security events and conditions.*
ACS81S	What system failures could cause some mission to be unaccomplished (mission failure)?	*identify security events and conditions.*
ACS82S	What breach of security attempts have been thwarted in the past?	*identify security events and conditions.*
ACS83S	What is the financial cost to the company of a data security breech?	*identify security risk.*
ACS84S	What is the cost of misuse of the data or product?	*identify security risk.*
ACS85S	What is the effect on competitive advantage due to misuse?	*identify security risk.*
ACS86S	What if a competitor obtained any data?	*identify security risk.*
ACS87S	What is the public perception cost to the company of a data security breech?	*identify security risk.*
ACS88S	What rules are in place for establishing and managing user/customer authentication?	*identify sources of authentication.*
ACS89R	What design and development methods are required to ensure the entire application meets security requirements?	*identify methodology constraints.*

5.1 ACS

PURPOSE (WHY?) (continued)

ID	Access Security Suggested Questions	Ask this to:
ACS90R	How is this project different from other projects with regard to security?	*identify security events and conditions.*
ACS91R	What measures have been taken to detect access security design flaws?	*identify security events and conditions.*
ACS92R	What security measures must be taken to protect the environment?	*identify security events and conditions.*
ACS93R	What hardware and equipment are the users of the system allowed to install?	*identify security risk.*
ACS94R	What software are the users of the system allowed to install?	*identify security risk.*
ACS95R	What security concerns are greater/less than those on other projects? Why?	*identify security risk.*
ACS96B	What else should I be asking about access security "purpose"?	*uncover additional requirements.*

TIMING (WHEN?)

ID	Access Security Suggested Questions	Ask this to:
ACS97S	What authorized users are authorized for access at all times?	*differentiate the user classes.*
ACS98S	Under what conditions are more than one approval required?	*identify security events and conditions.*
ACS99S	Who will be allowed to use the system when it is first installed?	*identify security events and conditions.*
ACS100S	How soon should the system time-out because of inactivity?	*identify security events and conditions.*
ACS101S	Specify conditions or circumstances that limit user authorization to access the system.	*identify security events and conditions.*
ACS102S	What events make the authorization conditional?	*identify security events and conditions.*
ACS103S	How long shall access be granted?	*identify security metrics.*
ACS104S	How promptly is approval needed?	*identify turnaround expectations.*
ACS105S	When should the system provide a user/customer lock session?	*identify types of usage.*

TIMING (WHEN?) (continued)

ID	Access Security Suggested Questions	Ask this to:
ASC106S	When are the periods of high or low usage by the user classes?	*identify usage patterns.*
ACS107S	Under what conditions could locked sessions be broken?	*identify types of usage.*
ACS108S	Specify the functions and data of the system that each user group is authorized to access.	*make certain all functions of the system are covered.*
ACS109R	When is it possible for any computers to be connected without following all company security policies?	*identify security events and conditions.*
ACS110R	At what points during use of the application should users re-authenticate themselves?	*identify security events and conditions.*
ACS111R	What system components must be locked up when not in use?	*identify security events and conditions.*
ACS112B	What else should I be asking about access security "timing"?	*uncover additional requirements.*

LOGISTICS (WHERE?)

ID	Access Security Suggested Questions	Ask this to:
ACS113S	How will access security be the same at all business locations?	*identify security events and conditions by location.*
ACS114S	What are different levels of security at each location where disaster recovery hardware, software, and other business artifacts are stored?	*identify security events and conditions by location.*
ACS115S	How is access security different for customers accessing information remotely?	*identify security events and conditions by location.*
ACS116S	What access security is needed for employees that work from home or other remote locations?	*identify security events and conditions by location.*
ACS117S	What access restrictions are necessary to the work areas where the application will be used?	*identify physical constraints.*
ACS118S	What security measures must be taken when accessing the application using public computers?	*identify potential holes.*
ACS119S	What resources are needed to secure each location?	*identify resources needed.*
ACS120S	How does access depend on the time of day or location of the user at the time of access?	*identify security dependencies.*

5.1 ACS

LOGISTICS (WHERE?) (continued)

ID	Access Security Suggested Questions	Ask this to:
ACS121R	What reasons are there for this application to run on computers that are not connected to the Internet?	identify location needs.
ACS122R	Where is information from the vendors of supplies for this system maintained?	identify regulation compliance.
ACS123R	Where is regulatory information maintained?	identify regulations.
ACS124R	What hardware/software is needed to secure each location?	identify resources needed.
ACS125R	What security measures are necessary as interfaces pass control through the system?	identify security events and conditions.
ACS126B	What else should I be asking about access security "logistics"?	uncover additional requirements.

PROCESS (HOW?)

ID	Access Security Suggested Questions	Ask this to:
ACS127S	What is the process flow of hardcopy from receipt to destruction?	identify hardcopy life-cycle limitations.
ACS128S	After denying access, what steps should be taken when a security breach is detected?	identify persistent attack.
ACS129S	How is access reset?	identify recovery.
ACS130S	What should be done when unauthorized access is recognized?	identify responses.
ACS131S	What procedures need to be in place to safely dispose of confidential documents, files, electronic storage devices, and other media?	identify security processes and procedures.
ACS132S	What happens when an approver denies approval?	identify security processes and procedures.
ACS133S	How do users provide identification (indicate to the system who they are)?	identify security processes and procedures.
ACS134S	What metrics of security need to be put in place?	identify security processes and procedures.
ACS135S	How do users provide authentication (indicate to the system that users are in fact who they claim to be)?	identify security processes and procedures.
ACS136S	If multiple means of authentication are offered, which one is the preferred or primary method?	prioritize authentication methods.

ID	Access Security Suggested Questions	Ask this to:
ACS137R	What different security measures must be developed?	estimate implementation effort.
ACS138R	How are users/customers authenticated?	identify authentication procedures.
ACS139R	How do the users purge confidential information?	identify extended process.
ACS140R	What routine audits are performed to detect improper usage, either by authorized or non-authorized users?	identify inspection criteria.
ACS141R	What integrity checks prevent unintentional misuse by authorized users?	identify integrity checks.
ACS142R	What security is in place to guard against abnormal events and conditions?	identify integrity checks.
ACS143R	How is hardcopy security monitored?	identify physical controls.
ACS144R	What means of authentication should be offered?	identify possible methods of authentication.
ACS145R	What security conventions apply to the development stages? Testing stages?	identify security events and conditions.
ACS146R	How do the users dispose of unused software? Hardware?	identify security processes and procedures.
ACS147R	How must the security measures be implemented?	identify security processes and procedures.
ACS148R	How do new users/customers self-enroll?	identify security processes and procedures.
ACS149R	How are users/customers removed from the system?	identify security processes and procedures.
ACS150R	How will this application be used on computers connected to a network or the Internet?	identify security processes and procedures.
ACS151R	What additional precautions should be taken with the hardware/software of the system?	identify security processes and procedures.
ACS152R	How can the system recognize legitimate users/customers?	identify security processes and procedures.
ACS153R	How do new users/customers get added to the system?	identify security processes and procedures.
ACS154R	What Quality Assurance (QA) measures must be followed to ensure proper security of the system?	identify security processes and procedures.
ACS155B	What else should I be asking about access security "processes"?	uncover additional requirements.

5.2 AVAILABILITY (AVL)

USER CONCERN:	How dependable is the system during normal operating times?
RELATED CATEGORIES:	Accessibility, Dependability, Maintainability, Reliability

5.2.1 Availability Definition

Availability is the degree to which users can depend on the system to be up (able to function) during "normal operating times."

5.2.2 Availability Discussion

Availability requirements describe:

(1) When the system is expected to be available for use. An enterprise should establish its "normal operating times." This is also referred to as the "availability window."

(2) What constitutes an acceptable amount of outage time or period of time when the system can be unavailable to users. This outage time, also referred to as the "unavailability window," takes into consideration periods of time for scheduled downtime, housekeeping, upgrades, and unexpected failure. The availability requirements should also define what the user can expect when the system is unavailable.

Generally, availability is measured by the probability that a system is operating satisfactorily at any point in time when used under stated conditions. Availability is usually described as a percentage as shown in some of the examples on page 142.

When eliciting availability requirements, consider the following aspects:

◆ DOWNTIME IMPACT ON THE BUSINESS. If the system is not available during normal operation, what is the disruption to business? Is a high degree of availability critical or just nice to have?

◆ PARTIAL AVAILABILITY IMPACT ON THE BUSINESS. What parts are critical to business continuity? What is the acceptable reduced level of service that the users will tolerate? What business components have an acceptable workaround?

◆ TRANSPARENT UNAVAILABILITY. What housekeeping tasks must be done during normal operation without user awareness? What degree of degraded performance is tolerable, if any?

◆ MINIMIZING UNAVAILABILITY (reducing downtime). Some might view these considerations to be reliability or maintainability or both, and that's okay with me as long as they are addressed somewhere. I've included them here because they often affect system availability.

◇ **Frequency and duration of maintenance**. Many companies run an "end-of-day" maintenance cycle. Does it have to run every day? Could the maintenance be subdivided and spread out across a day? What maintenance routines can run while the system is available to users?

◇ **Frequency and duration of periodic upgrades or releases**. The business nature of a particular upgrade can drive the timing of an upgrade. For example, an urgent production fix might mandate that an off-scheduled upgrade occur. It is common to execute system upgrades on a weekend when business is closed. Unfortunately, usually due to poor planning, I have seen upgrades last the entire weekend. Also included in the decision is business impact, users, and inter-related business processes.

◇ **Frequency and duration of unexpected system failures**. Failures can be due to accidents or deliberate acts. A quality system must address ways to prevent both types of failure. When the system cannot prevent failure, maintenance procedures must fix it as quickly as possible.

5.2.3 Availability Requirement Examples

5.2 AVL

a) The Online Payment System shall be available for use between the hours of 6:00 a.m. and 11:00 p.m. CST.

b) The Online Payment System shall achieve 100 hours MTBF (mean time between failure).

c) The CIF system shall achieve 99.5% up time.

d) The mortgage amortization schedule shall be available to the customer within 15 seconds for 95% of the times that it is requested. The remaining times it will be available within 20 seconds.

e) The Automated Teller Machine shall be at least 99.0 percent available on weekdays between 6:00 a.m. and 11:00 p.m. local time. The machine shall be at least 99.95 percent available on weekdays between 4:00 p.m. and 6:00 p.m. local time.

f) Unless the system is non-operational, the system shall present a user with notification informing them that the system is unavailable.

g) A new installation of the system shall be available for first-time use within 24 hours of the start of the install.

h) The online registration system shall permit backing up of the registration database while other registration activities are going on. (It is estimated that this requirement reduces duration for which the online registration system would be unavailable to students for maintenance by 15 minutes each calendar day.)

5.2.4 Availability Suggested Questions

DATA (WHAT?)   5.2 AVL

ID	Availability Suggested Questions	Ask this to:
AVL1S	What notification is needed when the system is completely down?	*identify availability data.*
AVL2S	What notification is needed when the system is partially down?	*identify availability data.*
AVL3S	What processes use data for business that can be recovered following a system outage?	*identify availability data.*
AVL4S	What processes use data for business that cannot be recovered following a system outage?	*identify availability data.*
AVL5S	What challenges do users have in inputting information or materials?	*identify barriers.*
AVL6S	What challenges do users have in retrieving information or materials?	*identify barriers.*
AVL7S	When are multiple means of notification used?	*identify notifications.*
AVL8S	What means of notification should be used?	*identify notifications.*
AVL9S	Which means of notification should be used by type of system outage?	*identify notifications.*
AVL10S	When the system is unavailable, what notification should be given to users attempting to access the system?	*identify notifications.*
AVL11S	What advanced warning to users of planned outage is expected?	*identify notifications.*
AVL12R	What information or materials are archived and stored off-site?	*identify availability data.*
AVL13R	What information or materials are difficult to retrieve?	*identify availability data.*
AVL14R	How does notification depend on type of error?	*identify notifications.*
AVL15R	After an outage, how should users be notified of system availability?	*identify notifications.*
AVL16B	What else should I be asking about availability "data"?	*uncover additional requirements.*

ROLES (WHO?)

ID	Availability Suggested Questions	Ask this to:
AVL17s	What emergency access should be extended to each user class?	*identify exceptions.*
AVL18s	What are the expectations on system availability?	*identify expectations.*
AVL19s	What emergency access is expected for each user class?	*identify forms of access.*
AVL20s	When should multiple people be notified?	*identify role priority.*
AVL21s	What users should have limited availability (access) to the system?	*identify role rankings.*
AVL22s	Who should receive notification when there are system failures?	*identify role responsibilities.*
AVL23s	Which people need to be notified when there is a serious error?	*identify role responsibilities.*
AVL24s	Who is authorized to access what data when the system is unavailable?	*identify role responsibilities.*
AVL25s	How should acknowledgment from someone taking responsibility for the problem be communicated?	*identify role responsibilities.*
AVL26s	What is the typical number of users accessing the system simultaneously?	*identify usage.*
AVL27s	What is the greatest number of simultaneous users during peak processing? Anticipated future usage?	*identify usage.*
AVL28r	Who performs routine maintenance?	*identify role responsibilities.*
AVL29r	Who gets called when the system is down?	*identify role responsibilities.*
AVL30r	What percent of problems reported to the first level support group (for example, help desk) should be handled by the first level support group?	*identify role responsibilities.*
AVL31r	Who supports the system during "after hours" or non-normal operation hours?	*identify role responsibilities.*
AVL32b	What else should I be asking about availability "roles"?	*uncover additional requirements.*

PURPOSE (WHY?)

ID	Availability Suggested Questions	Ask this to:
AVL33s	How would users describe availability?	*clarify terminology.*
AVL34s	Define availability in terms of functions that are performed.	*clarify terminology.*
AVL35s	Define availability in terms of users that perform the work.	*clarify terminology.*
AVL36s	What are the "normal" business hours of operation?	*establish business rules.*
AVL37s	What causes the most pain when the system is not available?	*identify effects.*
AVL38s	How long can the system be down before there is permanent business loss?	*identify assessments.*
AVL39s	What is an acceptable amount of time to detect an outage?	*identify detection timeframes.*
AVL40s	When should emergency access be extended to bypass normal access restrictions?	*identify events.*
AVL41s	What are the expectations of the availability of the system?	*identify expectations.*
AVL42s	What are the associated risks to conducting business "as usual" if the system/application is unavailable?	*identify limitations in alternatives.*
AVL43s	What is the acceptable effort required of users/customers to gain access to data?	*identify possible trade-offs.*
AVL44s	How much is the business (sponsor) willing to invest to reduce the chance of downtime or failure?	*identify possible trade-offs.*
AVL45s	What problems with availability have been experienced in the past?	*identify problems and lessons learned.*
AVL46s	What are the greatest concerns about availability?	*identify risk.*
AVL47s	What is the cost to the business for system downtime?	*identify risk.*
AVL48s	What constitutes a serious error?	*identify risk.*
AVL49s	How much permanent business loss is acceptable?	*identify risk.*
AVL50s	If the system is not available, how is the business affected?	*identify risk.*
AVL51s	What is an acceptable effect on system availability of background activity?	*identify tolerance metrics.*

5.2 AVL

PURPOSE (WHY?) (continued)

5.2 AVL

ID	Availability Suggested Questions	Ask this to:
AVL52s	What cost tolerance is acceptable to maintain the required level of availability?	*identify tolerance metrics.*
AVL53s	How does routine maintenance hinder or delay productivity?	*identify various types of maintenance.*
AVL54s	What processes are considered to be absolutely mission critical to the business?	*prioritize processes.*
AVL55s	What processes must be the last to fail or be unavailable?	*prioritize processes.*
AVL56R	What level of limited availability in a degraded mode is acceptable?	*identify graduations.*
AVL57R	What current availability issues must be avoided by this project?	*identify lessons learned.*
AVL58R	What level of performance constitutes available?	*identify performance levels.*
AVL59R	How do security devices or procedures hinder or delay access of information or materials?	*identify possible trade-offs.*
AVL60R	What hardware components are common sources of availability issues?	*identify sources of issues.*
AVL61R	What is the timeframe for problem resolution by the first-level support group?	*identify tolerance metrics.*
AVL62B	What else should I be asking about availability "purpose"?	*uncover additional requirements.*

TIMING (WHEN?)

ID	Availability Suggested Questions	Ask this to:
AVL63S	How does notification depend on time of day?	*identify graduations in notifications.*
AVL64S	What is the fallback position for partial availability?	*identify processing sequence.*
AVL65S	When can upgrades be scheduled?	*identify schedules.*
AVL66S	What special processes are executed for trade-shows, customer events or promotions?	*identify time-triggered events.*
AVL67S	What days during the week should the system be available?	*identify time-triggered events.*
AVL68S	What special processes run for week-end, month-end, and year-end?	*identify time-triggered events.*
AVL69S	What time-sensitive processing occurs? (daily, monthly, quarterly, annually, month-end, quarter-end, or year-end).	*identify time-triggered events.*
AVL70S	When do the users need access to the information and materials they want?	*identify time-triggered events.*
AVL71S	What specific periods are imperative to meet business or safety objectives?	*identify time-triggered events.*
AVL72S	If the system cannot be available "24/7" or "all the time," when are acceptable periods or conditions for the system to be unavailable?	*identify time-triggered events.*
AVL73S	How does availability vary by time of day?	*identify time-triggered events.*
AVL74S	When should the availability limitations be imposed?	*identify time-triggered events.*
AVL75S	When do the users need to prepare or enter inputs?	*identify time-triggered events.*
AVL76S	When do the users need to retrieve or get outputs?	*identify time-triggered events.*
AVL77S	When do the users need to perform their work?	*identify time-triggered events.*
AVL78S	When are users trying to do their jobs?	*identify time-triggered events.*
AVL79S	When are the most critical business periods? (time of day; busy season)	*identify time-triggered events.*
AVL80S	What time frame should be used when tracking the percentage of availability over an extended period? (day, week, month, quarter, year, or longer)	*identify tolerance metrics.*
AVL81S	When are periods of planned/expected peak usage?	*identify tolerance metrics.*
AVL82S	What is the expected availability during peak hours?	*identify tolerance metrics.*

5.2 AVL

TIMING (WHEN?) (continued)

ID	Availability Suggested Questions	Ask this to:
AVL83s	What is the acceptable availability during peak usage hours?	*identify tolerance metrics.*
AVL84s	What is the acceptable amount of time to react to an outage?	*identify tolerance metrics.*
AVL85s	When is the best time to perform maintenance?	*identify tolerance metrics.*
AVL86s	What is the accepted tolerance for system failure or unexpected downtime?	*identify tolerance metrics.*
AVL87s	What is an acceptable amount of time to correct a problem?	*identify tolerance metrics.*
AVL88s	What is a reasonable time to wait for retrieval of information or materials stored off-site?	*identify tolerance metrics.*
AVL89s	What is an acceptable amount of time to perform maintenance?	*identify various forms of maintenance.*
AVL90s	What activities or tasks are more time critical than others?	*prioritize activities.*
AVL91s	What time periods must be avoided for upgrades and maintenance?	*prioritize activities.*
AVL92s	Depending on time of day, which means of notification should be used?	*prioritize notifications.*
AVL93R	When should correction escalation be invoked?	*identify escalation triggers.*
AVL94R	When should notification escalation be invoked?	*identify escalations.*
AVL95B	What else should I be asking about availability "timing"?	*uncover additional requirements.*

LOGISTICS (WHERE?)

ID	Availability Suggested Questions	Ask this to:
AVL96S	What users access the system in a location that is susceptible to availability issues?	*identify availability needs by location.*
AVL97S	How does routine maintenance vary by business location?	*identify availability needs by location.*
AVL98S	How does system availability vary by business location?	*identify availability needs by location.*
AVL99S	How do users in varying business locations need access to the system differently?	*identify availability needs by location.*
AVL100S	What business locations must have access to the system?	*identify availability needs by location.*
AVL101S	What peak periods of usage vary by location?	*identify location restrictions.*
AVL102R	How does off-site storage hinder or delay productivity?	*identify location restrictions.*
AVL103R	What time periods must be avoided for upgrades and maintenance by business location?	*identify location restrictions.*
AVL104R	What processes are performed at each location?	*identify relationships between processes and location.*
AVL105R	What resources are needed at each business location to prevent downtime?	*identify resource needs.*
AVL106R	What hardware/software and people resources are needed at each location to perform routine maintenance?	*identify resource needs.*
AVL107R	How will system usage be monitored by location?	*identify usage.*
AVL108B	What else should I be asking about availability "logistics"?	*uncover additional requirements.*

PROCESS (HOW?)

ID	Availability Suggested Questions	Ask this to:
AVL109s	What processes are legally required?	*classify processes.*
AVL110s	What processes are required by contract obligation?	*classify processes.*
AVL111s	Which processes will be used by the most customers?	*classify processes.*
AVL112s	Which processes will be used by the most users?	*classify processes.*
AVL113s	What processes are most dependent on the system being available?	*evaluate processes.*
AVL114s	What processes may have diminished availability due to degradation?	*evaluate processes.*
AVL115s	If the system/application is not available, how is business conducted?	*identify alternative processes.*
AVL116s	How long are users able to conduct business if the system/application is down?	*identify alternative processes.*
AVL117s	What processes or procedures are followed to continue doing business due to system malfunction?	*identify alternative processes.*
AVL118s	What workarounds do the users use if the system is unavailable?	*identify alternative processes.*
AVL119s	What triggers availability limitations?	*identify events.*
AVL120s	What special processes run for government purposes?	*identify external factors.*
AVL121s	What uses of the system are most apt to have availability issues?	*identify processes.*
AVL122s	What business processes cannot be performed if the system is down?	*identify processes.*
AVL123s	Which processes are compromised by the loss of related processes?	*identify relationships.*
AVL124s	What events or conditions may occur that would delay access to inputs/outputs?	*identify various events and conditions.*
AVL125s	What events or conditions may occur that would prevent access to inputs/outputs?	*identify various events or conditions.*
AVL126s	Which functions of the system are most critical to the business?	*prioritize processes.*

PROCESS (HOW?) (continued)

ID	Availability Suggested Questions	Ask this to:
AVL127S	What processes must always be available?	prioritize processes.
AVL128S	Which processes cause the greatest loss of company productivity when unavailable?	prioritize processes.
AVL129S	Which processes produce the most revenue?	prioritize processes.
AVL130S	Which processes produce the least revenue?	prioritize processes.
AVL131S	Which processes manage the most time-sensitive data?	prioritize processes.
AVL132S	Which processes manage the least time-critical data?	prioritize processes.
AVL133S	What processes have the most recoverable data?	prioritize processes.
AVL134S	What processes have the least recoverable data?	prioritize processes.
AVL135R	Which processes are the most frequently used?	evaluate processes.
AVL136R	When availability of a process is lost, which processes take the longest to regain a normal state of productivity?	evaluate processes.
AVL137R	When availability of a process is lost, which processes are the quickest to regain a normal state of productivity?	evaluate processes.
AVL138R	Which processes are dependent on the most system resources?	evaluate processes.
AVL139R	What routine maintenance is performed on the system? When is it performed?	identify alternative processes.
AVL140R	When the system is not available, what alternatives are there?	identify alternative processes.
AVL141R	What means of notification escalation should be used?	identify escalation procedures.
AVL142R	What means of correction escalation should be used?	identify escalation procedures.
AVL143R	What external communications are the source of availability issues?	identify external factors.
AVL144R	How does availability vary by function?	identify processes.
AVL145R	What processes should have availability limitations?	identify restrictions.
AVL146R	How should availability limitations be imposed?	identify triggers.
AVL147B	What else should I be asking about availability "processes"?	uncover additional requirements.

5.2 AVL

5.3 EFFICIENCY (EFC)

USER CONCERN:	How fast does the system function? How many can be processed? How well does the system respond?
RELATED CATEGORIES:	Capacity, Performance, Responsiveness, Throughput

5.3.1 Efficiency Definition

Efficiency is the extent to which the software system handles capacity, throughput, and response time.

5.3.2 Efficiency Discussion

Efficiency is defined by some as "workability." Workability is the raw ability of the system to perform work. Efficiency requirements identify required functionality, indicating the strain or burden placed on current resources. These requirements identify the user needs to perform tasks in a given amount of time. Efficiency requirements express the expectations with regard to response time, throughput, and capacity:

- *Response time* or *Responsiveness* is the degree to which the system reacts to a single event or condition. Response time requirements specify how much time it takes the software system to act upon a user input or request.

- *Throughput* is the rate at which the system can perform input and output processing. Generally, throughput deals with how fast inputs can be taken in and how quickly the system can crank out the outputs.

◆ *Process capacity* is the ability to process units of work in specified units of time. Process capacity also deals with how many of a particular entity can be processed at the same time.

◆ *Storage capacity* is the ability of the system to store units of any defined entity.

When eliciting efficiency requirements, consider the following aspects:

◆ RESPONSE TIME.

◊ **Possible actions to improve response time**. Things that can be done to improve response time are dependent on the specifics of each system, and therefore not named here. It is up to the team to identify them.

◊ **Ways to measure response time.** What internal monitoring can be done by the system itself? What products and devices are available to monitor the system? What system responses can be watched by hand (monitored by a human)?

◊ **Minimizing user frustration while waiting for a response**. A quality system should notify the user of possible wait times, give progress information during the wait, and camouflage the wait if possible. For example, giving the user something to do while they wait can make the wait duration seem to take less time.

◆ THROUGHPUT.

◊ **Ways to monitor throughput.** Throughput measurements can be current-state (those taken to record what's happening right now) or historical (those recorded over a period of time in order to identify peak periods and trends).

◊ **Cause of throughput traffic and reasons to limit throughput**. Are there peak processing periods when it might be necessary to limit the number of users accessing the system? Can the business process be altered so that the work load is leveled out? For example, instead of having all employees trying to "punch out" on the time clock at 5:00 p.m., the quitting times could be staggered every 10 minutes from 4:30 p.m. to 5:30 p.m. (assuming the start time is also adjusted accordingly).

◊ **Possible actions to improve throughput**. What work can be done at other times or every other day? It is recommended that background processing run on separate systems.

◊ **Ways to organize user inputs and outputs** to optimize system processing of data validation, storage, and retrieval.

♦ PROCESS CAPACITY.

◊ **Number of simultaneous users**. When might it be necessary to limit the number of users logging in?

◊ **Ways to monitor usage**. What information might be helpful in monitoring user activity? It is generally helpful to track the number of users currently active, as well as the number and class of users on each system. Tracking the number of active users over a period of time can help identify peak processing periods.

◊ **Ways to free up system resources**. The development and system support teams should be on the lookout for ways to reduce system workloads.

◊ **Ways to optimize system resources around patterns of use or relationships**. The development and system support teams should look to relationships of data and resources to anticipate workloads for better resource balance.

♦ STORAGE CAPACITY.

◊ **Permanent or temporary storage**. Consider data longevity and data archiving needs. What procedures should be taken to prevent the system from getting over cluttered with inactive data?

◊ **Rate and frequency of retrieving stored entities**. Historical information can be tracked in order to identify performance metrics over time.

◊ **Contingency if storage capacity is exceeded**. Who should be notified? Is there a "warning" level before capacity is exceeded?

5.3.3 Efficiency Requirement Examples

a) At least 20 percent of the processor capacity and storage space available to the system shall be unused at peak load seasonal periods.

b) The system restart cycle must execute completely in less than 60 seconds.

c) System shall be able to process a notification in 1 second or less, and up to and including 100 notifications in 15 seconds or less.

d) The initial system shall be able to handle the entry of orders by customers at a minimum rate of 10 per second.

e) The system must accommodate 300 simultaneous users or less within the peak load period from 9:00 a.m. to 11:00 a.m. Maximum simultaneous user capacity loading at non-peak periods will be 150.

f) Any interface between a user and the automated system shall have a maximum response time of two seconds.

g) Complete report summaries of the current business day's trading shall be available one minute after the end-of-day close of trading.

h) Routine maintenance that is executed while users are active shall not cause a perceptible increase in response time for any function of more than 5% over the response time when no maintenance process is executing.

i) The system shall produce a storage capacity warning notification when the 65% capacity threshold is crossed with additional notifications issued thereafter at 5% threshold increments.

5.3.4 Efficiency Suggested Questions

DATA (WHAT?)

ID	Efficiency Suggested Questions	Ask this to:
EFC1S	What is the outgoing source of throughput peak volume?	*identify information sources.*
EFC2S	What is the incoming source of throughput peak volume?	*identify information sources.*
EFC3S	How much data should be retained for each user?	*identify retention needs.*
EFC4S	How much data should be retained for each customer?	*identify retention needs.*
EFC5S	How much data should be retained for each transaction?	*identify retention needs.*
EFC6S	How much data should be retained for each product?	*identify retention needs.*
EFC7S	How long should the data be retained?	*identify retention needs.*
EFC8S	How long should the data be retained for real-time access?	*identify retention needs.*
EFC9S	When is an acknowledgment before results an expected response?	*identify various communications.*
EFC10S	Which requests require indicators of progress while processing?	*identify various communications.*
EFC11S	Which requests require estimates of time remaining before completion?	*identify various communications.*
EFC12S	What warning thresholds can be set as capacity grows?	*identify warnings.*
EFC13S	What is the balance between incoming and outgoing throughput?	*prioritize information or materials.*
EFC14B	What else should I be asking about efficiency "data"?	*uncover additional requirements.*

ROLES (WHO?)

5.3 EFC

ID	Efficiency Suggested Questions	Ask this to:
EFC15s	What source can provide an accurate count of existing end users?	*identify additional stakeholders.*
EFC16s	What source can provide an accurate count of existing customers?	*identify additional stakeholders.*
EFC17s	What source can provide an accurate count of existing processes?	*identify additional stakeholders.*
EFC18s	What source can provide an accurate volume count of existing transactions?	*identify additional stakeholders.*
EFC19s	What are the expectations on system efficiency?	*identify expectations.*
EFC20s	What are the expectations on system response time?	*identify expectations.*
EFC21s	What are the expectations on system throughput?	*identify expectations.*
EFC22s	What are the expectations on system capacity?	*identify expectations.*
EFC23s	What users should have a need for greater efficiency than others?	*identify expectations.*
EFC24s	When should multiple people be notified?	*identify role responsibilities.*
EFC25s	Who should receive notification when there are system failures?	*identify role responsibilities.*
EFC26s	Which people need to be notified when there is a serious error?	*identify role responsibilities.*
EFC27s	Who is authorized to perform what functions?	*identify role responsibilities.*
EFC28s	Who is authorized to access what data?	*identify role responsibilities.*
EFC29s	Who (role) should receive warning messages as thresholds are exceeded?	*identify role responsibilities.*
EFC30s	What is the typical number of users accessing the system simultaneously?	*identify usage.*
EFC31s	What is the greatest number of simultaneous users during peak processing? Anticipated future usage?	*identify usage.*
EFC32s	What limits to the number of simultaneous users apply?	*identify usage.*
EFC33s	What forcible eject/reject requirements exist for users?	*identify user behavior.*
EFC34s	What types of users can be affected by traffic metering?	*identify users.*
EFC35r	Who performs routine performance tuning?	*identify role responsibilities.*

ROLES (WHO?) (continued)

5.3 EFC

ID	Efficiency Suggested Questions	Ask this to:
EFC36R	Who gets called when the system is not performing as expected?	*identify role responsibilities.*
EFC37B	Who should receive system performance audit reports?	*identify role responsibilities.*
EFC38B	What else should I be asking about efficiency "roles"?	*uncover additional requirements.*

PURPOSE (WHY?)

ID	Efficiency Suggested Questions	Ask this to:
EFC39S	How many things can the system cope with and work on at once?	*identify expectations.*
EFC40S	How critical is this performance factor?	*identify metrics.*
EFC41S	What demand spike can be anticipated?	*identify metrics.*
EFC42S	What response time expectations are there by function?	*identify metrics.*
EFC43S	What class or category levels of performance can be defined?	*identify metrics.*
EFC44S	Where did the tolerable response time come from?	*identify metrics.*
EFC45S	What level of throughput is expected of the system?	*identify metrics.*
EFC46S	What is the minimum number of events the system must store?	*identify metrics.*
EFC47S	What performance is measured?	*identify metrics.*
EFC48S	What timeframe does this performance requirement need to meet?	*identify metrics.*
EFC49S	What is the maximum acceptable response time end-to-end?	*identify metrics.*
EFC50S	What percentage of time is the stated response time expected?	*identify metrics.*
EFC51S	How will volume of activity be measured?	*identify metrics.*
EFC52S	What volume levels will be measured, and in what timeframes?	*identify metrics.*

5.3 EFC

ID	Efficiency Suggested Questions	Ask this to:
EFC53S	How can performance be measured?	*identify metrics.*
EFC54S	When does measurement start and stop?	*identify metrics.*
EFC55S	How should performance be monitored?	*identify metrics.*
EFC56S	How much resource should be allocated to monitoring?	*identify metrics.*
EFC57S	What performance indicators are most important to the business?	*identify metrics.*
EFC58S	On what basis is this performance goal specified?	*identify metrics.*
EFC59S	What is a tolerable length of response time?	*identify metrics.*
EFC60S	Please fill in the following: What is the expected response time in [*unit of measure*]?	*identify metrics.*
EFC61S	Please fill in the following: What is the expected throughput in [*unit of measure*]?	*identify metrics.*
EFC62S	Please fill in the following: What is the expected capacity in [*unit of measure*]?	*identify metrics.*
EFC63S	What is the expected (accepted) average response time?	*identify metrics.*
EFC64S	What is the expected (accepted) maximum response time?	*identify metrics.*
EFC65S	What is the expected (accepted) average throughput?	*identify metrics.*
EFC66S	What is the expected (accepted) minimum throughput?	*identify metrics.*
EFC67S	What is the expected (accepted) maximum throughput?	*identify metrics.*
EFC68S	What is the expected speed to complete the task?	*identify metrics.*
EFC69S	Why is this level of performance needed?	*identify metrics.*
EFC70S	What is an acceptable mode of operation when the system has been degraded in some manner?	*identify performance levels.*
EFC71S	At what load level can response begin to degrade?	*identify performance levels.*
EFC72S	What is acceptable degradation during peak times?	*identify performance levels.*
EFC73S	What have been barriers to expected performance?	*identify performance levels.*

PURPOSE (WHY?) (continued)

ID	Efficiency Suggested Questions	Ask this to:
EFC74S	What is the worst that can happen if the requirement is not met?	identify results (outcomes).
EFC75S	What are risks associated with performance problems?	identify risk.
EFC76S	How critical to the business are the performance requirements?	identify risk.
EFC77S	How much is acceptable to pay for this level of performance?	identify value.
EFC78S	What is an acceptable cost of monitoring?	identify value.
EFC79R	What is the capacity of the system to store events of a particular type?	identify events.
EFC80R	What functions are candidates for metering response time?	identify events.
EFC81R	What are the predictors of high volume activity?	identify events.
EFC82R	What circumstances or conditions must be met from the operating environment?	identify events.
EFC83R	What efficiency conditions might exist from vendor hardware?	identify resource needs.
EFC84R	What efficiency conditions might exist from vendor software?	identify resource needs.
EFC85B	What are the known constraints/restrictions imposed by the system?	identify possible trade-offs.
EFC86B	What time-accuracy trade-offs have been considered?	identify possible trade-offs.
EFC87B	What time-space trade-offs have been considered?	identify possible trade-offs.
EFC88B	What is the trade-off between efficiency and scalability?	identify possible trade-offs.
EFC89B	What is the trade-off between efficiency and maintainability?	identify possible trade-offs.
EFC90B	What is the trade-off between efficiency and reliability?	identify possible trade-offs.
EFC91B	What is the trade-off between efficiency and flexibility?	identify possible trade-offs.
EFC92B	What else should I be asking about efficiency "purpose"?	uncover additional requirements.

TIMING (WHEN?)

ID	Efficiency Suggested Questions	Ask this to:
EFC93s	When should inactive data be removed?	*identify data characteristics.*
EFC94s	How often should performance be measured?	*identify metrics.*
EFC95s	When should performance be measured?	*identify metrics.*
EFC96s	What is typical off-peak throughput? Peak throughput?	*identify metrics.*
EFC97s	When during the week, month, quarter, and year will peak times occur?	*identify system load cycles.*
EFC98s	What is the expected duration of peak use activity periods?	*identify system load durations.*
EFC99s	What time of day will peak usage occur?	*identify system load time periods.*
EFC100s	Which requests have maximum response time limits?	*identify time limitations.*
EFC101s	Which requests have minimum response time limits?	*identify time limitations.*
EFC102s	Which requests have maximum sequential response time limits? (The request is followed by sequentially timed responses.)	*identify time limitations.*
EFC103s	Which requests have minimum sequential response time limits?	*identify time limitations.*
EFC104s	Which requests are sequential with maximum time limits? (For example, user must enter password within *x time* of entering user identification.)	*identify time limitations.*
EFC105s	Which requests are sequential with minimum time limits? (For example, user cannot enter password within *x time* of entering user identification.)	*identify time limitations.*
EFC106s	Which requests require completion by the user within a set period of time? (For example, entry of data must complete from first to last within *x time*.)	*identify time limitations.*
EFC107s	Which requests require completion by the user after a set period of time? (For example, entry of menu choice cannot occur until *x time* has lapsed from menu display.)	*identify time limitations.*
EFC108s	What timeframe is this capacity expected?	*identify time limitations.*
EFC109s	How do peak activity periods compare to normal activity periods of use?	*identify various time periods.*
EFC110b	What should the balance be between primary and secondary processes?	*identify possible trade-offs.*
EFC111b	What are the most important activities to process during peak load times?	*identify possible trade-offs.*

TIMING (WHEN?) (continued)

ID	Efficiency Suggested Questions	Ask this to:
EFC112B	What activities can be reduced during peak load times?	*identify possible trade-offs.*
EFC113B	What else should I be asking about efficiency "timing"?	*uncover additional requirements.*

5.3 EFC

LOGISTICS (WHERE?)

ID	Efficiency Suggested Questions	Ask this to:
EFC114S	What users access the system in a location that is susceptible to efficiency issues?	*identify efficiency needs by location.*
EFC115S	How does routine performance tuning vary by business location?	*identify efficiency needs by location.*
EFC116S	How does system efficiency vary by business location?	*identify efficiency needs by location.*
EFC117S	What users in varying business locations need access to the system differently?	*identify efficiency needs by location.*
EFC118S	What business locations interface with the system?	*identify efficiency needs by location.*
EFC119S	What peak periods of usage vary by location?	*identify efficiency needs by location.*
EFC120S	Where is the greatest concentration of users?	*identify locations.*
EFC121S	How widely spread are the system users?	*identify user locations.*
EFC122S	What users spread across time zones?	*identify user locations.*
EFC123S	What users spread across the world?	*identify user locations.*
EFC124S	What part of the system do each of the performance requirements pertain?	*identify various components.*
EFC125R	How does off-site storage capacity hurt or help performance?	*identify location restrictions.*
EFC126R	What time periods must be avoided for performance tuning by business location?	*identify location restrictions.*
EFC127R	What processes are performed at each location?	*identify relationships between processes and location.*

LOGISTICS (WHERE?) (continued)

ID	Efficiency Suggested Questions	Ask this to:
EFC128R	What resources are needed at each business location to increase efficiency performance?	*identify resource needs.*
EFC129R	What hardware/software and people resources are needed at each location to execute performance tuning?	*identify resource needs.*
EFC130R	How will system throughput be monitored by location?	*identify usage.*
EFC131R	How will system capacity be monitored by location?	*identify usage.*
EFC132R	How will system response time be monitored by location?	*identify usage.*
EFC133B	What else should I be asking about efficiency "logistics"?	*uncover additional requirements.*

PROCESS (HOW?)

ID	Efficiency Suggested Questions	Ask this to:
EFC134S	What are acceptable response times during exception processing?	*identify exceptions.*
EFC135S	What is the anticipated growth?	*identify metrics.*
EFC136S	What peak load is anticipated?	*identify metrics.*
EFC137S	What time-critical processes are expected?	*identify processes.*
EFC138S	What makes these processes time critical?	*identify processes.*
EFC139S	What happens to the system during the time-critical processes when too much time is taken?	*identify processes.*
EFC140S	What processes include complex calculations?	*identify processes.*
EFC141S	What processes require large volumes of data?	*identify processes.*
EFC142S	What part of the system does this performance target apply to?	*identify processes.*

PROCESS (HOW?) (continued)

ID	Efficiency Suggested Questions	Ask this to:
EFC143s	What is the rate at which the system can process things?	*identify processing rates.*
EFC144s	How shall the system respond when warning thresholds are hit?	*identify system responses.*
EFC145s	What messages should be sent when warning thresholds are hit?	*identify system responses.*
EFC146s	What response is expected when stated capacities are exceeded?	*identify system responses.*
EFC147s	How long does it take the system to satisfy user requests?	*identify system responses.*
EFC148R	What exception processes must be considered?	*identify exceptions.*
EFC149R	When can traffic be metered for limiting access?	*identify metrics.*
EFC150R	What development techniques may be used to improve retrieval time?	*identify possible process improvement areas.*
EFC151R	What processing considerations (encryption, protocols, message sets) must be included in the application?	*identify processes.*
EFC152R	What operations are dependent upon vendor software?	*identify processes.*
EFC153R	How much main memory is needed to support the system?	*identify resource needs.*
EFC154R	What is the average expected hardware configuration?	*identify resource needs.*
EFC155R	What vendor software is under the company's control?	*identify resource needs.*
EFC156R	When should text versus graphical design considerations be used?	*identify resource needs.*
EFC157R	How much secondary storage space is needed to support the system?	*identify resource needs.*
EFC158R	What are the minimum hardware specifications expected for implementation to support the performance requirements?	*identify resource needs.*
EFC159R	What hardware could constrain development?	*identify resource needs.*
EFC160R	What is the lowest common denominator for design consideration of user equipment?	*identify resource needs.*
EFC161R	What are known resource limitations?	*identify resource needs.*
EFC162R	What can be done if the performance cannot be met?	*identify types of adjustments.*
EFC163R	What can be done if the performance is not met?	*identify types of adjustments.*
EFC164B	What else should I be asking about efficiency "processes"?	*uncover additional requirements.*

The Quest for Software Requirements

5.3 EFC

5.4 INTEGRITY (INT)

> USER CONCERN: How accurate and authentic are the data?
> RELATED CATEGORIES: Accuracy, Completeness, Confidentiality, Data
>   Authenticity, Data Integration, Data Security

5.4.1 Integrity Definition

Integrity is the degree to which the data maintained by the software system are accurate, authentic, and without corruption.

5.4.2 Integrity Discussion

The term "integrity" is used in this book to mean consistency, accuracy, and correctness of the data. Integrity is an indicator of the user's trust in the system's data. This book treats the terms *data* and *information* as synonymous. The integrity of information must be preserved (identically maintained) during operations in which information is transferred, stored, and retrieved.

Integrity requirements describe the ability of the system to survive threats to its data integrity. Threats are potential attacks on the system integrity, both accidental and intentional. A threat to the system integrity is measured by an estimated probability of an attack of a specific type occurring within a particular time frame. Meanwhile, the potential to counteract threats on system integrity can be measured as the probability of counteracting attacks of a particular type.

Integrity is also viewed as the degree to which the system is free from any sorts of intentional attacks (for example, thieves and saboteurs) or non-malicious events (for example, failing hardware, transmission errors, and accidental physical file destruction by the operator). Integrity is also the degree to which data are both untouched by any sort of corruption, removal, change, or addition, and are not penetrated by unauthorized people or processes for any purpose.

Integrity is a close relative of security. Some authors use the term integrity to encompass a variety of *security* issues, such as blocking unauthorized access to system functions (also called *access security* or *access control*, as explained earlier in subsection 5.1), and ensuring that the software is protected from virus infection, as well as disaster and recovery of software and hardware. As stated earlier, these are not included in the scope of integrity as referenced in this book.

5.4 INT

When eliciting integrity requirements, consider the following aspects:

♦ REGULAR AND CONSISTENT BACKUPS OF THE SYSTEM'S DATA HELP TO PREVENT DATA LOSS. In the event of system failure (due to any reason), the challenge lies in being able to restore all of the lost information to its original state with 100-percent accuracy.

♦ BACKING UP TO THE SAME DRIVE AS THE NATIVE DATA IS USELESS; a hard-drive crash can mean losing everything. Backup software should allow the possibility for storing data to a variety of media (external to the original data store). Backup archives are also dependent on the type of medium chosen and its long-term shelf-life.

♦ DATA RESTORE PROCEDURES SHOULD BE TESTED FREQUENTLY TO VERIFY THAT STORAGE HARDWARE IS WORKING PROPERLY. A faulty hard-drive may reproduce corrupt backup archives no matter how good the backup software is.

♦ DATA AUTHENTICITY: maintaining the data and representing the data in accord with the original data source.

◊ **Data precision**: specifying the degree of numeric precision in calculations, storage, and presentation.

◊ **Accuracy of information portrayed**: presenting information as intended by the originating source.

◊ **Authentic relationships**: maintaining data relationships as defined by the originating sources.

◊ **True to the source of the data**, ensuring the data are consistently stored, presented, and maintained with respect to the originating source.

◊ **Data encryption methods**.

5.4.3 Integrity Requirement Examples

5.4 INT

a) All monetary amounts must be accurate to two decimal places.

b) Accuracy of warehouse temperature readings will be within plus or minus two degrees Celsius.

c) Whenever a change is made to information stored in Microsoft Word® , the fact of the change shall be recorded in a database or equivalent technology that is routinely backed up. This is intended to identify changed documents in the event of the loss of a disk.

d) The loan origination system shall perform all calculations with rounding to five (5) decimal places before rounding for presentation to two decimal places (dollars and cents).

e) The integrity of the system data area must be checked by the internal audit system twice per second; if inconsistencies in the data are detected, the system operation should be disabled.

f) The precision of calculations with derived data shall be at the same degree of precision as the originating source data.

g) Derived totals and sub-totals shall be considered transient data and never committed to permanent storage.

h) Tallies and totals shall acknowledge the source of record when presented without supporting detail.

i) Presentation of earned premium shall be relative to presentation date, policy renewal date, and payment posted date calculated to a whole day.

5.4.4 Integrity Suggested Questions

DATA (WHAT?)

ID	Integrity Suggested Questions	Ask this to:
INT1S	What causes information to be created?	*correlate information and events.*
INT2S	What causes information to be updated?	*correlate information and events.*
INT3S	What causes information to be deleted?	*correlate information and events.*
INT4S	What causes a change in status to information?	*correlate information and events.*
INT5S	What is the response from the event?	*determine information that is output from the event.*
INT6S	What is the reaction of the system to each business event?	*determine information that is output from the event.*
INT7S	What is the response to each business event?	*determine information that is output from the event.*
INT8S	How does the business event get triggered?	*determine what information is received to initiate the event.*
INT9S	Who owns the existing information?	*identify additional stakeholders.*
INT10S	What do internal users need to do their jobs?	*identify correlations between information and users.*
INT11S	What information is each user looking for?	*identify correlations between information and users.*
INT12S	What are concerns for the wholeness or completeness of the information?	*identify data security needs.*
INT13S	If information exists within another system, what is the condition of the data?	*identify effort to clean existing data.*
INT14S	What information already exists within another system?	*identify effort to create data.*
INT15S	How does the existing data need to change in the system under development?	*identify effort to create data.*
INT16S	Who triggers the business event?	*identify information input sources.*

ID	Integrity Suggested Questions	Ask this to:
INT17s	What information is needed to perform the process?	*identify information input sources.*
INT18s	Who is the recipient of the business event?	*identify information output sources.*
INT19s	Who should be notified if a failure occurs?	*identify information output sources.*
INT20s	What is the output of the process?	*identify information output sources.*
INT21s	What is the relationship of each information group with other groups?	*identify information relationships.*
INT22s	What kinds of user activities cause data corruption?	*identify problematic uses.*
INT23s	What multi-part information entry applications should the user/customer be allowed to recommence entry?	*identify process activities.*
INT24s	How does each business policy affect information groups?	*identify relationships between data and rules.*
INT25s	What information is needed to enforce business policies?	*identify relationships between data and rules.*
INT26s	How long should backed-up data be retained?	*identify retention levels.*
INT27s	What data must be archived?	*identify retention levels.*
INT28s	How long will data be stored to allow user/customer to complete entry in a multi-part entry system?	*identify retention levels.*
INT29s	How long should transaction history be retained?	*identify retention periods.*
INT30s	How long should archived data be retained?	*identify retention periods.*
INT31s	What multi-part information should be retained if a failure occurs partway through the entry?	*identify retention types.*
INT32s	How long should the system retain partial data from interrupted entry?	*identify retention types.*
INT33s	What records of events happening are needed?	*identify retention.*
INT34s	What history of changed data is needed?	*identify retention.*
INT35s	When data are changed, how long should the previous value be retained?	*identify retention.*

5.4 INT

DATA (WHAT?) (continued)

ID	Integrity Suggested Questions	Ask this to:
INT36s	When data are changed, how many generations of previous values need to be retained?	*identify retention.*
INT37s	What errors must be tracked?	*identify retention.*
INT38s	In addition to the company security, what must this application do to protect the data?	*identify security events and conditions.*
INT39s	What are concerns for the authenticity of the information?	*identify security events and conditions.*
INT40s	What are information concerns for the genuineness or faithfulness of true representation?	*identify security events and conditions.*
INT41s	What other steps must be taken to protect information?	*identify security events and conditions.*
INT42s	What availability or assured service of information must be maintained? Assured service is guarding against interruption of service.	*identify security risk.*
INT43s	What data are not made available for hardcopy reports?	*identify types of access.*
INT44s	What data should be backed up?	*identify types of backup.*
INT45s	What are the expectations for data backup? Backing up is the act of making a copy at a specific point in time.	*identify types of backups.*
INT46s	What are the expectations for data recovery? Recovery is the act of bringing the restored data up to date, usually using an update log of the changes made since the back-up was taken.	*identify types of recovery.*
INT47s	What is needed to do each user's job?	*identify user information needs.*
INT48s	What kinds of audit trails or logs are kept?	*identify various controls and retention.*
INT49r	What data are stored locally (user's computer) while using the application?	*identify data security issues.*
INT50r	What is the cardinality between related information? (Cardinality is the number—minimum or maximum—of times a relationship occurs.)	*identify optional data and volume.*
INT51r	What controls over data mining of the application data must be put in place?	*identify possible access combinations.*
INT52r	What derived data are stored?	*identify sources of data.*

5.4 INT

DATA (WHAT?) (continued)

ID	Integrity Suggested Questions	Ask this to:
INT53R	What data are received from other systems, stored by this system, and must not be changed by this system?	*identify sources of data.*
INT54R	Which data elements must always be encrypted to all users?	*identify types of controls.*
INT55R	Which data elements must always be encrypted to all access attempts?	*identify types of controls.*
INT56R	Which data elements are completely blocked from unauthorized access?	*identify types of data.*
INT57R	Which data elements are partially blocked from unauthorized access?	*identify types of data.*
INT58R	What if data became corrupted?	*identify types of monitoring and verification.*
INT59R	What safeguards must be put in place for information that resides externally?	*identify uncontained information.*
INT60B	What else should I be asking about integrity "data"?	*uncover additional requirements.*

5.4 INT

ROLES (WHO?)

ID	Integrity Suggested Questions	Ask this to:
INT61S	How does each business policy affect each user class?	*correlate users and business rules.*
INT62S	Who should not trigger this event?	*identify access security requirements.*
INT63S	What would be the risk to the business if an unauthorized user triggered the event?	*identify access security requirements.*
INT64S	Who should be denied access through each communication type?	*identify access security requirements.*
INT65S	Who has authority to trigger the process?	*identify access security requirements.*
INT66S	Once verified, how is externally sourced data changed?	*identify authority.*
INT67S	Which users initiate which business events?	*identify correlations between users and events.*

ROLES (WHO?) (continued)

ID	Integrity Suggested Questions	Ask this to:
INT68S	Under what conditions can approval decisions be overridden?	*identify levels of authority.*
INT69S	What should happen when another component/system has not completed its responsibility?	*identify levels of responsibility.*
INT70S	Who triggers each event?	*identify relationships between users and events.*
INT71S	Who gets the response from the event?	*identify relationships between users and events.*
INT72S	How does the process differ by user class?	*identify restrictions by user.*
INT73S	Who (user/customer role) is authorized to delete data?	*identify role authority levels.*
INT74S	What component/system is authorized to change data?	*identify role authority levels.*
INT75S	What component/system is authorized to delete data?	*identify role authority levels.*
INT76S	When a multiple data store application is used, who (what component/system) is responsible for monitoring the other components/systems?	*identify role authority levels.*
INT77S	What combinations of data elements must not be shown to any group of people except the highest authorized?	*identify role levels of authority.*
INT78S	Who (user role) is responsible for the data?	*identify role responsibilities.*
INT79S	Who should know about changes made to data?	*identify role responsibilities.*
INT80S	Who has the authority to verify derived data?	*identify role responsibilities.*
INT81S	Who has the authority to override approval decisions?	*identify role responsibilities.*
INT82S	What users must see data only related to their roles?	*identify role responsibilities.*
INT83S	Who owns the interface between components/systems?	*identify role responsibilities.*
INT84S	What roles are constrained to particular high-level analytics?	*identify role responsibilities.*
INT85S	What roles have access to reporting system data but will be restricted from access to analytic system data?	*identify role responsibilities.*
INT86S	What component/system is responsible for the data?	*identify role responsibilities.*
INT87S	What information must be protected from which user classes at all costs?	*identify security issues.*

ROLES (WHO?) (continued)

ID	Integrity Suggested Questions	Ask this to:
INT88s	How are high-level analytics constrained by role?	*identify usage.*
INT89s	What is the impact on the customer's business if the information is out of date?	*identify usage.*
INT90s	What consequences are there for two different users having two different versions of the data?	*identify usage.*
INT91s	How will the information be used?	*identify usage.*
INT92s	What data elements must be presented in combination and not as individual elements?	*identify usage.*
INT93s	How many users need access at each location?	*identify users.*
INT94s	How are data levels of access granted?	*identify various authorizers.*
INT95s	Which data elements require a higher level of security to access?	*identify various levels of access.*
INT96r	How many levels of data access exist?	*identify various levels of access.*
INT97r	What control is required to authorize changes to data?	*identify various types of authorization.*
INT98r	How many concurrent users are there for each communication type?	*identify need to add resources.*
INT99r	Who will need access during backup/restore procedures?	*identify role responsibilities.*
INT100r	Who has authority to override backup/restore procedures?	*identify role responsibilities.*
INT101r	What user audit processes are in place currently?	*identify role responsibilities.*
INT102r	What could be done to improve user audit controls?	*identify role responsibilities.*
INT103b	What else should I be asking about integrity "roles"?	*uncover additional requirements.*

5.4 INT

PURPOSE (WHY?)

5.4 INT

ID	Integrity Suggested Questions	Ask this to:
INT104s	What are legal concerns in performing this process? Not performing the process?	*correlate processes and business rules.*
INT105s	How does this event conflict with business policies?	*correlate processes and business rules.*
INT106s	How is this event triggered by business policies?	*correlate processes and business rules.*
INT107s	How does each business policy affect business events?	*correlate processes and business rules.*
INT108s	What restrictions need to be applied to each user class?	*correlate users and business rules.*
INT109s	What are the effects on business if a user class does not have access to requested information?	*identify business risks.*
INT110s	How is the business policy dependent on another policy?	*identify relationships among business rules.*
INT111s	How does the satisfaction of this business policy affect another policy?	*identify relationships among business rules.*
INT112s	What makes that data necessary to protect?	*identify risk.*
INT113s	What would be the effect on business if a user class does not have access for a few days, or a few weeks?	*identify tolerance of system downtime.*
INT114s	What audit trail of access to sensitive or confidential data should be kept?	*identify types of monitoring and verification.*
INT115s	What audit trail of unsuccessful data access should be maintained?	*identify types of monitoring and verification.*
INT116s	What audit trail of failed user actions should be kept?	*identify types of monitoring and verification.*
INT117s	What security violations that the system detects should be recorded?	*identify types of monitoring and verification.*
INT118s	What record of incorrect authentication (for example, password) entry should be kept?	*identify types of monitoring and verification.*
INT119s	What combination of data would cause serious damage to the business if made available?	*identify various data combinations.*

ID	Integrity Suggested Questions	Ask this to:
INT120s	What data must always be presented together for an accurate representation of the business?	*identify various data relationships.*
INT121s	How much data can be lost?	*identify various levels of data.*
INT122s	What restrictions should be placed on modifying timed changes?	*identify various types of controls.*
INT123s	What audit trail of user actions should be kept?	*identify various types of monitors.*
INT124s	What record should be kept of the frequency that data are viewed? Changed?	*identify various types of monitors.*
INT125s	What audit trail of error conditions detected by the system shall be recorded?	*identify various types of monitors.*
INT126s	What information must be captured when approval decisions are overridden?	*identify various types of monitors.*
INT127s	What log of changes should be maintained?	*identify various types of monitors.*
INT128s	What evidence of processes being run or executed are necessary?	*identify various types of monitors.*
INT129s	What transaction history is needed? A transaction is a representation of an event or occurrence that happens at a point in time.	*identify various types of monitors.*
INT130s	What audit trail of significant system events should be kept?	*identify various types of monitors.*
INT131s	How will data access be audited?	*identify various types of monitors.*
INT132s	What audits must be in place to detect unintentional or unauthorized changes to data?	*identify various types of monitors.*
INT133s	What should be known about data changes?	*identify various types of monitors.*
INT134s	What steps should be taken to audit data quality?	*identify various types of monitors.*
INT135s	What data functions must have time of activity recorded?	*identify various types of monitors.*
INT136s	What audits must be in place to detect improper usage of data by either authorized or unauthorized users/customers?	*identify various types of monitors.*
INT137s	What audits must be in place to detect improper usage of data by either authorized or unauthorized components/systems?	*identify various types of monitors.*
INT138s	What integrity checks must be in place to validate data after a restore?	*identify various types of verification.*

5.4 INT

PURPOSE (WHY?) (continued)

5.4 INT

ID	Integrity Suggested Questions	Ask this to:
INT139s	What integrity checks must be in place to validate data after recovery?	*identify various types of verification.*
INT140s	What integrity checks must be in place to validate data after an abnormal event?	*identify various types of verification.*
INT141s	What data must be available for high-level analytics of the business?	*identify various usages.*
INT142s	How should the system prompt the user to verify data when an interrupted entry is resumed?	*identify verification types.*
INT143s	What are the greatest concerns regarding access to reports produced by the analytic system?	*identify vulnerabilities.*
INT144s	What information will provide user with confidence that the system is working?	*prioritize processes.*
INT145s	In what business areas would failure to perform hurt the business the most?	*prioritize requirements.*
INT146s	Where would users hate to see something go wrong?	*prioritize requirements.*
INT147s	If the users were away for two weeks, what would be the first things they checked upon returning?	*prioritize requirements.*
INT148b	What else should I be asking about integrity "purpose"?	*uncover additional requirements.*

TIMING (WHEN?)

ID	Integrity Suggested Questions	Ask this to:
INT149s	What should happen if a user is in the middle of entering a timed change when its time is reached?	*correlate processes and business rules.*
INT150s	What should happen to a timed change that needs approval but hasn't been approved by the time it's due?	*correlate processes and business rules.*
INT151s	When the user is interrupted during data entry, where does the user expect to resume entry?	*correlate processes and business rules.*

ID	Integrity Suggested Questions	Ask this to:
INT152s	Where should users recommence entering information later on, from the point they had reached previously?	*correlate processes and business rules.*
INT153s	When should data be backed up?	*identify business cycles.*
INT154s	How frequently should data backups be taken?	*identify business cycles.*
INT155s	How frequently should data be archived?	*identify business cycles.*
INT156s	Explain the order, if any, of the list of business events.	*identify event dependencies.*
INT157s	What are the expectations for data restore? (Restore is the act of copying from a back-up when the main data are lost.)	*identify levels of restore.*
INT158s	What sequence must the process follow?	*identify process dependencies.*
INT159s	Why would each user interact with the system?	*identify standard triggers of events.*
INT160s	What stimulates the business event to occur?	*identify standard triggers of events.*
INT161r	At what logical points or triggers should the user be aware that information entered has been retained?	*identify communication types.*
INT162r	When will data quality be measured?	*identify metrics.*
INT163r	When will data security be measured?	*identify metrics.*
INT164r	How long is the current communication response time?	*identify need to add resources.*
INT165r	What timed changes to information occur? (A timed change is a change to information at a precise, predetermined moment in time.)	*identify process activities.*
INT166r	What coordinated changes to information occur? (A coordinated change is a collection of related changes that all need to be applied at exactly the same time.)	*identify process activities.*
INT167r	What incremental changes of data should be stored between backups?	*identify process cycles.*
INT168r	When should changes to data be committed?	*identify process cycles.*
INT169b	What else should I be asking about integrity "timing"?	*uncover additional requirements.*

5.4 INT

LOGISTICS (WHERE?)

ID	Integrity Suggested Questions	Ask this to:
INT170S	Who needs access to the information at each business location?	*identify communication locations.*
INT171S	What users access the system in a location that is susceptible to data corruption?	*identify integrity needs by location.*
INT172S	How does data transmission vary by business location?	*identify integrity needs by location.*
INT173S	How do integrity needs vary by business location?	*identify integrity needs by location.*
INT174S	How do users in varying business locations access information differently?	*identify integrity needs by location.*
INT175S	What business locations must have access to the system?	*identify integrity needs by location.*
INT176S	What information audits should be performed at each business location?	*identify integrity needs by location.*
INT177S	What are the peak periods of usage that vary by location?	*identify location restrictions.*
INT178S	What geographic dependencies are there to the business events?	*identify relationships between locations and events.*
INT179S	How are business policies geographically dependent?	*identify relationships between locations and rules.*
INT180S	How does the process vary by geographic location?	*identify restrictions by location.*
INT181S	What data are stored in multiple places?	*identify storage locations.*
INT182S	What data will be stored locally?	*identify various data types.*
INT183R	How should the coordination of data stored in multiple data stores be managed?	*identify location controls.*
INT184R	How should data stored in multiple data stores be recovered?	*identify location controls.*
INT185R	How does off-site storage help or hurt integrity?	*identify location restrictions.*
INT186R	What time periods must be avoided for backup/restore procedures by business location?	*identify location restrictions.*
INT187R	What data manipulation processes are performed at each location?	*identify relationships between processes and location.*
INT188R	What resources are needed at each business location to safeguard integrity?	*identify resource needs.*

5.4 INT

LOGISTICS (WHERE?) (continued)

ID	Integrity Suggested Questions	Ask this to:
INT189R	What hardware/software and people resources are needed at each location to perform audit processes?	*identify resource needs.*
INT190R	How will system usage be monitored by location?	*identify usage.*
INT191B	What else should I be asking about integrity "logistics"?	*uncover additional requirements.*

5.4 INT

PROCESS (HOW?)

ID	Integrity Suggested Questions	Ask this to:
INT192S	How does processing differ between deleting and canceling information?	*clarify terminology.*
INT193S	What functions should each user class be allowed to perform?	*correlate users and processing.*
INT194S	What types of technology equipment are currently used?	*define current resources.*
INT195S	What types of communication are currently used?	*define current resources.*
INT196S	What is the relationship between business events?	*determine workflow dependencies.*
INT197S	Where does the output from the process go?	*identify additional processes or processes that aren't needed.*
INT198S	What happens to the output from the process?	*identify additional processes or processes that aren't needed.*
INT199S	What are the current responsibilities of the users?	*identify additional processes.*
INT200S	Who can best describe the process?	*identify additional stakeholders.*
INT201S	What steps are needed to ensure data are represented in the manner intended by the source/authority?	*identify integrity checks.*
INT202S	What steps are needed to ensure data are maintained in the manner intended by the source/authority?	*identify integrity checks.*
INT203S	How are derived data verified before presentation?	*identify integrity checks.*

PROCESS (HOW?) (continued)

5.4 INT

ID	Integrity Suggested Questions	Ask this to:
INT204s	What areas cause bottlenecks or issues?	*identify possible process improvement areas.*
INT205s	How would the users like the system to work?	*identify possible process improvement areas.*
INT206s	What information must be updated by a particular user class while other users are viewing the information?	*identify process relationships.*
INT207s	What entry of information could be disrupted?	*identify processes.*
INT208s	How is access of sensitive data controlled?	*identify types of control.*
INT209s	How is externally sourced data verified?	*identify types of monitoring and verification.*
INT210s	How should coordinated changes be managed? (multi-site, multi-platform, multi-system)	*identify various activities or actions.*
INT211r	What happens if either the system or an external interface system fails during the transmission of data?	*correlate processes and business rules.*
INT212r	What controls must be in place when transforming data from reporting systems to analytic data stores?	*correlate processes and business rules.*
INT213r	What steps should be taken to deal with loss of data from multi-part entry?	*correlate processes and business rules.*
INT214r	What processes or procedures need to be in place to protect software from viruses that can cause data loss or corruption?	*correlate processes and business rules.*
INT215r	What processes or procedures need to be in place to protect hardware?	*correlate processes and business rules.*
INT216r	When a failed component/system returns, what initiates recovery?	*correlate processes and business rules.*
INT217r	How will data security be measured?	*identify metrics.*
INT218r	What support processes might be affected by the system?	*identify process dependencies.*
INT219b	What else should I be asking about integrity "processes"?	*uncover additional requirements.*

5.5 RELIABILITY (REL)

> USER CONCERN: How immune is the system to failure?
> RELATED CATEGORIES: Availability, Dependability, Fault Tolerance, Maintainability, Survivability

5.5.1 Reliability Definition

Reliability is the extent to which the software system consistently performs the specified functions without failure.

5.5.2 Reliability Discussion

Reliability might be the most important dynamic characteristic of a software system. The reason for this is that the costs associated with system failure often far exceed development costs.

Informally, the reliability of a software system is the degree to which users think the system provides the services that they require. Reliability is the extent to which the system is doing what it ought to or doing the right thing, as opposed to something else such as producing a wrong answer or producing nothing. "Ought to" or "right thing" must be clearly defined before trying to measure reliability.

Fault avoidance is a term that might be used instead of reliability. Fault avoidance is a strategy applied to the design and development of a system that is *fault-free*. Fault-free software means that the software conforms to its requirement specifications. Because there may be errors in the specifications, or the requirements may not reflect the user's real needs, fault-free software doesn't necessarily mean that the system works as the user wants. In statistical terms, reliability is defined as the probability of failure-free operation of a software system in a specified environment for a specified time.

Reliability requirements describe the degree to which the system operates as expected to deliver the service to the end-users. As such, reliability requirements are closely related to availability and maintainability. For instance, if the system does experience a failure, the system is *unavailable* for its intended work tasks. The system remains unavailable based on the ability to find and fix the error quickly (*maintainability*).

> The zeroth law of reliability generalized:
> You can reach almost any ambitious level
> if you are willing to sacrifice all the other attributes.
> —Tom Gilb, author of *Principles of*
> *Software Engineering Management* [Gilb, 1988]

5.5 REL

When eliciting reliability requirements, consider the following aspects:

- ◆ POSSIBLE CAUSES OF SYSTEM FAILURE.
  - ◊ Poor development or testing practices.
  - ◊ Missed requirements.
  - ◊ Incorrect assumptions regarding system requirements.
  - ◊ Poor user interface.
  - ◊ Faulty hardware.
  - ◊ Inadequate user training (user error).

- ◆ PREVENTATIVE ACTIONS OR PROCEDURES NECESSARY TO AVOID FAILURE.
  - ◊ Acceptable data values are defined.
  - ◊ Exception handling for invalid data values is defined.
  - ◊ Functions: algorithms, calculations, and computations are defined and verified.
  - ◊ Combinations, sequences, or series of events are defined.

♦ FAILURE CLASSES [Sommerville, 2007].

◊ Transient—occurs only with certain inputs.

◊ Permanent—occurs with all inputs.

◊ Recoverable—system can recover without operator intervention.

◊ Unrecoverable—operator intervention needed to recover from failure.

◊ Non-corrupting—failure does not corrupt system state or data.

◊ Corrupting—failure corrupts system state or data.

5.5 REL

♦ RELIABILITY METRICS.

◊ **POFOD** (Probability of failure on demand): a measure of the likelihood that the system will fail when a service request is made. For example, a POFOD of 0.002 means that 2 out of 1000 service requests may result in failure.

◊ **ROCOF** (Rate of failure occurrence): a measure of the frequency of occurrence with which unexpected behavior is likely to occur. For example, a ROCOF of 5/100 means that 5 failures are likely to occur in each 100 operational time units.

◊ **MTTF** (Mean time to failure): a measure of the time between observed system failures. For example, an MTTF User forgets password.

5.5.3 Reliability Requirement Examples

a) The Automated Teller Machine (ATM) probability of failure on demand (POFOD) shall be 0.001 (1 out of 1000) when reading the magnetic stripe data on an undamaged card.

b) The rate of failure occurrence (ROCOF) per ATM shall be 1/1000 (1 occurrence in 1000 days). Failure means the ATM fails to operate with any card inserted, and the software must be restarted to correct the failure.

c) The mean time to failure (MTTF) of the ATM timing out due to user inactivity shall be 1/1000 (1 occurrence in 1000 transactions). Failure means the ATM must cancel the transaction, and the software must allow the user to start over.

5.5 REL

d) The account update process shall roll back all related updates when any update fails to commit.

e) The authorization transaction match process shall require a 100-percent match to post a transaction.

f) The data transmission process shall confirm the receiving terminal is in a ready state prior to the start of transmission.

g) The point-of-sale terminal shall have a mean time to failure (MTTF) of 1/10,000 (1 occurrence in 10,000 transactions) in a rate of failure occurrence (ROCOF) of 1/30 (1 occurrence in 30 days). Failure is defined as an invalid transaction presented for processing.

5.5.4 Reliability Suggested Questions

DATA (WHAT?)

ID	Reliability Suggested Questions	Ask this to:
REL1S	What are the classifications for found defects?	*classify defects.*
REL2S	What is considered a critical bug or defect?	*classify defects.*
REL3S	What acknowledgment is required indicating that someone has taken responsibility for the problem?	*identify communication needs.*
REL4S	What notifications are necessary at the time of system failure?	*identify communication needs.*
REL5S	What means of notification are currently used?	*identify communication needs.*
REL6S	What training and documentation must be provided for the critical components?	*identify communication needs.*
REL7S	What types of reports or validations are available or necessary to monitor system accuracy?	*identify communication needs.*
REL8S	What system failure reports are needed?	*identify information.*
REL9S	What system failure data are captured currently?	*identify information.*
REL10S	What system performance data are needed by auditors?	*identify information.*
REL11S	What error messages and error detection information trails are provided by the system?	*identify resources.*
REL12S	What alternate, cross-check calculations can be performed to validate derived data?	*identify verifications.*
REL13S	What components manage unrecoverable data?	*identify weaknesses or gaps.*
REL14R	What should the system maintain on an event log?	*identify information.*
REL15R	What data exist for use in rigorous testing to achieve the level of desired reliability?	*identify testing techniques.*
REL16B	What else should I be asking about reliability "data"?	*uncover additional requirements.*

5.5 REL

ROLES (WHO?)

5.5 REL

ID	Reliability Suggested Questions	Ask this to:
REL17s	What source can provide an accurate count of existing end-users?	*identify additional stakeholders.*
REL18s	What source can provide an accurate count of existing customers?	*identify additional stakeholders.*
REL19s	What source can provide an accurate count of existing processes?	*identify additional stakeholders.*
REL20s	What source can provide an accurate volume count of existing transactions?	*identify additional stakeholders.*
REL21s	What are the user expectations for system reliability?	*identify expectations.*
REL22s	What are the customer expectations for system reliability?	*identify expectations.*
REL23s	What users have a need for greater reliability than others?	*identify expectations.*
REL24s	Who is responsible for monitoring system errors and outages?	*identify responsibilities.*
REL25s	Who is responsible for reliability of purchased software and hardware?	*identify responsibilities.*
REL26s	Who should receive notification when there are system outages?	*identify role responsibilities.*
REL27s	Who should receive notification when there are system errors?	*identify role responsibilities.*
REL28s	Which user classes need to be notified when there is a serious error?	*identify role responsibilities.*
REL29s	Who is authorized to perform what functions on the system?	*identify role responsibilities.*
REL30s	Who is authorized to access what data?	*identify role responsibilities.*
REL31s	Who should receive warning messages when errors occur?	*identify role responsibilities.*
REL32s	What is the typical number of users accessing the system simultaneously?	*identify usage.*
REL33s	What is the greatest number of simultaneous users during peak processing? Anticipated future usage?	*identify usage.*
REL34s	What limits apply to the number of simultaneous users?	*identify usage.*
REL35s	What types of users can be affected by error and failure metering?	*identify users.*
REL36R	What skill level of technician is required in an outage?	*identify responsibilities.*
REL37R	How much in-house support for purchased software and hardware is necessary?	*identify responsibilities.*

ROLES (WHO?) (continued)

ID	Reliability Suggested Questions	Ask this to:
REL38R	Who performs system upgrades and releases?	*identify role responsibilities.*
REL39R	Who gets called when system outages occur?	*identify role responsibilities.*
REL40B	Who receives system error/failure audit reports?	*identify role responsibilities.*
REL41B	What else should I be asking about reliability "roles"?	*uncover additional requirements.*

5.5 REL

PURPOSE (WHY?)

ID	Reliability Suggested Questions	Ask this to:
REL42S	Define "system failure."	*clarify terminology.*
REL43S	Define "repaired."	*clarify terminology.*
REL44S	What is the acceptable level of known bugs or defect rate allowed to migrate into production?	*classify defects.*
REL45S	What service agreements are in place with vendors of purchased hardware and software?	*identify agreements.*
REL46S	What is the cost of lost/incorrect data?	*identify business impacts.*
REL47S	What is the business benefit of the expected level of reliability?	*identify business value.*
REL48S	What is the cost of lost business when the expected level of reliability is not achieved?	*identify business value.*
REL49S	What system components must run for extended periods of time without failure?	*identify components.*
REL50S	At the time of a problem, what component(s) must receive immediate attention?	*identify components.*
REL51S	What degree of recovery or restart is expected of failed components?	*identify deliverables.*
REL52S	Under what circumstances would the whole system be required to shut down?	*identify events.*

PURPOSE (WHY?) (continued)

ID	Reliability Suggested Questions	Ask this to:
REL53s	What is the expected rate of reliability?	*identify metrics for the expected level of reliability.*
REL54s	What are the success factors for the level of desired reliability?	*identify metrics for the expected level of reliability.*
REL55s	What is the severity of impact if failures occur?	*identify metrics.*
REL56s	What is the measurement of defect rate?	*identify metrics.*
REL57s	What is the acceptable spending limit for this level of reliability?	*identify possible trade-offs.*
REL58s	What components are most critical to the business?	*identify priorities.*
REL59s	What components manage the most expensive/critical business elements?	*identify priorities.*
REL60s	What functions do customers rely on the most?	*identify priorities.*
REL61s	What functions do users rely on the most?	*identify priorities.*
REL62s	What components can be sacrificed, temporarily, for the more critical components?	*identify priorities.*
REL63s	What are the criteria defining classes of errors?	*identify tolerance levels.*
REL64s	What tolerance for error is acceptable?	*identify tolerance levels.*
REL65r	What purchased software and hardware are being used?	*identify components.*
REL66r	What different measures (expectations) exist for the hardware than for the software?	*identify failure types.*
REL67r	How wide is the exposure to error on the network?	*identify integration.*
REL68r	What has been the history of releases from the vendors?	*identify lessons learned.*
REL69r	What is the history/track record for similar installations of vendor components?	*identify lessons learned.*
REL70r	Why are there different measures needed for hardware than software?	*identify metrics.*
REL71r	How is the monitoring system audited?	*identify possible trade-offs.*
REL72r	What software and hardware is considered outdated?	*identify resources.*

5.5 REL

PURPOSE (WHY?) (continued)

ID	Reliability Suggested Questions	Ask this to:
REL73R	What hardware components should be replaced?	*identify resources.*
REL74B	What are business consequences when system failure occurs?	*identify deliverables.*
REL75B	What is the trade-off between reliability and efficiency?	*identify possible trade-offs.*
REL76B	What is the trade-off between reliability and availability?	*identify possible trade-offs.*
REL77B	What is the business cost of less than that level of reliability?	*identify possible trade-offs.*
REL78B	What is the cost of achieving that level of reliability?	*identify possible trade-offs.*
REL79B	What else should I be asking about reliability "purpose"?	*uncover additional requirements.*

5.5 REL

TIMING (WHEN?)

ID	Reliability Suggested Questions	Ask this to:
REL80S	What is the required interval for system checking?	*identify intervals.*
REL81S	What is the minimum expected time duration between outages caused by defects?	*identify metrics.*
REL82R	What is the maximum acceptable time duration to fix defects?	*identify metrics.*
REL83S	When is the system *most* reliable?	*identify metrics.*
REL84S	When is the system *least* reliable?	*identify metrics.*
REL85S	What is the expected mean time between system failures?	*identify metrics.*
REL86S	What is the expected mean time to repair the system?	*identify metrics.*
REL87S	What components must be available during an outage?	*prioritize components.*
REL88S	During what time periods is system reliability most critical?	*prioritize usage.*
REL89R	When are system upgrades and fixes migrated into production?	*identify timing restrictions.*
REL90B	What else should I be asking about reliability "timing"?	*uncover additional requirements.*

LOGISTICS (WHERE?)

ID	Reliability Suggested Questions	Ask this to:
REL91s	What are the peak periods of usage that vary by location?	identify location restrictions.
REL92s	What expected users of the application are localized? Dispersed?	identify locations.
REL93s	What locations require reliability the most?	identify locations.
REL94s	What users access the system in a location that is susceptible to reliability issues?	identify reliability needs by location.
REL95s	How does system reliability vary by business location?	identify reliability needs by location.
REL96s	How do users in varying business locations experience system failure more than other locations?	identify reliability needs by location.
REL97s	What business locations must have access to the system?	identify reliability needs by location.
REL98s	What remote access facilities are in place/necessary?	identify types of accesses.
REL99s	What environmental conditions must be created to simulate the planned installation environment for testing to achieve that level of reliability?	identify verifications.
REL100R	How does off-site processing help or hurt reliability?	identify location restrictions.
REL101R	What time periods must be avoided for upgrades and maintenance by business location?	identify location restrictions.
REL102R	How will system errors and outages be monitored by location?	identify monitoring controls.
REL103R	Where are known weak points in the network?	identify possible process improvement areas.
REL104R	What processes are performed at each location?	identify relationships between processes and location.
REL105R	How do releases of production fixes vary by location?	identify reliability needs by location.
REL106R	What resources are needed at each business location to restore a system?	identify resource needs.
REL107R	What resources are needed at each business location to prevent system failure?	identify resource needs.
REL108R	What hardware/software and people resources are needed at each location to perform routine maintenance?	identify resource needs.
REL109R	What is the measure of accuracy with which a given algorithm is being implemented for a specific software and hardware environment?	identify verifications.
REL110B	What else should I be asking about reliability "logistics"?	uncover additional requirements.

5.5 REL

PROCESS (HOW?)

ID	Reliability Suggested Questions	Ask this to:
REL111S	What monitoring tools must be in place?	*identify methods of monitoring.*
REL112S	What measures of reliability need to be tracked?	*identify metrics.*
REL113S	What ensures the accuracy of range and value checks?	*identify procedural checks.*
REL114S	What metrics are used to ensure that all the numeric fields are the right (same) size?	*identify procedures.*
REL115S	What ensures that all the artificial limits on size and number are eliminated?	*identify procedures.*
REL116S	What ensures the completeness of test cases?	*identify procedures.*
REL117S	What escalation procedures are required during an outage?	*identify procedures.*
REL118S	What alternatives are available during an outage?	*identify procedures.*
REL119S	What fault-tolerance does the application require?	*identify procedures.*
REL120S	What off-site redundant implementation procedures are required?	*identify procedures.*
REL121S	What access control extensions are necessary and permissible to address the problem?	*identify procedures.*
REL122S	What vendor access is necessary for problem resolution?	*identify procedures.*
REL123S	How should the system respond under stress?	*identify procedures.*
REL124S	How will the algorithm be tested to confirm it works as intended?	*identify procedures.*
REL125S	What configuration management steps are in place for production control?	*identify procedures.*
REL126S	What procedures need to be in place to address any failures that occur?	*identify procedures.*
REL127S	What ensures a high degree of confidence in the accuracy of the information?	*identify process controls.*
REL128S	What should be in place for the system to detect and then prevent unauthorized access?	*identify process controls.*
REL129S	What procedures are used to ensure that all the data is edited properly?	*identify process controls.*
REL130S	What process steps can be taken to verify information accuracy?	*identify process controls.*
REL131S	What will show that mathematical functions are within real number tolerances?	*identify process controls.*

5.5 REL

PROCESS (HOW?) (continued)

5.5 REL

ID	Reliability Suggested Questions	Ask this to:
REL132S	Compared to how it works in the real world, how will users know an algorithm does what it should?	*identify process controls.*
REL133S	What sources of information are available to validate the values for derived data?	*identify process controls.*
REL134S	What is the measure of adequacy with which the implemented algorithm relates to real-world interactions?	*identify process controls.*
REL135S	What test plan should the Quality Assurance testing group follow?	*identify process controls.*
REL136S	What can be done to reduce exposure to components that run for extended periods of time and cannot fail?	*identify process controls.*
REL137S	What are the appropriate locations and intervals to check critical data elements for accuracy?	*identify process controls.*
REL138S	How frequently are system enhancements expected?	*identify rates of change.*
REL139S	What response time to outages is required?	*identify responses.*
REL140S	What response time to defects (errors not causing outages) is required?	*identify responses.*
REL141S	What functions in the production environment should be replicated in a test environment?	*identify verifications.*
REL142S	What amount of regression testing is minimal when repairing defects?	*identify verifications.*
REL143S	What amount of regression testing is minimal when making enhancements?	*identify verifications.*
REL144R	What are known weak points in the network?	*evaluate design.*
REL145R	How can the known weak points in the network be avoided by this system?	*identify alternate processes.*
REL146R	How is the system monitored for detection of errors that do not cause an outage?	*identify monitoring techniques.*
REL147R	How is the system precision and accuracy monitored?	*identify monitoring techniques.*
REL148R	What systematic error detection and correction monitoring is required?	*identify monitoring techniques.*
REL149R	How fail safe is the monitoring system?	*identify monitoring techniques.*
REL150R	How should defects be handled, as "fixed as found" or packaged into releases?	*identify processes.*

PROCESS (HOW?) (continued)

ID	Reliability Suggested Questions	Ask this to:
REL151R	What tools do users need to monitor the system?	*identify processes.*
REL152R	What procedures must be in place to ensure that the data are backed up correctly and are recoverable?	*identify processes.*
REL153R	What control over vendor software do users have?	*identify verifications.*
REL154R	What is the plan to manage vendor upgrade releases?	*identify verifications.*
REL155R	What measures of control are in place on vendor software update releases?	*identify verifications.*
REL156R	What stress tests can be applied?	*identify verifications.*
REL157B	What else should I be asking about reliability "processes"?	*uncover additional requirements.*

5.5 REL

5.6 SURVIVABILITY (SRV)

USER CONCERN:	How resilient is the system from failure?
RELATED CATEGORIES:	Availability, Dependability, Fault Avoidance, Maintainability, Reliability, Robustness

5.6 SRV

5.6.1 Survivability Definition

Survivability is the extent to which the software system continues to function and recovers in the presence of a system failure.

5.6.2 Survivability Discussion

Survivability requirements identify the ability of the system to respond reasonably to unexpected events. The system must have a degree of stability to withstand unexpected business situations and conditions. Survivability of a system is demonstrated by its ability to continue to deliver essential, mission-critical functionality to authorized users while it is under attack or after a portion of the system has been damaged as a result of an attack or system failure.

Robert Ellison, Software Engineering Institute (SEI), and colleagues [Ellison, 2002] define survivability as "the capability of a system to fulfill its mission, in a timely manner, in the presence of attacks, failures, or accidents." Ellison, et al. created a method called Survivable Systems Analysis to assess vulnerabilities in systems. This method of achieving survivability depends on three strategies:

♦ RESISTANCE involves avoiding faults or failures by building capabilities into the system to thwart off attacks. For example, a system might use voice recognition to authenticate users as a way to make it more difficult, albeit not impossible, for unauthorized users to gain entry.

♦ RECOGNITION consists of detecting faults or failures by building capabilities into the system to do so and assess the resulting damage. For example, the system might add check digits on account numbers so that corruption to the data can be detected.

♦ RECOVERY means tolerating faults or failures by building capabilities into the system to continue providing essential functionality while under attack and to restore full functionality after an attack. For example, business-critical systems might have software and hardware that execute in parallel in order to pick up processing in the event of a system outage.

Survivability is also referred to as *fault tolerance*, which indicates the degree to which techniques are applied to prevent system faults from resulting in system errors, or system errors from resulting in system failures. Moreover, survivability requirements may also be called *robustness* requirements, as they reflect the ability to continue to deliver essential business-critical services to legitimate users while the system is under attack, or after part of the system has been damaged as a consequence of an attack or a system failure. As such, survivability requirements are closely related to reliability, availability, and maintainability as these nonfunctional requirements are compromised by system failures.

5.6 SRV

A *fault-tolerant* system can continue in operation after some system faults have occurred. According to Ian Sommerville [Sommerville, 2007], there are four aspects to fault-tolerance:

♦ FAULT DETECTION involves checking that the system state is consistent, and identifying a failure has occurred or will result in a system failure.

♦ DAMAGE ASSESSMENT consists of assessing the parts of the system state that have been affected by a fault.

♦ FAULT RECOVERY includes actions to modify the state of the system so that the effects of the fault are minimized. Forward recovery involves correcting the damaged system, while backward recovery restores the system to its normal "safe" state.

♦ FAULT REPAIR involves making modifications to the system so that the fault does not occur again.

When eliciting survivability requirements, consider the following aspects:

♦ FAILURE PREVENTION AND DAMAGE ASSESSMENT TECHNIQUES.

◊ Exception handling.

◊ Check-sums in data exchange.

◊ Check digits in numeric data.

5.6 SRV

♦ FAULT RECOVERY TECHNIQUES.

◊ Forward error recovery (correcting the damaged system).

◊ Backward error recovery (restoring the system).

5.6.3 Survivability Requirement Examples

a) If the audit trail function fails before the user saves updates to the contract, the system shall be able to recover all changes made in the contract being updated up to one minute prior to the failure.

b) When an update failure is detected, all updates performed during the failed session shall be rolled back to restore the data to pre-session condition.

c) All data recovered in a roll-back condition shall be recorded for use in forward recovery under user control.

d) When operating after a failure, the user shall be informed the application is operating in a "safe mode" and all data are available for review without update.

e) The system shall prevent access to failed functions while providing access to all currently operational functions.

f) All transactions shall pass three-way hash routine validation before committing transaction update.

g) All hardware components of the assembly operation shall be replicated, such that failure of any one hardware component shall not render the assembly operation unavailable to end-users. It is acceptable for system performance to be poorer than normal for up to 3 business days following the failure and replacement of a piece of hardware.

h) All software modules shall pass check-sum verification every time the module is initiated.

i) The system shall prevent subsequent updates to an account when an update failure has been detected until the failure has been corrected.

j) The system shall verify all assigned confirmation numbers using dual-verify check digit routines. All confirmation numbers are unique in the system and never re-used.

5.6.4 Survivability Suggested Questions

DATA (WHAT?)

5.6 SRV

ID	Survivability Suggested Questions	Ask this to:
SRV1S	What is the most likely source of corrupt data?	*identify problem sources.*
SRV2S	What measures can be taken to reduce, eliminate, or cleanse corrupt data?	*identify recovery measures.*
SRV3S	What is the predictability of corrupt data?	*identify validations.*
SRV4S	What is the expected level of precision on calculations?	*identify validations.*
SRV5S	What ranges of valid values are known?	*identify validations.*
SRV6S	How can the calculations be validated?	*identify validations.*
SRV7S	What are the applicable limitations for the formulas?	*identify validations.*
SRV8S	What validation edits are in place for the calculation variables?	*identify validations.*
SRV9S	What are the numeric data attributes that must be enforced consistently?	*identify various attributes.*
SRV10S	What date, time, date and time attributes must be enforced consistently?	*identify various attributes.*
SRV11S	What time standard has been established?	*identify various attributes.*
SRV12S	What time zone is the standard for the system?	*identify various attributes.*
SRV13S	What are the data type attributes that must be enforced consistently?	*identify various attributes.*
SRV14S	What default values must be applied for variables when invalid/missing data are found?	*identify various attributes.*
SRV15S	How much data can be recovered when problems occur?	*qualify data loss.*
SRV16S	How much data can be lost when problems occur?	*qualify data loss.*
SRV17S	How should the system correct/reject nonconforming data?	*qualify data loss.*
SRV18S	How many attempts at resolution of bad data should be provided?	*quantify responses.*
SRV19R	What date management and terminology will be used consistently by the system?	*identify date specific details.*
SRV20R	What check digit routines will be used by the system?	*identify fault detection procedures.*

DATA (WHAT?) (continued)

ID	Survivability Suggested Questions	Ask this to:
SRV21R	What volatile interfaces can be eliminated?	*identify interfaces.*
SRV22R	What are the test plans for the calculations?	*identify validations.*
SRV23B	What else should I be asking about survivability "data"?	*uncover additional requirements.*

ROLES (WHO?)

ID	Survivability Suggested Questions	Ask this to:
SRV24S	What is the expected growth rate of the number of users, customers, transactions, and products?	*assess magnitude of usage patterns.*
SRV25S	What authorization is necessary to use default values?	*identify access security requirements.*
SRV26S	When default values are substituted for invalid data, who needs to be alerted?	*identify access security requirements.*
SRV27S	Who can validate the calculations?	*identify additional stakeholders.*
SRV28S	What is the source of calculation formulas?	*identify additional stakeholders.*
SRV29S	What are the user expectations for system survivability?	*identify expectations.*
SRV30S	What are the customer expectations for system survivability?	*identify expectations.*
SRV31S	Who should receive notification when there are system faults?	*identify role responsibilities.*
SRV32S	Who should receive notification when there are system recoveries or repairs?	*identify role responsibilities.*
SRV33S	Who needs to be notified when there are serious damages?	*identify role responsibilities.*
SRV34S	Who is authorized to perform recovery procedures?	*identify role responsibilities.*
SRV35S	Who should receive warning messages when system faults are encountered?	*identify role responsibilities.*
SRV36S	What are the conditions under which more than one approval is required?	*identify role responsibilities.*
SRV37S	Who will be allowed to restore or recover the system?	*identify role responsibilities.*
SRV38S	What faults, conditions, or events make the authorization conditional?	*identify role responsibilities.*

5.6 SRV

ROLES (WHO?) (continued)

ID	Survivability Suggested Questions	Ask this to:
SRV39S	What types of extreme user behaviors can be expected?	*identify usage.*
SRV40S	What is the typical number of users accessing the system simultaneously?	*identify usage.*
SRV41S	What is the greatest number of simultaneous users during peak processing? Anticipated future usage?	*identify usage.*
SRV42S	What types of users can be affected by fault and repair monitoring?	*identify users.*
SRV43R	Who is responsible for monitoring system faults, recoveries, and repairs?	*identify responsibilities.*
SRV44R	Who is responsible for survivability aspects of purchased software and hardware?	*identify responsibilities.*
SRV45R	What skill level of technician is required to recover or restore the system?	*identify responsibilities.*
SRV46R	Who is authorized to perform system backups and restores?	*identify role responsibilities.*
SRV47R	Who gets called when system failures occur?	*identify role responsibilities.*
SRV48B	Who receives system fault/repair audit reports?	*identify role responsibilities.*
SRV49B	What else should I be asking about survivability "roles"?	*uncover additional requirements.*

5.6 SRV

Purpose (Why?)

ID	Survivability Suggested Questions	Ask this to:
SRV50s	Define "recovery."	*clarify terminology.*
SRV51s	Define "system restore."	*clarify terminology.*
SRV52s	What are the business rules for the calculations used?	*identify applicable standards.*
SRV53s	How much can be afforded to make the system as sturdy as requested?	*identify possible trade-offs.*
SRV54s	What is the cost to the company if there are some failures due to survivability issues?	*identify possible trade-offs.*
SRV55s	What aspects must be "fool resistant"?	*identify vulnerable components.*
SRV56s	What is the impact of a failed device?	*qualify devices.*
SRV57R	What extreme conditions of implementation can be expected?	*identify implementations.*
SRV58R	What is the expected operating environment of the system?	*identify implementations.*
SRV59R	What technology is planned for this project?	*identify technical environments.*
SRV60B	What is the acceptable trade-off between survivable and available?	*identify possible trade-offs.*
SRV61B	What is the acceptable trade-off between survivable and maintainable?	*identify possible trade-offs.*
SRV62B	What is the acceptable trade-off between survivable and reliable?	*identify possible trade-offs.*
SRV63B	What is the acceptable trade-off between survivable and flexible?	*identify possible trade-offs.*
SRV64B	What else should I be asking about survivability "purpose"?	*uncover additional requirements.*

5.6 SRV

TIMING (WHEN?)

ID	Survivability Suggested Questions	Ask this to:
SRV65S	When are the periods of high or low usage by the user classes?	*identify fault patterns.*
SRV66S	When are the periods of high or low occurrences of system faults?	*identify fault patterns.*
SRV67S	When can system restores be run?	*identify time sensitive processes.*
SRV68S	When are disaster recovery plans tested?	*identify time sensitive processes.*
SRV69S	How frequently should fault detection processes run?	*identify time-triggered processes.*
SRV70S	When can system backups be run?	*identify time-triggered processes.*
SRV71R	What types of preventative maintenance schedule need to be established for the software and hardware?	*identify fault detection procedures.*
SRV72R	How often are inspections of hardware and software conducted?	*identify routine inspections.*
SRV73R	What hardware and software must be locked up when not in use?	*identify security events and conditions.*
SRV74R	How frequently are repairs migrated into production?	*identify time-triggered processes.*
SRV75R	How much time is required to recover the system?	*identify turnaround expectations.*
SRV76R	How much time is required to do a system restore?	*identify turnaround expectations.*
SRV77B	What else should I be asking about survivability "timing"?	*uncover additional requirements.*

5.6 SRV

LOGISTICS (WHERE?)

ID	Survivability Suggested Questions	Ask this to:
SRV78S	How will access security be the same at all business locations?	*identify fault risks by location.*
SRV79S	What are the different levels of security at the location where disaster recovery hardware, software, and other business artifacts are stored?	*identify fault risks by location.*
SRV80S	How is access security different for users accessing information remotely?	*identify fault risks by location.*
SRV81S	What access security is needed for employees that work from home or other remote locations?	*identify fault risks by location.*
SRV82S	What access restrictions are necessary to the work areas where this application will be used?	*identify fault risks by location.*
SRV83S	What security measures must be taken when accessing the application using public computers?	*identify fault risks by location.*
SRV84S	Where is regulatory information maintained?	*identify regulations.*
SRV85R	What resources are needed to recover/restore each location?	*identify resources needed.*
SRV86R	Where is backup software and hardware kept?	*identify resources needed.*
SRV87R	Where is backup information stored?	*identify resources needed.*
SRV88B	What else should I be asking about survivability "logistics"?	*uncover additional requirements.*

5.6 SRV

PROCESS (HOW?)

ID	Survivability Suggested Questions	Ask this to:
SRV89S	In similar applications, where have there been points of failure that should have been more robust?	*identify alternative processes.*
SRV90S	What alternatives exist for processing without the corrupt data?	*identify alternative processes.*
SRV91S	What does the current technology prohibit or hinder?	*identify capabilities.*
SRV92S	What recovery capability from errors is expected?	*identify capabilities.*
SRV93S	When extreme input is encountered, how fast must the system respond and recover?	*identify fault detection procedures.*
SRV94S	How should the system respond to input errors?	*identify fault detection procedures.*
SRV95S	How should the system react to unusual error conditions?	*identify fault detection procedures.*
SRV96S	Which interfaces are critical to business continuity when faults occur?	*identify interfaces.*
SRV97S	What is the practical minimum number of transactions and events the system must handle?	*identify measures.*
SRV98S	What is the practical minimum number of users and customers the system must handle?	*identify measures.*
SRV99S	What procedures are necessary to "show your work" on calculations?	*identify procedures.*
SRV100S	Which processes must continue to function or survive with reduced capability when faults occur?	*identify processes.*
SRV101S	Which processes should terminate gracefully when faults occur?	*identify processes.*
SRV102S	What should the process do to terminate gracefully?	*identify processes.*
SRV103S	If there are failures due to unexpected corrupt data or hardware failures, what lost business can be recovered?	*identify recovery measures.*
SRV104S	What workaround is available for a failed hardware device?	*identify recovery measures.*
SRV105S	Which processes performed by the system have manual workarounds?	*identify risk areas.*
SRV106S	How should the system respond to extreme conditions?	*identify types of responses.*
SRV107S	What types of error conditions might the system encounter?	*identify various conditions.*

5.6 SRV

The Quest for Software Requirements

PROCESS (HOW?) (continued)

ID	Survivability Suggested Questions	Ask this to:
SRV108R	What can be done to make the hardware devices more robust?	*identify alternative processes.*
SRV109R	What software and hardware has a history of failures?	*identify alternative processes.*
SRV110R	What alternatives exist for software and hardware that have a history of failures?	*identify alternative processes.*
SRV111R	What alternatives exist for any devices currently used?	*identify alternative processes.*
SRV112R	What design considerations should be made to reduce the impact of anticipated trouble spots?	*identify configurations.*
SRV113R	What design considerations should be made to improve the robustness of anticipated trouble spots?	*identify configurations.*
SRV114R	What hardware fault tolerance is acceptable?	*identify configurations.*
SRV115R	What hardware redundancy is necessary?	*identify configurations.*
SRV116R	Which hardware devices must be the most robust?	*identify configurations.*
SRV117R	How can the system predict a hardware device failure?	*identify configurations.*
SRV118R	What is the response plan for a failed device?	*identify fault detection procedures.*
SRV119R	Which interfaces have the highest degree of volatility?	*identify interfaces.*
SRV120R	What alternates are there for the volatile interfaces?	*identify interfaces.*
SRV121R	How can the volatile interfaces be reduced in priority?	*identify interfaces.*
SRV122R	What is the cause of volatility in any interfaces?	*identify interfaces.*
SRV123R	What measures are in place to safeguard software and hardware from natural disasters?	*identify security needs.*
SRV124R	What measures are in place to safeguard software and hardware from unauthorized access?	*identify security needs.*
SRV125R	What measures are in place to recover software and hardware from natural disasters?	*identify security needs.*
SRV126R	What measures are in place to recover software and hardware from unauthorized access?	*identify security needs.*
SRV127B	What else should I be asking about survivability "processes"?	*uncover additional requirements.*

5.6 SRV

5.7 USABILITY (USE)

> USER CONCERN: How easy is it to learn and operate the system?
> RELATED CATEGORIES: Human Engineering, Operability,
>   User-friendliness

5.7.1 Usability Definition

Usability is the ease with which the user is able to learn, operate, prepare inputs, and interpret outputs through interaction with a software system.

5.7.2 Usability Discussion

5.7 USE

Usability requirements indicate how well people are able and willing to use the system. Usability requirements are concerned with the user interface and end-user interaction with the system. *User-friendliness* and *human engineering* are terms often associated with usability, and describe the user's desire for a system that is easy to interact with and use. The usability of a system has an effect on productivity, error rates, and acceptance of the system. Usability requirements are often compromised by trade-offs between what the project sponsor is trying to achieve (business objective) and what the users expect (functionality to get their work done).

> If the system does not work as intended by the programmer, we
> have a program error—a bug. If it is impossible to carry out the
> task, we have a requirement defect—missing functionality.
> If the system works as intended by the programmer, and it can
> support the task, yet the user cannot figure out how to do it
> or doesn't like the system, we have a usability problem.
> —Soren Lauesen, author of *Software Requirements:*
> *Styles and Techniques* [Lauesen, 2002]

When eliciting usability requirements, consider the following aspects:

♦ EASE OF ENTRY: the extent that the system accounts for the human requirements for success in inputting information or materials into the system. It is often expressed in physical requirements (such as vision, hearing, and manual dexterity), and in terms of educational, intelligence, vocational, or cultural requirements.

♦ EASE OF LEARNING: the degree to which the system provides resources to help the user attain some measurable level of capability. The learning ability would be expected to vary with the capability of the individual user (such as previous experience with similar systems) and other human factors.

♦ EASE OF HANDLING: the extent to which the system aids the user in productivity. This is usually measured over time by a reduction in end-user errors. The ease of handling also will vary for specific classes of users.

♦ LIKABILITY: the measure of how well people like to use the system. One common way of measuring likability is user opinion surveys.

5.7 USE

♦ POSSIBLE USABILITY METRICS [Lauesen, 2002]:

◊ **Problem counts:** metric for ease of learning.

◊ **Task time:** metric for ease of learning and task efficiency.

◊ **Keystroke counts:** metric for task efficiency for experienced users.

◊ **Opinion poll:** subjective metric for user satisfaction.

◊ **Score for understanding:** subjective metric for understandability.

◊ **Design-level requirements:** metric descriptions regarding the user interface.

◊ **Product-level requirements:** metric for ease of remembering entry values.

◊ **Guideline adherence:** metric for the general appearance and response on the user interface.

◊ **Development process requirements:** metric for specifics applied to the development process.

5.7.3 Usability Requirement Examples

a) The new product shall be easy to use by adult members (age 18 to 80) of the public who may only have one hand free.

b) The vending product shall be able to be used by adult members of the public without training. A panel representative of at least 95 percent of the general public shall successfully purchase a product from the vending product on their first encounter.

c) The product shall be self-explanatory and intuitive such that a service agent shall be able to produce a price quote within 10 minutes of encountering the product for the first time.

d) The new policy management system shall be evaluated by 90 percent of the user community to be at least as easy to use as the existing system.

e) A trained order-entry clerk shall have the ability to submit a complete order for a product chosen from a supplier catalog in a maximum of 7 minutes, with an average order entry time of 4 minutes.

f) People with no training and no understanding of English shall be able to use the product.

g) A new warehouse clerk shall be able to enter a customer order on the system within a typical 8-hour business day.

h) The system shall be useable by program developers after five weeks of training.

5.7 USE

5.7.4 Usability Suggested Questions

DATA (WHAT?)

ID	Usability Suggested Questions	Ask this to:
USE1s	What are the institutional shorthand notations for common data elements?	*identify various types of data.*
USE2s	What natural clustering of information exists in the business area?	*identify business areas.*
USE3s	Where can the specific wording for the error messages, descriptions, and definitions be obtained?	*identify communications sources.*
USE4s	What confirmation of progress is expected?	*identify levels of communication.*
USE5s	What levels of user help are necessary?	*identify levels of help.*
USE6s	What levels of user interactive help are expected?	*identify levels of help.*
USE7s	What degree of interactive help is expected?	*identify levels of help.*
USE8s	What level(s) of error message information is expected?	*identify message levels.*
USE9s	How interactive is the process for data entry between data input and data contained in the system?	*identify processes.*
USE10s	What options should be available to turn on or turn off help features?	*identify types of help.*
USE11s	When is it acceptable to use the common shorthand notations?	*identify usage habits.*
USE12s	When is it not acceptable to use the common shorthand notations?	*identify usage habits.*
USE13s	How frequently do current help features get used?	*identify usage patterns.*
USE14s	What is the maximum number of keystrokes and presentation controls acceptable during data input?	*identify user interfaces.*
USE15s	What informative warning messages and error messages are needed?	*identify various communications.*
USE16s	What input/output devices will be supported?	*identify various devices.*
USE17s	What sort of input/output devices for the human interface are available and what are their characteristics?	*identify various devices.*

5.7 USE

DATA (WHAT?) (continued)

ID	Usability Suggested Questions	Ask this to:
USE18S	What specific terms, symbols, or expressions are commonly used by the users that need to be incorporated?	*identify various dialects.*
USE19S	How many types of help are expected?	*identify various forms of help.*
USE20S	Where do the users typically look first for help?	*identify various forms of help.*
USE21S	What "help" facilities or features are needed?	*identify various forms of help.*
USE22S	Where do the users expect to find help?	*identify various forms of help.*
USE23S	How appealing is the presentation of the information?	*identify various presentation styles.*
USE24S	Specify the existence and required features of online help systems, wizards, tool tips, context-sensitive help, user manuals, and other forms of documentation and assistance.	*identify various types of communication.*
USE25S	What expectations are there for error messages, descriptions, and definitions in varying lengths depending upon user?	*identify various types of communications.*
USE26S	What are the different lengths of error messages, descriptions, and definitions?	*identify various types of communications.*
USE27S	What data elements are repetitive and may be shortcut during data input?	*identify various types of data.*
USE28S	How complex is the combination of data during data entry?	*identify various types of data.*
USE29S	What "help" documentation is available to the user?	*identify various types of documentation.*
USE30S	What information or materials do the end users need in order to do their jobs?	*identify various types of information or material.*
USE31S	What history records of user injuries exist?	*identify various types of injuries.*
USE32S	How much data must be presented in common presentations?	*identify various types of presentations.*
USE33S	What clues for use are the users accustomed to having in their applications?	*identify various types of user guides.*
USE34R	What historical data are never retrieved by users?	*identify data cleansing areas.*
USE35R	What duplication of input could be eliminated or reduced?	*identify data cleansing areas.*
USE36R	What data labels are inconsistent or confusing?	*identify data cleansing areas.*

5.7 USE

The Quest for Software Requirements

DATA (WHAT?) (continued)

ID	Usability Suggested Questions	Ask this to:
USE37R	Regarding what data and functions does the help desk get repeated calls from users?	*identify types of help.*
USE38R	What additional data could be pre-populated for the user and reduce data entry time and amount?	*identify types of help.*
USE39R	What data are most frequently retrieved by each user class?	*identify various types of data.*
USE40R	What data are viewed the most by each user class?	*identify various types of data.*
USE41B	What else should I be asking about usability "data"?	*uncover additional requirements.*

ROLES (WHO?)

5.7 USE

ID	Usability Suggested Questions	Ask this to:
USE42S	What type of users are the end users?	*classify users.*
USE43S	What prior experience are users expected to have?	*classify users.*
USE44S	What is the range in years of experience of the end users?	*classify users.*
USE45S	What is the range in education level of the end users?	*classify users.*
USE46S	What different access levels will be offered to power users and casual users?	*classify users.*
USE47S	Who is the intended audience of the system?	*classify users.*
USE48S	What are the data throughput expectations per user role in the department?	*classify users.*
USE49S	What aspects of the system must be foolproof?	*identify access security risks.*
USE50S	What are the expectations regarding training on the new system?	*identify levels of training.*
USE51S	How much training is expected?	*identify levels of training.*
USE52S	What level of training will be provided, offered, or made available?	*identify levels of training.*
USE53S	What are the expectations for allowing users to alter their presentation formats?	*identify levels of usage.*
USE54S	What user access control preferences must be retained?	*identify preference types.*

ROLES (WHO?) (continued)

ID	Usability Suggested Questions	Ask this to:
USE55s	What user access control profiles must be retained?	*identify profile types.*
USE56s	What experience does the staff have in developing solutions for users with specific needs?	*identify resource needs.*
USE57s	What is the skill level of the target user group?	*identify skill levels.*
USE58s	What is the skill level of the majority of the primary users?	*identify skill levels.*
USE59s	What percentage of users will have specific needs?	*identify specific needs.*
USE60s	How does using the system change between skill levels of the users?	*identify system usages.*
USE61s	What training will be necessary before using the system?	*identify types of training.*
USE62s	What is the accessibility for handicapped users?	*identify types of usage.*
USE63s	What are the expectations for allowing users to filter out data?	*identify types of usage.*
USE64s	Describe the typical usage of novice users. Expert users.	*identify user capabilities.*
USE65s	How rapidly are users expected to advance from one category to the next?	*identify user capabilities.*
USE66s	How important is it for the system to be understandable by the users?	*identify user capabilities.*
USE67s	How many categories of user types are there? (novice, experienced, power)	*identify user categories.*
USE68s	Who is the expected user audience?	*identify user groups.*
USE69s	What do the users consider to be "stressful" aspects of their work?	*identify user perceptions.*
USE70s	What do users commonly express as "frustrations" with using the system?	*identify user perceptions.*
USE71s	Describe the typical user of the system.	*identify user types.*
USE72s	Describe the "novice" or "beginner" user.	*identify user types.*
USE73s	Describe the "expert" or "power" user.	*identify user types.*
USE74s	How much user to user collaboration happens while using the system?	*identify user usages.*
USE75s	What are the expectations for users to learn the system without providing training?	*identify user usages.*

5.7 USE

ROLES (WHO?) (continued)

ID	Usability Suggested Questions	Ask this to:
USE76S	How do different levels of users view the relationships within the data?	*identify user views.*
USE77S	How well will the users remember how to use the low-frequency features?	*identify various features.*
USE78S	How do the users "feel" about the system?	*identify various perceptions.*
USE79S	What specific needs of the prospective users must be met?	*identify various user needs.*
USE80R	What user classes require more help than others?	*identify levels of training.*
USE81R	What particular sequence should be used to train the users?	*identify levels of training.*
USE82R	What user classes have the most volume of data entry errors?	*identify levels of training.*
USE83R	What volume of users are there currently? Expected in the future?	*identify resource needs.*
USE84R	What users input the most data?	*identify user usages.*
USE85R	What usability characteristics are requested by novice users? By expert users?	*identify user usages.*
USE86R	What help features are most frequently used? What features are not used?	*identify various features.*
USE87R	What user classes use existing help features?	*identify various features.*
USE88B	Who is responsible for training the users?	*identify role responsibilities.*
USE89B	Who is responsible for supporting the users?	*identify role responsibilities.*
USE90B	What else should I be asking about usability "roles"?	*uncover additional requirements.*

5.7 USE

PURPOSE (WHY?)

ID	Usability Suggested Questions	Ask this to:
USE91S	What similar systems are available that the users are familiar with and like to use?	*identify comparatives.*
USE92S	What similar systems are available that the users are familiar with and do not like to use?	*identify comparatives.*
USE93S	What other interfaces are similar to that used in this system with which the users are familiar?	*identify comparatives.*
USE94S	What similar systems do the users complain about?	*identify comparatives.*
USE95S	Describe the usability of the proposed system with other state-of-the-art systems that the user community knows and likes.	*identify comparatives.*
USE96S	What other system could be used as a model for "ease of use"?	*identify comparatives.*
USE97S	What other system could be used as a model for "easy to learn"?	*identify comparatives.*
USE98S	What recognizable system can be used as a model or pattern?	*identify comparatives.*
USE99S	What are examples of good designs to emulate?	*identify comparatives.*
USE100S	What must be included beyond company usability design standards?	*identify exceptional standards.*
USE101S	What current company usability standards are not adequate?	*identify existing standards.*
USE102S	What usability laws or standards must be adhered to?	*identify laws or standards.*
USE103S	What usability improvements have been implemented in the past?	*identify lessons learned.*
USE104S	What is the importance that the system is easy to learn?	*identify metrics.*
USE105S	What is an allowable amount of time needed before users can successfully use the product?	*identify metrics.*
USE106S	Specify the required training time for users to become minimally productive (able to accomplish simple tasks) and operationally productive (able to accomplish normal, day-to-day tasks).	*identify metrics.*
USE107S	What are learning rate requirements?	*identify metrics.*
USE108S	How will learning rate be measured?	*identify metrics.*

5.7 USE

ID	Usability Suggested Questions	Ask this to:
USE109s	Describe characteristics to measure "easy to learn."	*identify metrics.*
USE110s	How are users measured on "ability to learn quickly"?	*identify metrics.*
USE111s	Once users have been trained to perform routine tasks, how long should it take them to perform a typical task or transaction?	*identify metrics.*
USE112s	How will the usability of the system be evaluated?	*identify metrics.*
USE113s	What metrics for user productivity are used?	*identify metrics.*
USE114s	What are entry rate requirements?	*identify metrics.*
USE115s	How will entry rate be measured?	*identify metrics.*
USE116s	What productivity gains are expected from using the system?	*identify metrics.*
USE117s	What productivity rate increase, in what timeframe, is expected from the system?	*identify metrics.*
USE118s	Specify measurable task times for typical tasks or transactions.	*identify metrics.*
USE119s	Please fill in the following: A user shall produce a [*specified result*] within [*specified time*] of beginning to use the product, without having to reference the user's manual.	*identify metrics.*
USE120s	Please fill in the following: After receiving [*number of hours*] training a user shall be able to produce [*quantity of specified outputs*] per [*unit of time*].	*identify metrics.*
USE121s	Please fill in the following: [*Agreed percentage*] of a test panel shall successfully complete [*specified task*] within [*specified time limit*].	*identify metrics.*
USE122s	Please fill in the following: After [*specified time duration, e.g., one month*], usage of the product shall result in a total error rate of less than [*an agreed-upon percentage*].	*identify metrics.*
USE123s	Please fill in the following: An anonymous survey shall show that [*an agreed percentage*] of the users are regularly using the product after [*an agreed time*] familiarization period.	*identify metrics.*

5.7 USE

PURPOSE (WHY?) (continued)

ID	Usability Suggested Questions	Ask this to:
USE124S	Please fill in the following: The users shall achieve [*agreed percentage*] pass rate from the final examination of the training.	*identify metrics.*
USE125S	What are handling or error rate requirements?	*identify metrics.*
USE126S	What error rate decrease, in what timeframe, is expected from the users of the system?	*identify metrics.*
USE127S	What is an acceptable user error rate when working at normal speed?	*identify metrics.*
USE128S	What reduction rate of user errors is expected?	*identify metrics.*
USE129S	How should acceptance of usability be measured?	*identify metrics.*
USE130S	How will user satisfaction be measured?	*identify metrics.*
USE131S	How is "likability" measured?	*identify metrics.*
USE132S	How are user errors measured?	*identify metrics.*
USE133S	What is the rate of errors by the users?	*identify metrics.*
USE134S	How will error rate be measured?	*identify metrics.*
USE135S	What standards/guidelines for navigation apply?	*identify navigation standards.*
USE136S	What complaints are heard most often from the users about systems they use on a regular basis?	*identify pain points.*
USE137S	What is the trade-off between "easy to use" and "easy to learn"?	*identify perspectives.*
USE138S	What standards/guidelines for amount of data on a presentation or the number of presentations apply?	*identify presentation standards.*
USE139S	What government or other regulatory compliance standards must be applied regarding user safety?	*identify safety standards.*
USE140S	What style guidelines should be followed?	*identify styles.*
USE141S	What will it take to make a successful system for the user?	*identify success criteria.*
USE142S	What conventions and standards developed for the human-to-machine interface must be applied?	*identify types of interfaces.*

5.7 USE

The Quest for Software Requirements

ID	Usability Suggested Questions	Ask this to:
USE143s	What accident prevention requirements must be considered?	*identify types of safety.*
USE144s	What global safety requirements or constraints must the system satisfy?	*identify types of safety.*
USE145s	What safety issues and concerns must users be educated about?	*identify types of safety.*
USE146s	How important is it to develop the system so that it minimizes user errors? What is the importance that users be protected from making errors?	*identify various conditions / events.*
USE147s	What are examples of bad designs to avoid? .	*identify various designs.*
USE148s	What will aid in user orientation and recognition when first exposed to the new system?	*identify various presentation styles.*
USE149s	What safety risks need to be addressed?	*identify various risks.*
USE150s	In terms of usability, what would make this system better than a competing one?	*identify various usability comparatives.*
USE151s	What is the user trying to achieve by using the system?	*identify various user goals.*
USE152R	What advanced technology could help users be more productive?	*identify improvement areas.*
USE153R	What usability design changes are recommended?	*identify improvement areas.*
USE154R	What could be done to improve usability?	*identify improvement areas.*
USE155R	In what way does training hinder usability?	*identify improvement areas.*
USE156R	In what way do user help components hinder usability?	*identify improvement areas.*
USE157R	In what way do current system features hinder usability?	*identify improvement areas.*
USE158R	What business policies put constraints on usability design?	*identify pain points.*
USE159R	What design standards constrain usability design?	*identify pain points.*
USE160R	What usability issues are potential business risks?	*identify pain points.*
USE161B	What design standards must be applied to ensure consistency?	*identify design standards.*
USE162B	What else should I be asking about usability "purpose"?	*uncover additional requirements.*

5.7 USE

TIMING (WHEN?)

ID	Usability Suggested Questions	Ask this to:
USE163S	What is the rate of acceptance by the users?	*assess acceptance.*
USE164S	What is a typical learning curve?	*assess learning.*
USE165S	What duration of time is an acceptable learning period?	*assess learning.*
USE166S	How long should it take to complete a process?	*identify process guidelines.*
USE167S	While entering data, how much time do the users spend reviewing, analyzing, or verifying the data?	*identify process interactions.*
USE168S	How important is it to complete a process quickly and easily?	*identify process performance levels.*
USE169S	When processing work, where are the breaks in sequence?	*identify process sequences.*
USE170S	What sequencing of activities is common to the business area?	*identify related activities.*
USE171S	What amount of time is required for a reply?	*identify response to events.*
USE172S	How long before re-prompt and time out?	*identify response to events.*
USE173S	What on-going user training must be provided?	*identify training needs.*
USE174S	What incremental user training should be provided?	*identify training needs.*
USE175S	How long should it take first-time users to learn the system to a proficient level?	*identify types of users.*
USE176S	How long should it take experienced users to learn the system?	*identify types of users.*
USE177S	What timing constraints are there on completion of a transaction?	*identify usage events.*
USE178S	How frequently will most functions be used?	*identify usage frequencies.*
USE179S	Which functions will be used the least frequently?	*identify usage frequencies.*
USE180S	What tasks are performed infrequently?	*identify usage patterns.*
USE181S	When there are breaks in the sequence of the work, how long are the breaks?	*identify usage patterns.*
USE182S	When there are breaks in the sequence of the work, how is the system expected to resume processing?	*identify usage patterns.*

5.7 USE

TIMING (WHEN?) (continued)

ID	Usability Suggested Questions	Ask this to:
USE183s	How quickly must users learn to use the most frequented features?	*identify various features.*
USE184R	When should users be trained?	*assess learning.*
USE185R	How long would it take the average user to get up to speed?	*assess learning.*
USE186R	When do most data entry errors occur?	*identify usage patterns.*
USE187R	When does the help desk receive the most calls?	*identify usage patterns.*
USE188B	During which peak periods is usability critical?	*identify usage patterns.*
USE189B	How often is user help updated?	*assess acceptance.*
USE190B	What else should I be asking about usability "timing"?	*uncover additional requirements.*

5.7 USE

LOGISTICS (WHERE?)

ID	Usability Suggested Questions	Ask this to:
USE191s	What are user needs to switch between multiple currencies?	*identify conversion combinations.*
USE192s	What multiple currencies must be supported?	*identify currencies.*
USE193s	What expectations are there for the system to be used by people who do not speak the language of the country where the system is used?	*identify distribution.*
USE194s	Describe the work environment adjacent to the specific area being considered.	*identify environment types.*
USE195s	Describe the typical environment in which the users do their work.	*identify environments.*
USE196s	Describe the ergonomic usage of the system.	*identify ergonomic levels.*
USE197s	What multiple languages must be supported?	*identify languages.*
USE198s	What is the sound quality of the system?	*identify sound levels.*

LOGISTICS (WHERE?) (continued)

ID	Usability Suggested Questions	Ask this to:
USE199S	What special environmental conditions must be considered?	*identify types of environments.*
USE200S	What special lighting needs are there?	*identify types of lighting.*
USE201S	What multiple currencies must be available in the same instance of the system?	*identify various combinations.*
USE202S	What external devices must be used in concert to provide accessibility?	*identify various combinations.*
USE203S	What geographical or logistical constraints impact the user's ability to use the system?	*identify various constraints.*
USE204S	What textual and graphical visual interfaces are needed?	*identify visual interface types.*
USE205R	What level of user support is needed at each business location?	*identify resource needs.*
USE206R	What usability issues vary by business location?	*identify types of environments.*
USE207R	Where does each user class do its work?	*identify types of environments.*
USE208R	What different levels of help information are needed at different locations?	*identify usability needs.*
USE209R	What could be done to improve usability at each location?	*identify usability needs.*
USE210B	What locations can accommodate user training?	*identify resource needs.*
USE211B	What else should I be asking about usability "logistics"?	*uncover additional requirements.*

5.7 USE

The Quest for Software Requirements

PROCESS (HOW?)

ID	Usability Suggested Questions	Ask this to:
USE212s	What features of the current technology constrain usability?	*assess technology.*
USE213s	What characteristics are needed to make the system "easy" to use?	*classify characteristics.*
USE214s	What features/functions are critical to enabling users to perform their jobs?	*classify features.*
USE215s	Which features are used for high volume data input?	*classify features.*
USE216s	What makes the product safe to use? Unsafe?	*classify safety.*
USE217s	How necessary is it for the system to lead users through the task?	*identify activities.*
USE218s	What must be put in place to avoid hazards?	*identify hazards.*
USE219s	What must be put in place to minimize accidents if hazards arise?	*identify hazards.*
USE220s	What is necessary to ensure safe operation?	*identify levels of safety.*
USE221s	What makes the information easy to read?	*identify presentation styles.*
USE222s	How many variations in presentation exist within user roles?	*identify presentation types.*
USE223s	What procedures must be taken in the event of an accident?	*identify procedures.*
USE224s	What are the routines (process flow) followed in the business area?	*identify processes.*
USE225s	How does the business area react to disruption of their normal routine?	*identify scenarios.*
USE226s	How does the system conform to any established user interface standards?	*identify standards.*
USE227s	What user tasks show the highest incidences of accidents?	*identify types of accidents.*
USE228s	What workers compensation claims have been made in the past?	*identify types of accidents.*
USE229s	What hazard identification and analysis is needed?	*identify types of hazards.*
USE230s	What should the system do to "remember" where users have been and assist in their return?	*identify usage patterns.*
USE231s	What different components have specific access procedures?	*identify various access processes.*
USE232s	Describe unacceptable or undesirable system behavior.	*identify various behaviors.*

5.7 USE

PROCESS (HOW?) (continued)

ID	Usability Suggested Questions	Ask this to:
USE233s	What benchmark system or metric will be used?	*identify various benchmarks.*
USE234s	What user-defined control functions are needed?	*identify various controls.*
USE235s	How many different ways are expected in order to accomplish the same function?	*identify various function usages.*
USE236s	What are the expectations for multiple ways to complete the same task?	*identify various scenarios.*
USE237s	What type of navigation is expected?	*identify various types of navigation.*
USE238s	What current workarounds are performed to improve usability?	*identify various types of workarounds.*
USE239s	What user workarounds are performed to offset system deficiencies?	*identify various types of workarounds.*
USE240r	What processes should be changed to improve usability?	*identify process improvement areas.*
USE241r	What process areas experience the most data entry errors?	*identify process improvement areas.*
USE242r	What processes or procedures affect usability?	*identify process improvement areas.*
USE243r	What manual workarounds could be automated?	*identify process improvement areas.*
USE244r	What processes are typically performed by novice users? Expert users?	*identify processes.*
USE245r	What are procedures for users to get help?	*identify processes.*
USE246r	What are procedures for users to get help desk support?	*identify processes.*
USE247r	What processes present user safety concerns?	*identify processes.*
USE248b	What processes or procedures require the most user training?	*identify processes.*
USE249b	What else should I be asking about usability "processes"?	*uncover additional requirements.*

5.7 USE

5.8 SUGGESTED READING

Handbook of Software Reliability Engineering, Michael R. Lyu (editor), [Lyu, 1996]. This is a comprehensive collection of articles on the subject of *software reliability*, and an article on *fault-tolerance* system architectures.

Non-functional Requirements in Software Engineering, by Lawrence Chung, et al., [Chung, 2000]. This book includes a concentrated discussion on cataloguing methods and non-functional requirement types, and a thorough perspective on accuracy (**integrity**), security, and performance (*efficiency*).

Requirements Engineering: Processes and Techniques, by Gerald Kotonya and Ian Sommerville, [Kotonya, 1998]. Non-functional requirements are discussed in Chapter 8 including *reliability*, security, safety, *usability*, and performance (*efficiency*).

Security in Computing, 3rd Edition, by Charles P. Pfleeger and Shari Lawrence Pfleeger, [Pfleeger, 2003]. This book is devoted entirely to the exploration of *security* for computer-based systems.

Software Engineering, 8th Edition, by Ian Sommerville, [Sommerville, 2007]. Chapter 3 deals with critical systems and discusses four dimensions of system dependability: *availability, reliability,* safety, and security. Chapter 20 covers the development of fault tolerant systems and some techniques for *fault avoidance*, while Chapter 30 deals with system *survivability*.

Software Fault Tolerance Techniques and Implementation, by Laura Pullum, [Pullum, 2001]. This is a comprehensive book on the subject of software fault tolerance (*survivability*).

Software Quality Engineering, by Jeff Tian, [Tian, 2005]. Chapter 22 introduces the general topic of software *reliability* engineering.

Software Reliability Engineering: More Reliable Software Faster and Cheaper, 2nd Edition, by John D. Musa, [Musa, 2004]. This book is a classic guide to the time-saving practice of *reliability*.

Software Requirement Patterns, by Stephen Withall, [Withall, 2007]. Chapter 11 of this book presents *access control* as its own domain category consisting of five requirement patterns: user registration, user authentication, user authorization (specific authorization and configurable authorization), and approval. Chapter 9, section 5, includes a discussion on *availability*.

Software Requirements, 2nd Edition, by Karl Wiegers, [Wiegers, 2003]. Chapter 12 provides an overview of several software quality attributes including robustness (*survivability*).

Software Requirements: Objects, Functions, & States, by Alan M. Davis, [Davis, 1993]. Davis discusses portability, *reliability, efficiency*, and human engineering (*usability*) in Chapter 5, "Specifying Nonbehavioral Requirements."

Software Requirements: Styles and Techniques, by Soren Lauesen, [Lauesen, 2002]. Chapter 6 presents a variety of categories, including *efficiency* and *usability*.

System Requirements Analysis, Jeffrey O. Grady, [Grady, 2006]. Although Grady's book focuses on system requirements instead of business requirements, Chapter 3.7, "Specialty Engineering Requirements Analysis," includes a discussion on *reliability* and maintainability engineering.

6 REVISION REQUIREMENTS

HOW EASY IS IT TO CORRECT ERRORS AND ADD ON FUNCTIONS?

Revision requirements define how efficiently the software system can be corrected or fixed when errors occur, and how easily new features can be added. Revision requirements are generally of greater concern to the users who read the software system documentation to understand the design and usage of the system, and change source code or data that drive the system. As such, the user's view of *quality* is a system that is easy to maintain and easy to demonstrate that performance requirements are being met.

The revision group of nonfunctional categories encompasses the concerns of the users supporting a system in a production environment. Revision requirements answer user concerns for the following software qualities:

- ♦ FLEXIBILITY. How easy is it to modify the system to work in different environments?

- ♦ MAINTAINABILITY. How easy is it to upkeep and repair the system?

- ♦ SCALABILITY. How easy is it to expand or upgrade the capabilities of the system?

- ♦ VERIFIABILITY. How easy is it to show the system performs its functions?

In the same order as listed above, this chapter presents the following for each revision category: definition, brief discussion, examples of requirements, and suggested elicitation questions. The introduction to Part Two explains the anatomy of a category and provides guidance for how to use the suggested questions.

6.1 FLEXIBILITY (FLX)

> **USER CONCERN:** How easy is it to modify the system to work in different environments?
>
> **RELATED CATEGORIES:** Adaptability, Extendability, Interchangeability, Multiplicability, Tailorability

6.1.1 Flexibility Definition

Flexibility is the ease with which the software can be modified to adapt to different environments, configurations, and user expectations.

6.1.2 Flexibility Discussion

Flexibility concerns the built-in ability of the system to adapt or to be adapted by the users to meet business conditions without major reconstruction of the core system.

Flexibility is often subdivided into the following attributes:

6.1 FLX

♦ EXTENDABILITY: concerned with the ability to extend the existing software by "plugging in" (also called "plug-and-play") extra components. Examples are as follows:

   a) It shall be possible to add a new delivery option for customer mailing method by developing and "plugging in" the functionality necessary to support that delivery option. The new delivery option shall not require changes to the core software of the system to allow its introduction.

   b) It shall be possible to deliver mail to customers via United Parcel Service (UPS). To send mail via UPS, the customer must have a valid residential or business address. (UPS will not deliver to post office boxes.)

   c) There shall be a maintenance function to allow the entry of details about a new delivery option and the editing of existing delivery options.

- ◆ INTERCHANGEABILITY: concerned with the ability to modify the system to switch from using a specific set of components to using another set. For example, the security software shall be configured to switch from workday mode to weekend mode.

- ◆ MULTIPLICABILITY: concerned with the ability of the system to handle multiple objects at the same time, each of which typically has its own user interface with data that are distinctly separate from the others. For example, a multi-lingual system will have different user interfaces for each language supported.

Flexibility is generally more applicable when building commercial-off-the-shelf (COTS) software or a software product that is intended to be sold to multiple organizations. It makes it easier to tailor (hence, the term "tailorability") or customize the software for each organization without affecting core functionality. For example, a word processing software package should be able to adapt to different kinds of printers.

6.1 FLX

When eliciting flexibility requirements, consider the following aspects:

- ◆ DIFFERENT ORGANIZATIONS. This might literally be organizations that the software is sold to. It might also be various divisions within a large corporation. Even internal departments or business silos within an organization could have difference business practices. Consider the following differences:
    - ◊ Data types and display format
    - ◊ Organization structure or hierarchy
    - ◊ Employee roles and job descriptions
    - ◊ Accounting and General Ledger entries
    - ◊ Interfaces with external systems
    - ◊ Terminology

♦ **DIFFERENT INDUSTRIES.** Is the system being built going to be used in multiple industries? Minor differences such as terminology can affect the flexibility of the software.

♦ **DIFFERENT COUNTRIES.** Not only do different languages and currencies exist, but processing differences occur across physical land boundaries and governances. Consider the following differences:

◊ Currency

◊ Numeric display format

◊ Date display format

◊ Language

◊ Dialect

◊ Time zone

◊ Financial year

◊ Calendar

◊ Geographic regions (for example, states, territories, and provinces)

◊ Postal codes

◊ Address format

◊ Telephone numbers

◊ Measurement system

◊ Grammatical punctuation

◊ Cultural differences

◊ Tax, regulatory, and legal regimes

◊ Calculations (for example, bank interest)

6.1 FLX

- ◆ SINGLE SITE. If you are building software for one specific site or location, this must be clearly communicated or documented as an assumption. In other words, call attention to it to confirm this.

- ◆ DIFFERENT SITES. If the software is intended to be used in multiple departments, business silos, divisions, and so on, it is important to identify any diversity or difference between them.

6.1.3 Flexibility Requirement Examples

a) Provisions shall be made for the future usage of multiple languages. Provision shall include at least the following: 1) The structure of the data store shall be such that multi-lingual support shall not necessitate additional components or the need to replace current components, and 2) A user shall be able to nominate their preferred language when entering their personal information.

b) No piece of text that might be displayed to a user shall reside in program source code. Every piece of text that a user might see must be modifiable without changing source code. That is, no user-visible text will be "hard-coded."

6.1 FLX

c) The billing system shall be able to process invoices and payments in multiple different currencies. (Currency conversion calculations are to be detailed in business rules and enforced by functional requirements.)

d) The course curriculum management system shall allow multiple independent courses to be offered with multiple scheduled offerings. Information about courses shall be rigorously separated from each other, and no user shall be able to view or otherwise access information about a course with which they are not connected.

e) The employee benefits system shall be suitable for use by any ABC Corporation office in any country in which ABC Corporation operates. (It is assumed that all users of the system speak a common language so translation into multiple languages for user interfaces, reports, documentation, and other business materials is not necessary.)

f) The system shall have the ability to add a new user notification method by developing and "plugging in" the software necessary to support the new method. A new user notification method shall not require changes to the core software of the system to allow its introduction.

6.1.4 Flexibility Suggested Questions

DATA (WHAT?)

ID	Flexibility Suggested Questions	Ask this to:
FLX1S	What information is updated based on the event?	*correlate information and events.*
FLX2S	How long must the information be available to the user?	*determine amount of history storage needs.*
FLX3S	What information history is customized by the user?	*determine customization needs.*
FLX4S	How does the quantity of instances vary by specific user?	*determine customization needs.*
FLX5S	In what level of detail is history needed?	*determine if summarization history is needed.*
FLX6S	What information is needed to monitor adherence to business policies?	*identify processing.*
FLX7S	What types of notification methods can be anticipated?	*identify response rates.*
FLX8R	What information is passed with the system response?	*correlate information and events.*
FLX9R	What information is heavily accessed?	*determine flexibility metrics.*
FLX10R	How often can a calculated result change?	*identify need to refresh information.*
FLX11R	What calculations on the data are performed?	*identify calculations that can be stored.*
FLX12R	What special information is needed to add a new interface?	*identify configurations.*
FLX13R	How would users like to see or view information?	*identify formats for displaying information.*
FLX14R	How would users like to access information?	*identify formats for displaying information.*
FLX15R	Under what circumstances should information *not* be transferred?	*identify geographic or device restrictions in transmitting data.*
FLX16R	How is the information used?	*identify how information is manipulated.*
FLX17R	What information is needed about each business object?	*identify information attributes.*

6.1 FLX

DATA (WHAT?) (continued)

ID	Flexibility Suggested Questions	Ask this to:
FLX18R	Where does information come from?	*identify information input sources.*
FLX19R	Where does information go?	*identify information output sources.*
FLX20R	Who views information?	*identify information output sources.*
FLX21R	What information is needed to facilitate user customization?	*identify information to personalize the user's experience.*
FLX22R	What information is needed about each user class?	*identify information to request from users.*
FLX23R	How often is the calculated result needed?	*identify need to store information.*
FLX24R	What additional information about each business object would be nice to know?	*identify optional data.*
FLX25R	What information requires quick access?	*identify response time.*
FLX26R	What encryption algorithms can be anticipated?	*identify security requirements.*
FLX27R	What quantity of data can be transmitted at one time?	*identify the maximum data capacity by device type or function.*
FLX28R	What information do users need to perform a process?	*identify user information needs.*
FLX29R	What information is captured or modified by this process?	*identify user information needs.*
FLX30R	What error, informational, and help messages do users need?	*identify user information needs.*
FLX31R	What additional input file formats can be anticipated?	*identify various interfaces.*
FLX32R	What additional output file formats can be anticipated?	*identify various interfaces.*
FLX33R	What other processes receive the same information requests from the users?	*minimize the need to enter information multiple times.*
FLX34B	What else should I be asking about flexibility "data"?	*uncover additional requirements.*

6.1 FLX

The Quest for Software Requirements

ROLES (WHO?)

ID	Flexibility Suggested Questions	Ask this to:
FLX35S	Why should users be allowed to set their preferred date presentation?	*identify controls extended to users.*
FLX36S	Why should users be allowed to set their preferred presentation standards?	*identify controls extended to users.*
FLX37S	How diverse are individual users allowed to make their system profile?	*identify controls extended to users.*
FLX38S	What system settings could be added at the user level?	*identify controls extended to users.*
FLX39S	Who enforces the adherence to business policies?	*identify role responsibilities.*
FLX40S	Who is responsible for knowing the special information?	*identify role responsibilities.*
FLX41S	What are the expectations of the role for the one entering special information about the configuration?	*identify training needs.*
FLX42S	What dialects within languages must be supported?	*identify users.*
FLX43S	What types of new customers might be added?	*identify users.*
FLX44S	What is the expectation for adding new types of users?	*identify users.*
FLX45S	How do these new types of users differ from current users?	*identify users.*
FLX46S	What types of new users might be added?	*identify users.*
FLX47S	What is the skill level of those users in remote locations for managing installations and upgrades?	*identify users.*
FLX48R	Who determines the amount of history to be kept?	*determine amount of history storage needs.*
FLX49R	Who can validate the information during a test?	*identify additional stakeholders.*
FLX50R	Who can validate that the process works correctly?	*identify additional stakeholders.*
FLX51R	What configuration settings are established at the user level?	*identify controls extended to users.*
FLX52R	Who (role) is responsible for the underlying infrastructure?	*identify role responsibilities.*
FLX53R	When doing new installations, what is the expected level of expertise for the installer?	*identify role responsibilities.*
FLX54R	Who (role) is responsible for entering the special information in the configuration?	*identify role responsibilities.*
FLX55B	What else should I be asking about flexibility "roles"?	*uncover additional requirements.*

6.1 FLX

PURPOSE (WHY?)

ID	Flexibility Suggested Questions	Ask this to:
FLX56s	How mature is the business for this application?	*assess maturity.*
FLX57s	How does adherence to business policies vary by user class?	*determine customization needs.*
FLX58s	What is the range of the degree a business policy might be broken?	*determine flexibility metrics.*
FLX59s	During what times can the business policy be broken with no action required?	*identify business rules.*
FLX60s	What is the extent to which the business policy might be broken?	*identify business rules.*
FLX61s	Which features/functions could be affected by regulatory control?	*identify change severities.*
FLX62s	Which features/functions must be most flexible to respond to business changes?	*identify change velocity.*
FLX63s	How frequently can additions be expected?	*identify change velocity.*
FLX64s	How quickly must the company respond to customer feedback?	*identify channels of communication.*
FLX65s	How aggressive are the competitors in the same market space?	*identify competitors.*
FLX66s	What interfaces with external systems can be anticipated?	*identify configurations.*
FLX67s	How fast must enhancements be completed?	*identify enhancements.*
FLX68s	What external factors cause business change?	*identify external factors.*
FLX69s	Which features/functions are most susceptible to external changes?	*identify external factors.*
FLX70s	As the business evolves, how might this system be affected?	*identify longevities.*
FLX71s	What is the value of being first to market with an innovation?	*identify market pressure.*
FLX72s	What user frustrations must be addressed, from the current release, to promote wide-spread use of the system?	*identify obstacles/barriers to implementation.*
FLX73s	What types of new products might be added?	*identify possibilities.*
FLX74s	What types of new services might be added?	*identify possibilities.*
FLX75s	What is the performance expectation for extending the system?	*identify possible extensions.*

6.1 FLX

ID	Flexibility Suggested Questions	Ask this to:
FLX76s	What enhancement capabilities can be expected?	*identify potential requests.*
FLX77s	How many different types of features/functions are anticipated?	*identify processing.*
FLX78s	How large could the change be as a result of a regulatory change?	*identify regulatory controls.*
FLX79s	What is the anticipated rate of requests for the addition of new features/functions?	*identify scope of change.*
FLX80s	What should be the measurement of a feature added to the product?	*identify sizing metrics.*
FLX81s	What is the date presentation standard?	*identify standards.*
FLX82R	How does the additional infrastructure alter the project scope?	*assess impact.*
FLX83R	How different will these new features/functions be from those expected in this release?	*evaluate solutions.*
FLX84R	What levels of restricted access to any information exist?	*identify access security requirements.*
FLX85R	What additional devices can be anticipated?	*identify configurations.*
FLX86R	What considerations need to be given for configuration information?	*identify configurations.*
FLX87R	How much configuration special information is managed by the system?	*identify configurations.*
FLX88R	How quickly should new devices be made available to users?	*identify configurations.*
FLX89R	How much effort is expected for adding new, common devices?	*identify configurations.*
FLX90R	What expectations are there for uninstalling the whole system?	*identify configurations.*
FLX91R	What expectations are there for uninstalling system components?	*identify configurations.*
FLX92R	What expectations are there for re-installing alternate configurations?	*identify configurations.*
FLX93R	When external factors cause change, which factors require a system response?	*identify external factors.*
FLX94R	What is expected for adding a new instance?	*identify implementations.*
FLX95R	Provide details of hardware and software that are currently used.	*identify interfaces.*

6.1 FLX

PURPOSE (WHY?) (continued)

ID	Flexibility Suggested Questions	Ask this to:
FLX96R	How will the system manage software license expiration?	*identify licensing.*
FLX97R	What licensing controls should be implemented?	*identify limitations.*
FLX98R	What simplifications of multiples are acceptable?	*identify limitations.*
FLX99R	What means for extending features are available in the current design?	*identify limitations.*
FLX100R	What design considerations need to be made for adding physical devices?	*identify possible devices.*
FLX101R	How easy should it be to "plug in" a new interface?	*identify possible interfaces.*
FLX102R	What is the trade-off between innovative and incremental releases?	*identify types of change.*
FLX103R	What is the expected combination of modifying existing features and adding new features?	*identify types of change.*
FLX104R	How difficult is it to modify or extend the application to meet specific needs?	*identify various extensions.*
FLX105R	What will be the user acceptance test criteria?	*prioritize requirements and identify test considerations.*
FLX106R	What is the trade-off between flexibility and performance?	*relate categories.*
FLX107B	What else should I be asking about flexibility "purpose"?	*uncover additional requirements.*

6.1 FLX

TIMING (WHEN?)

ID	Flexibility Suggested Questions	Ask this to:
FLX108s	What fiscal reporting periods will the system be expected to support?	identify business cycles.
FLX109s	How long is the system expected to be in use?	identify life expectancy.
FLX110s	How often are new sites added for installation?	identify pace of change.
FLX111s	How rapidly is the business changing or evolving?	identify rate of change.
FLX112s	How tolerant of change are the users/customers of the system?	identify rates of change.
FLX113s	What is the trade-off between small, quick changes and large, more time-consuming feature changes?	identify rates of change.
FLX114s	How frequently will different currencies be added?	identify rates of change.
FLX115s	How quickly must new features/functions be completed?	identify rates of change.
FLX116s	What is the lead time notice of regulation change?	identify regulatory compliance.
FLX117s	What is the rate of regulation change?	identify regulatory controls.
FLX118s	When should users be notified that a business policy might potentially be broken?	identify time-triggered events.
FLX119R	How long should information be kept?	determine amount of history storage needs.
FLX120R	When is the expected peak period for each user class?	determine capacity requirements.
FLX121R	When is the expected peak period for each business event?	determine capacity requirements.
FLX122R	When is the expected peak period for each business location?	determine capacity requirements.
FLX123R	What would be the expected performance for peak periods?	determine flexibility metrics.
FLX124R	When is information needed?	determine information supply strategy.
FLX125R	How soon is the history needed for analysis?	determine optional archival methods.
FLX126R	How often is information transmitted?	determine traffic patterns.
FLX127R	How often must the information be uploaded?	determine traffic patterns.
FLX128R	When is the peak period that data transmission occurs?	determine traffic patterns.

6.1 FLX

TIMING (WHEN?) (continued)

ID	Flexibility Suggested Questions	Ask this to:
FLX129R	At what specific time must downloaded information be available?	*determine traffic patterns.*
FLX130R	What information transmissions vary by user class?	*determine traffic patterns.*
FLX131R	What information transmissions vary by device type?	*determine traffic patterns.*
FLX132R	What is the expected volume growth of information over the next year? Five years? Ten years?	*identify expandability requirements.*
FLX133R	How often must the information be updated?	*identify how often information should be refreshed.*
FLX134R	How fast must installations be completed?	*identify installations.*
FLX135R	During what time periods is information accessed more than others?	*identify patterns in retrieving information.*
FLX136R	What history information will be accessed immediately?	*identify patterns in retrieving information.*
FLX137R	What are the considerations for making upgrades by skipping release levels?	*identify rates of change.*
FLX138R	What is the sequence in which the events must occur?	*identify time-triggered events.*
FLX139R	At what point in the process is the information needed?	*minimize the need to carry information throughout the process.*
FLX140B	What else should I be asking about flexibility "timing"?	*uncover additional requirements.*

6.1 FLX

LOGISTICS (WHERE?)

ID	Flexibility Suggested Questions	Ask this to:
FLX141S	What kinds of things should the system be able to support multiples of?	*identify configurations.*
FLX142S	What level of support for multiple features is expected?	*identify configurations.*
FLX143S	What is different (how diverse) about each new site?	*identify diversity.*
FLX144S	What other related business areas might this system support?	*identify extensions.*

LOGISTICS (WHERE?) (continued)

ID	Flexibility Suggested Questions	Ask this to:
FLX145S	How does the system need to support currency conversion?	*identify interface dependencies.*
FLX146S	What are the plans for installation at remote locations?	*identify location complexities.*
FLX147S	In what sites will the system be installed?	*identify possible breadth.*
FLX148S	How rapidly will languages be added?	*identify speed of changes.*
FLX149S	What current languages are supported?	*identify users.*
FLX150S	What nationalities and languages must be supported?	*identify users.*
FLX151S	How broad (and how limited) is the set of environments for which the system should be suitable?	*identify various environments.*
FLX152S	What are possible new sites in the same industry?	*identify various extensions.*
FLX153S	What currencies must be supported?	*identify various installations.*
FLX154S	What are possible new sites in the same country?	*identify various location combinations.*
FLX155S	What are possible new sites within the organization?	*identify various locations.*
FLX156R	What would be the priority by geographic location and business processes?	*determine traffic patterns.*
FLX157R	What is the availability time frame at each location?	*determine when backups can be initiated.*
FLX158R	How much information would be retrieved by each business location?	*identify amount of data transmitted by device type.*
FLX159R	How much information is uploaded by each business location?	*identify amount of data transmitted by device type.*
FLX160R	What are the possible variations within a single installation?	*identify configurations.*
FLX161R	What additional/alternate database platforms can be anticipated?	*identify configurations.*
FLX162R	What type of information is transferred by each business location?	*identify graphical and textual information transmitted.*
FLX163B	What else should I be asking about flexibility "logistics"?	*uncover additional requirements.*

6.1 FLX

PROCESS (HOW?)

ID	Flexibility Suggested Questions	Ask this to:
FLX164s	Describe the current workflow.	*define current processes.*
FLX165s	How does the process work today?	*define current processes.*
FLX166s	Why does the process work that way?	*define current processes.*
FLX167s	Where will the system need agility to remain viable with the expected business growth?	*identify areas of rapid response.*
FLX168s	What additional functions/features can be anticipated?	*identify possible extensions.*
FLX169s	How will the system monitor adherence to business policies?	*identify processing.*
FLX170s	What should occur if a business policy is not followed?	*identify processing.*
FLX171R	How will the system know that users are who they claim to be?	*identify access security requirements.*
FLX172R	What combinations of information and processing requires special access privileges?	*identify access security requirements.*
FLX173R	What are the exceptions to user actions?	*identify additional processes.*
FLX174R	What is done when an exception occurs?	*identify additional processes.*
FLX175R	What are exceptions to the normal workflow?	*identify alternative processes.*
FLX176R	How does the process vary by user?	*identify alternative processes.*
FLX177R	What alternatives are there to this process?	*identify alternative processes.*
FLX178R	What other processes are there?	*identify alternative processes.*
FLX179R	What specific processing limits need to apply to each user class?	*identify capacity metrics.*
FLX180R	What conditions must be met for this event to occur?	*identify event dependencies.*
FLX181R	What happens if the conditions are not met?	*identify event dependencies.*
FLX182R	What would users like changed in the current workflow?	*identify possible process improvement areas.*

6.1 FLX

PROCESS (HOW?) (continued)

ID	Flexibility Suggested Questions	Ask this to:
FLX183R	When is the process reusable?	*identify possible process improvement areas.*
FLX184R	How are users added, changed, deleted, reviewed, and monitored?	*identify processing restrictions.*
FLX185R	What is the system response from the event?	*identify processing.*
FLX186R	What actions take place when the event is triggered?	*identify relationships between events and processes.*
FLX187R	How does the activity differ in terms of which user initiates the event?	*identify relationships between users and events.*
FLX188R	During what processes is information reusable?	*identify reusable components.*
FLX189R	What would prevent implementing changes in the current workflow?	*identify risks and issues.*
FLX190B	What else should I be asking about flexibility "processes"?	*uncover additional requirements.*

6.1 FLX

6.2 MAINTAINABILITY (MNT)

> USER CONCERN: How easy is it to upkeep and repair the system?
> RELATED CATEGORIES: Correctiveness, Modifiability, Reliability,
> Repairability, Supportability

6.2.1 Maintainability Definition

Maintainability is the ease with which faults in a software system can be found and fixed.

6.2.2 Maintainability Discussion

Maintainability is an indicator of how quickly an unreliable system (one in a failed state) can be brought to a reliable state. Maintainability depends on how easily the software can be understood, changed, and tested.

In general, maintainability requirements need to consider not only the repair of the defect or fault, but recovery from the effects of the fault, so that the system is ready again to do its intended work (see also *reliability* in Chapter 5, "Operation Requirements").

Software engineers usually differentiate between four kinds of maintenance requirements:

6.2 MNT

- ♦ CORRECTIVE MAINTENANCE: concerned with correcting known defects in the system. Changes are made to the software to remove faults (defects in the code).

- ♦ PREVENTATIVE MAINTENANCE: concerned with correcting defects that haven't caused problems yet, but might later on. Changes are made to the software to make it more maintainable.

- ♦ PERFECTIVE MAINTENANCE: concerned with expanding the system to meet additional business needs. Changes and enhancements are made to the software as a result of user requests.

♦ ADAPTIVE MAINTENANCE: concerned with modifying the system to accommodate technology. Changes are made to the software as a consequence of operated system, hardware, or other technical-oriented changes.

The intent of maintainability engineering is to integrate maintainability requirements with system requirements and design parameters to increase the likelihood that the software and hardware are readily maintainable within the designated performance levels at the lowest possible system life-cycle cost. The maintainability requirements are often design criteria or constraints on how the system is to be developed. Such design criteria includes modularization, standardization, accessibility, interchangeability, repair guidance, discard guidance, and test checkpoint placement and quantity. These criteria are stated in both qualitative and quantitative parameters, and are used as guidelines by the design and development team.

As an aid to specifying maintainability requirements, let's turn our attention to several maintainability metrics, which are commonly stated in time parameters (usually in hours). Maintenance time criteria must be carefully defined and agreed upon by the stakeholders. Commonly used maintainability parameters are listed in Table 6-1.

Table 6-1 Maintainability Parameters

6.2 MNT

Parameter	Description	Meaning
MTTR	Mean time to repair	How long it takes to repair the item on average
MTRR	Mean time to remove and replace	Item removal and installation time
MTBM	Mean time between maintenance	Time between maintenance actions
MCT	Mean corrective maintenance time	Time to repair a failure on average (such as MTTR)
MPT	Mean preventative maintenance time	Time required for preventive action

When eliciting maintainability requirements, consider the following aspects:

♦ MAINTENANCE PERFORMANCE METRICS (refer to Table 6-1). These deal with how long it takes to perform maintenance activities.

♦ MAINTENANCE SUPPORT FEATURES. Support features usually specify things to happen during system maintenance without regard to how much time it takes to do them. For example, "The software vendor shall assign a dedicated resource to perform onsite maintenance."

♦ SYSTEM MAINTENANCE FEATURES. Software vendors might build features into the product itself or the support tools to help satisfy maintenance performance requirements with less effort. For example, "The system shall log all user actions," or "The system shall provide remote diagnostic functions."

♦ SYSTEM COMPLEXITY. Some developers contend that maintainability can be measured by the source code. For example, a requirement might state, "The cyclomatic complexity of the source code shall not exceed 6. No method in any object shall exceed 200 lines of code." Assuming that a source program with 12 nested loops is more difficult to maintain than one with 3 or 4, the cyclomatic complexity measure of code essentially counts the levels of nesting. However, experienced developers find these counts of little value toward predicting maintainability.

♦ DEVELOPMENT PROCESS. What assessment methods or standards can be used to measure the maintainability of source code? For example, International Organization for Standardization (ISO) programming standards might be applied.

♦ MAINTENANCE PROCESS CYCLE.

◊ **Reporting.** Notification that a defect or fault has been encountered. Who gets notified? What information is needed to report a problem?

◊ **Analysis.** The problem report is reviewed, and an investigation of the cause of the problem is conducted. Where is the defect that caused the problem? What would it cost to repair the problem? What would happen if nothing was done about the problem?

6.2 MNT

◊ **Decision**. Based upon the analysis of the problem, what are possible solutions? Is there a work-around? What actions should be taken to keep users informed? Is additional user training needed as part of the solution? Should the problem be dismissed (it isn't worth fixing)? Is there enough known about the problem and the possible solutions to make a decision? If it is decided to fix the problem, when should it be fixed? Immediately? Fix it in the next release?

◊ **Reply**. Report the outcome of the analysis and decision to affected users, business areas, and other stakeholders.

◊ **Test the solution**. If it is decided to apply a work-around or a system repair, test that it works. Look for related defects that might also be corrected (preventative maintenance).

◊ **Follow through on the decision**. Implement approved changes, repairs, or fixes. Regardless of the decision (for example, repair or don't repair), communicate follow-through actions to affected users and stakeholders.

♦ POSSIBLE PROBLEMS.

◊ **Programming error**. The system doesn't work as intended by the developer.

◊ **Requirement violation**. The system doesn't work as described by the requirements.

6.2 MNT

◊ **Change request**. The issue was not an expectation of the system (excluded from the scope) at the start of the development or installation project.

◊ **Usability error**. The system can perform what the user wants, but the user cannot operate the system. This might be a user training issue, or the user interface needs to be improved.

◊ **Unstated user expectation**. In practice, it is likely that requirements are missed. If the user has a reasonable expectation regarding the system functions, then such missing requirements are generally viewed as defects.

6.2.3 Maintainability Requirement Examples

a) The customer service call center shall analyze 95% of the problem reports within 2 hours. Items classified as "urgent" shall be repaired within 3 business days in 98% of the reported cases.

b) The application development process must have a regression test procedure that allows complete re-testing within two business days.

c) A maintenance developer shall be able to modify existing statements to conform to revised regulations from the federal government with 24 labor hours or less of development and testing effort.

d) A new consumer type code must be able to be added to the product within 12 business hours.

e) The system must maintain a service log and, on system start-up, must check if system service is due. If a scheduled service session has not been carried out within 5 calendar days of the scheduled date, the system should discontinue operation.

f) A development programmer who has at least one year of experience supporting this software application shall be able to add a new product feature, including source code modifications and testing, with no more than one week of labor.

g) The system shall not be shut down for maintenance more than once in a 24-hour period.

6.2 MNT

6.2.4 Maintainability Suggested Questions

DATA (WHAT?)

ID	Maintainability Suggested Questions	Ask this to:
MNT1s	What concerns exist about vendor-supplied documentation?	*identify concerns.*
MNT2s	What data elements must have unique values?	*identify data needs.*
MNT3s	What are special handling requirements for certain data types?	*identify exceptions.*
MNT4s	What control parameters will be stored and maintained?	*identify various controls.*
MNT5s	What standards for managing common data elements like name and address fields apply?	*maintain compliance with standards.*
MNT6s	What date, time, date and time, attributes must be enforced consistently?	*maintain compliance with standards.*
MNT7s	What is the expected level of precision on calculations?	*maintain compliance with standards.*
MNT8r	What check digit routines will be used by the system?	*identify variety of routines.*
MNT9r	What data access methods must be used?	*identify various methodologies.*
MNT10r	What are the data type attributes that must be enforced consistently?	*maintain compliance with standards.*
MNT11r	What are the numeric data attributes that must be enforced consistently?	*maintain compliance with standards.*
MNT12r	What numeric standards apply for: signed, unsigned, units, and rounding?	*maintain compliance with standards.*
MNT13b	What maintenance records should be kept?	*identify maintenance data.*
MNT14b	What messaging formats must be used?	*identify various formats.*
MNT15b	What maintenance schedule information do users need?	*identify various methodologies.*
MNT16b	What else should I be asking about maintainability "data"?	*uncover additional requirements.*

6.2 MNT

ROLES (WHO?)

ID	Maintainability Suggested Questions	Ask this to:
MNT17s	Who should be notified if scheduled maintenance will be delayed or not performed?	*identify role responsibilities.*
MNT18s	Who supports the users when maintenance is performed?	*identify role responsibilities.*
MNT19s	Who needs access security to perform system maintenance?	*identify security levels.*
MNT20s	What effect do maintenance activities have on customers?	*identify users.*
MNT21s	What effect do maintenance activities have on users?	*identify users.*
MNT22R	Who should be notified when time-triggered maintenance tasks fail?	*identify role responsibilities.*
MNY23R	Who performs routine maintenance?	*identify role responsibilities.*
MNT24R	Who performs system upgrades?	*identify role responsibilities.*
MNT25R	Who migrates enhancement releases?	*identify role responsibilities.*
MNT26R	Who owns the points of interface?	*identify role responsibilities.*
MNT27R	Who is responsible when an interface with a device fails?	*identify role responsibilities.*
MNT28R	Who is responsible for the interface?	*identify role responsibilities.*
MNT29R	Who (what role) will be performing the maintenance?	*identify role responsibilities.*
MNT30R	Who (role) will be authorized to manage control parameters?	*identify role responsibilities.*
MNT31R	Who sets the rules for the interface?	*identify role responsibilities.*
MNT32R	What is the expected skill level of the maintenance team?	*identify skills.*
MNT33R	How much experience does the current staff have with the devices?	*identify skills.*
MNT34R	What points of interface exist with vendor components?	*identify software interfaces.*
MNT35R	What level of access is expected of the maintenance staff?	*identify various levels.*
MNT36B	Who should be notified of maintenance tasks and schedules?	*identify role responsibilities.*
MNT37B	Who needs to monitor maintenance records?	*identify role responsibilities.*
MNT38B	What else should I be asking about maintainability "roles"?	*uncover additional requirements.*

6.2 MNT

PURPOSE (WHY?)

ID	Maintainability Suggested Questions	Ask this to:
MNT39s	How quickly must enhancements be added?	*establish expectations related to flexibility.*
MNT40s	What response time is expected for adding simple, moderate, or complex enhancements?	*establish expectations related to flexibility.*
MNT41s	What is the expected skill level of the enhancement development team?	*establish expectations.*
MNT42s	How easy should it be to change devices?	*establish expectations.*
MNT43s	What preventative maintenance should be applied?	*identify anticipated actions.*
MNT44s	What external mandates for upgrades or changes impact the project?	*identify external factors.*
MNT45s	What features are most likely to change?	*identify potential changes.*
MNT46s	What proposed standards or changes to existing standards exist?	*identify potential changes.*
MNT47s	What anticipated new releases expand functionality?	*identify scope of change.*
MNT48s	How are early adopters in this line of business served?	*identify service expectations.*
MNT49s	What are the drivers of business change?	*identify sources for change.*
MNT50s	What changes to the business organization could affect the system?	*identify sources of impact.*
MNT51s	How mature is the line of business this application is being built to support?	*identify sources of information.*
MNT52s	How mature is the industry in this line of business?	*identify sources of knowledge.*
MNT53s	What types of mandatory changes can be expected?	*identify types of changes and reduce response.*
MNT54s	What business rules could change that would affect the system?	*identify volatile business rules to ease maintenance for change.*
MNT55s	What date management and terminology will be used consistently by the system?	*maintain compliance with standards.*
MNT56r	What degree of complexity is anticipated for add-on enhancements?	*identify complexities.*
MNT57r	What is the importance of staying on current releases?	*identify configurations.*
MNT58r	What hardware devices or software features are expected to require the most frequent maintenance?	*identify points of failure.*
MNT59r	What audits are performed on maintenance service levels?	*identify standards.*

6.2 MNT

PURPOSE (WHY?) (continued)

ID	Maintainability Suggested Questions	Ask this to:
MNT60R	How stable is the configuration environment?	*identify various configurations and possible impacts.*
MNT61R	What user interface and presentation design standards should be in place?	*maintain compliance with standards.*
MNT62R	What are standard display formats for all data attribute types?	*maintain compliance with standards.*
MNT63R	What file format and database interface standards must be in place?	*maintain compliance with standards.*
MNT64R	What are the industry standard messaging formats?	*maintain compliance with standards.*
MNT65R	What protocols must be used?	*maintain compliance with standards.*
MNT66R	What are the industry standards for the protocols?	*maintain compliance with standards.*
MNT67B	What will be needed to keep business running while software or hardware is being replaced or upgraded?	*identify business impacts.*
MNT68B	What concerns exist about vendor supplied software?	*identify concerns.*
MNT69B	What are the cost expectations for maintenance enhancements?	*identify constraints.*
MNT70B	What are the known industry standards?	*identify controlling standards.*
MNT71B	What trade-offs are there between maintenance and availability?	*identify possible trade-offs.*
MNT72B	What trade-offs are there between maintenance and reliability?	*identify possible trade-offs.*
MNT73B	What trade-offs are there between maintenance and flexibility?	*identify possible trade-offs.*
MNT74B	What elements must be defined to develop an acceptable service-level agreement?	*identify priorities.*
MNT75B	What changes in the regulations could affect the system?	*identify regulations.*
MNT76B	What service level agreements are in place with the customers?	*identify various agreements.*
MNT77B	What vendor agreements are in place on the software?	*identify various agreements.*
MNT78B	What regulations govern this application?	*identify various regulations.*
MNT79B	What else should I be asking about maintainability "purpose"?	*uncover additional requirements.*

6.2 MNT

TIMING (WHEN?)

ID	Maintainability Suggested Questions	Ask this to:
MNT80S	During what time frames is routine maintenance unacceptable?	*identify effects on availability.*
MNT81S	When should routine maintenance be performed?	*identify effects on availability.*
MNT82S	How frequently will enhancements be added to the system?	*identify rates of change related to flexibility.*
MNT83S	How fast-paced are the competitors' responses?	*identify response rates.*
MNT84S	What lead-time notice is there for mandatory changes?	*identify response to demand.*
MNT85S	What are the seasons in this line of business?	*identify seasonality and understand the impacts.*
MNT86S	What time standard has been established?	*identify timing expectations.*
MNT87S	When could future installations happen?	*identify timing.*
MNT88S	What are the responses necessary due to seasonality?	*identify timing.*
MNT89S	What industry changes are anticipated?	*identify trends that could impact implementation.*
MNT90S	What changes are anticipated in the industry or organization?	*identify trends.*
MNT91S	What elements or features change frequently due to external events, decisions, or regulations?	*identify volatility and reduce impact.*
MNT92R	When will it be necessary to perform maintenance on hardware devices?	*clarify timing.*
MNT93R	How frequently do the devices require repair?	*identify frequency of failure.*
MNT94R	How often are maintenance releases expected?	*identify frequency.*
MNT95R	What specific time frames during the day should maintenance activities be avoided?	*identify maintenance schedule concerns.*
MNT96R	What peak periods in processing cause maintenance concerns?	*identify maintenance schedule concerns.*
MNT97R	What maintenance is triggered by time of day?	*identify maintenance schedule concerns.*
MNT98R	What maintenance is triggered by events?	*identify maintenance schedule concerns.*

6.2 MNT

TIMING (WHEN?) (continued)

ID	Maintainability Suggested Questions	Ask this to:
MNT99R	What maintenance is performed automatically by the system?	*identify maintenance schedule concerns.*
MNT100R	How often do upgrades to interfaces get released?	*identify pace of change.*
MNT101R	How often do upgrades to components get released?	*identify rates of change.*
MNT102B	How often do regulations change?	*identify frequency.*
MNT103B	What else should I be asking about maintainability "timing"?	*uncover additional requirements.*

LOGISTICS (WHERE?)

ID	Maintainability Suggested Questions	Ask this to:
MNT104S	What time zone is the standard for the system?	*identify locations.*
MNT105S	Where is the most maintenance needed?	*identify locations.*
MNT106S	What maintenance support is expected at each location?	*identify locations.*
MNT107S	What maintenance is performed at each location?	*identify locations.*
MNT108R	Where is the source code escrowed to prevent emergency situations from vendor-supplied software?	*identify emergency recovery.*
MNT109R	What changes in the configuration environment could affect the system?	*identify environmental impacts.*
MNT110R	What will be the environment of use?	*identify environments.*
MNT111R	What will be the development environment used?	*identify environments.*
MNT112R	What level of maintenance is required at each business location?	*identify locations.*
MNT113R	What routine maintenance is performed at each business location?	*identify locations.*
MNT114R	What maintenance is performed offsite?	*identify locations.*
MNT115R	What is the schedule for upgrades or releases at each location?	*identify locations.*

6.2 MNT

LOGISTICS (WHERE?) (continued)

ID	Maintainability Suggested Questions	Ask this to:
MNT116R	What time-triggered maintenance is performed at each location?	*identify maintenance activities by location.*
MNT117R	What event-triggered maintenance is performed at each location?	*identify maintenance activities by location.*
MNT118R	By location, what maintenance is done manually?	*identify maintenance activities by location.*
MNT119R	By location, what maintenance is automated?	*identify maintenance activities by location.*
MNT120R	On what types of operating environments/hardware configurations will this system be deployed?	*identify various configurations.*
MNT121B	What else should I be asking about maintainability "logistics"?	*uncover additional requirements.*

PROCESS (HOW?)

ID	Maintainability Suggested Questions	Ask this to:
MNT122S	Under what events or conditions should this system deviate from any standard?	*identify potential challenges.*
MNT123S	Under what conditions is the industry standard messaging format not adequate?	*identify potential for noncompliance.*
MNT124S	Under what conditions is the industry standard protocol not adequate?	*identify potential for noncompliance.*
MNT125S	What features are strongest from the competitors?	*identify pressured features.*
MNT126S	What features are most appealing to the customers?	*identify priority features.*
MNT127S	What workaround processes are performed while the system is being maintained?	*identify process impact.*
MNT128S	What functions are limited or unavailable during maintenance?	*identify process impact.*
MNT129R	What types of support is needed from the vendors?	*identify dependencies.*
MNT130R	What vendor devices will be used in this system?	*identify device interfaces.*
MNT131R	What types of harsh conditions are hardware components subject to that could cause frequent failure?	*identify exposure.*

6.2 MNT

PROCESS (HOW?) (continued)

ID	Maintainability Suggested Questions	Ask this to:
MNT132R	What provisions exist for modification of the industry standard messaging format?	*identify potential changes.*
MNT133R	What provisions exist for modification of the industry standard protocol?	*identify potential changes.*
MNT134R	What are current procedures and processes for system maintenance?	*identify processes.*
MNT135R	What maintenance activities are performed automatically?	*identify processes.*
MNT136R	What maintenance activities are performed manually?	*identify processes.*
MNT137R	What is the expected interruption when adding, changing, or repairing a hardware device?	*identify response expectations.*
MNT138R	What types and varieties of hardware devices will be used on the system?	*identify various devices.*
MNT139B	What is the expectation for repairing related, non-repaired defects?	*identify various defects and level expectations.*
MNT140B	What else should I be asking about maintainability "processes"?	*uncover additional requirements.*

6.2 MNT

6.3 SCALABILITY (SCL)

USER CONCERN:	How easy is it to expand or upgrade the system's capabilities?
RELATED CATEGORIES:	Augmentability, Expandability, Flexibility

6.3.1 Scalability Definition

Scalability is the degree to which the software system is able to expand its processing capabilities upward and outward to support business growth.

6.3.2 Scalability Discussion

Scalability requirements specify a way in which a system must be able to expand without significant impact, usually to accommodate growth in business volume. The system must scale to handle increased usage without a proportional increase in all the supporting elements.

Scalability is the degree to which the system is capable of taking on more when the load increases, and having ways to react without turning to drastic means for change. Scalability means that the development of a system (software and hardware) must not restrict the business to any particular level of volume. That is, development of the system should take into account any possibility of future changes, and make adequate provisions for that eventuality. The users should identify the most likely areas for future growth.

6.3 SCL

When eliciting scalability requirements, consider the following aspects:

- ABILITY TO COPE WITH INCREASING PROCESSING LOAD.
    - ◊ Effect on data inquiries and report generation.
    - ◊ Maintenance and administration tasks.
    - ◊ Frequency, timing, and resources needed for installations and upgrades.

◊ Spreading the processing load across multiple systems or platforms (expand outward).

◊ Boosting the processing power of a specific system (expand upward).

♦ EXPANDING BUSINESS LOCATIONS.

◊ Minimize redundant processing and administration.

◊ Coordination of resources (data, people, software, and hardware).

♦ POSSIBLE CAUSE FOR DEGRADATION.

◊ Support resources.

◊ Downtime for routine maintenance.

◊ Duration of processing (how long does it take?).

◊ Contention for resources.

♦ RECYCLE HARDWARE TO MINIMIZE WASTE.

◊ Ability to add hardware instead of replacing hardware.

6.3 SCL

6.3.3 Scalability Requirement Examples

a) The elapsed duration of time required to produce any statement or report showing information about transactions shall be based upon how much data are presented rather than the total quantity of stored data.

b) The effort needed to administer the payroll system (as measured in hours per month of system administrators' time) shall not increase with an increase in the number of employees. If there is a significant increase in system operation work, it shall be proportionately less than an increase in the number of employees.

c) The payroll system shall be scalable to support unlimited growth in the number of employees.

d) The business rules repository shall be scalable to manage an unrestricted number of additional rules.

e) The travel reservation system shall be scalable to accommodate its use by an unlimited number of agency offices world wide.

f) The claims system shall support all assigned adjustors following any catastrophic event.

g) The account management system shall support unlimited customer, account, and transaction relationships.

h) The transaction authorization system shall scale to potential hourly spikes of 1,000% in authorization requests during peak holiday shopping.

6.3 SCL

6.3.4 Scalability Suggested Questions

DATA (WHAT?)

ID	Scalability Suggested Questions	Ask this to:
SCL1S	What scalability data history must be stored?	*identify historical data.*
SCL2S	What analysis reporting of history data is needed?	*identify historical data.*
SCL3S	What scalability data are input to the system?	*identify inputs/outputs.*
SCL4S	What scalability data are output from the system?	*identify inputs/outputs.*
SCL5S	What scalability data do management request?	*identify reporting needs.*
SCL6S	What scalability data are necessary for audit purposes?	*identify reporting needs.*
SCL7S	What scalability data are necessary for regulatory and compliance purposes?	*identify reporting needs.*
SCL8S	What demographic reporting is needed?	*identify reporting needs.*
SCL9R	What sources could provide analysis data?	*identify historical data.*
SCL10R	What historical data are stored currently?	*identify historical data.*
SCL11R	What volume data are tracked currently?	*identify reporting needs.*
SCL12B	What data would help to identify growth trends or patterns?	*identify historical data.*
SCL13B	What else should I be asking about scalability "data"?	*uncover additional requirements.*

6.3 SCL

ROLES (WHO?)

ID	Scalability Suggested Questions	Ask this to:
SCL14S	Who audits system growth and expansion?	*identify additional stakeholders.*
SCL15S	What regulatory or government agencies must be notified of expansion?	*identify additional stakeholders.*
SCL16S	Who should receive scalability reports?	*identify role responsibilities.*
SCL17S	Who is responsible for the business architecture?	*identify role responsibilities.*
SCL18R	Who is responsible for monitoring software and hardware expansion?	*identify additional stakeholders.*
SCL19R	What sources could provide analysis data?	*identify additional stakeholders.*
SCL20R	Who interfaces with the system that is being upgraded?	*identify additional stakeholders.*
SCL21R	Who is responsible for the system architecture?	*identify role responsibilities.*
SCL22B	Who should participate in a system inspection/review?	*identify additional stakeholders.*
SCL23B	Who monitors growth trends and patterns?	*identify role responsibilities.*
SCL24B	What else should I be asking about scalability "roles"?	*uncover additional requirements.*

6.3 SCL

PURPOSE (WHY?)

ID	Scalability Suggested Questions	Ask this to:
SCL25S	How elastic is the anticipated scalability?	*identify combinations of metrics or indicators.*
SCL26S	How easy must it be to expand the system?	*identify concerns.*
SCL27S	What product or feature is most likely to stimulate growth?	*identify functions.*
SCL28S	What is the extreme scale of system components?	*identify functions.*
SCL29S	What is the extreme scale of system features?	*identify functions.*
SCL30S	What is the extreme scale of system functions?	*identify functions.*
SCL31S	What magnitude of increase in customers is expected?	*identify growth potential.*
SCL32S	What magnitude of increase in users is expected?	*identify growth potential.*
SCL33S	What magnitude of increase in products is expected?	*identify growth potential.*
SCL34S	What magnitude of increase in sales is expected?	*identify growth potential.*
SCL35S	What magnitude of increase in transactions is expected?	*identify growth potential.*
SCL36S	What magnitude of increase in inputs is expected?	*identify growth potential.*
SCL37S	What magnitude of increase in outputs is expected?	*identify growth potential.*
SCL38S	How rapidly might business volume increase?	*identify growth potential.*
SCL39S	Why is this level of scalability needed?	*identify influencing activity.*
SCL40S	What is the current maximum number of: users, customers, accounts, and transactions?	*identify metrics.*
SCL41S	What is the basis for scalability projections?	*identify metrics.*
SCL42S	What business loss would result from not being scalable?	*identify risks.*
SCL43S	What business could be lost due to expansion?	*identify risks.*
SCL44S	What feature of the business is most likely to grow the fastest?	*identify trends or patterns.*
SCL45S	What is the most probable source for growth: users, customers, transactions?	*identify trends or patterns.*

6.3 SCL

ID	Scalability Suggested Questions	Ask this to:
SCL46s	How might business spurts be one-time events or sustainable?	*identify trends or patterns.*
SCL47s	How might business spurts be sporadic or on-going occurrences?	*identify trends or patterns.*
SCL48s	What feature of the business is most likely to grow the most?	*identify trends or patterns.*
SCL49R	What will enable an expansion of the software without a disproportionate increase in hardware?	*identify configurations.*
SCL50R	What will enable an expansion of the software without a disproportionate increase in support personnel?	*identify constraints.*
SCL51R	What is the affect of vertical (software) scaling?	*identify growth potential.*
SCL52R	What is the affect of horizontal (hardware) scaling?	*identify growth potential.*
SCL53B	What indicators of growth should be monitored?	*identify cycles.*
SCL54B	How can the system scale and continue to meet performance and reliability requirements?	*identify possible trade-offs.*
SCL55B	What is the trade-off between scalability and maintainability?	*identify possible trade-offs.*
SCL56B	What is the trade-off between scalability and flexibility?	*identify possible trade-offs.*
SCL57B	What is the trade-off between scalability and efficiency?	*identify possible trade-offs.*
SCL58B	What else should I be asking about scalability "purpose"?	*uncover additional requirements.*

6.3 SCL

TIMING (WHEN?)

ID	Scalability Suggested Questions	Ask this to:
SCL59s	How soon after implementation might business volume increase?	*identify cycles.*
SCL60s	How long does the peak volume last?	*identify cycles.*
SCL61s	What response time expectations are there for peak periods?	*identify metrics.*
SCL62s	How are peak usage volumes measured?	*identify metrics.*
SCL63s	What noticeable difference between peak periods and normal activity is acceptable?	*identify metrics.*
SCL64s	What event could cause that surprise development?	*identify metrics.*
SCL65s	How fast could a surprise happen?	*identify metrics.*
SCL66s	When do peak processing volumes occur?	*identify processing volumes.*
SCL67s	What throughput volumes are expected during peak periods?	*identify processing volumes.*
SCL68s	How fast does the volume change from peak to normal levels?	*identify rates of change.*
SCL69r	When are additions or upgrades typically implemented?	*identify processing cycles.*
SCL70r	When should system expansions be avoided if possible?	*identify processing cycles.*
SCL71r	When have upgrades been scheduled in the past?	*identify processing cycles.*
SCL72r	What is the average duration of an upgrade install?	*identify processing time.*
SCL73b	When are specific periods when additions or upgrades should be avoided?	*identify processing cycles.*
SCL74b	What else should I be asking about scalability "timing"?	*uncover additional requirements.*

6.3 SCL

LOGISTICS (WHERE?)

ID	Scalability Suggested Questions	Ask this to:
SCL75S	What locations could be problematic with sudden increase in business volume?	*identify location issues.*
SCL76S	What types of problems could arise due to variances in locations?	*identify location issues.*
SCL77S	What types of organizational structures are needed to be aware of as the system scales?	*identify organizational units.*
SCL78S	What area has been the most constrained so far but is building momentum?	*identify organizational units.*
SCL79S	What area has been dismissed for growth potential but could be a surprise development?	*identify organizational units.*
SCL80S	What could cause volume projections to change in a particular location?	*identify rates of change.*
SCL81S	What locations could increase in volume faster than other locations?	*identify volumes and locations.*
SCL82S	What locations appear to have static volume?	*identify volumes and locations.*
SCL83R	Where will additional software/hardware be needed to expand the business?	*identify location resources.*
SCL84R	Where will additional maintenance and administering be needed to expand the business?	*identify location resources.*
SCL85R	Where can software be installed on an existing machine?	*identify location resources.*
SCL86R	Where can software be upgraded on an existing machine?	*identify location resources.*
SCL87B	Where might corporate restructuring take place to accommodate growth?	*identify organizational units.*
SCL88B	What else should I be asking about scalability "logistics"?	*uncover additional requirements.*

6.3 SCL

PROCESS (HOW?)

ID	Scalability Suggested Questions	Ask this to:
SCL89s	What system component is the most critical to growth of the business?	*identify critical components.*
SCL90s	In what ways must the system keep performing just as well as it grows?	*identify critical components.*
SCL91s	What component will be the greatest challenge to scale?	*identify functions.*
SCL92s	What specific features are needed so that the system will continue to be as easy to use as volumes grow?	*identify functions.*
SCL93s	What specific features cannot degrade as the system scales?	*identify functions.*
SCL94s	What aspect of the system needs to be scalable?	*identify functions.*
SCL95s	What business activity could lead to rapid increase in business volume?	*identify influencing activity.*
SCL96s	What processes in which locations are most susceptible to peak volume pressure?	*identify process and location relationships.*
SCL97s	What business processes are vulnerable to volume pressure?	*identify process and volume relationships.*
SCL98s	What events could cause sudden increase in business volume?	*identify rates of change.*
SCL99R	What will enable an expansion of the software without a disproportionate increase in ancillary system support? (backup, security, restore, recovery)	*identify configurations.*
SCL100R	How dynamically can the system be expanded?	*identify configurations.*
SCL101R	What third-party components are in use/planned for use that will have scalability issues?	*identify functions.*
SCL102R	What architectural feature could be the most difficult to scale?	*identify functions.*
SCL103R	Where are the weak points in the architecture?	*identify functions.*
SCL104R	What is the difference between peak maximum and "normal" volumes in a process cycle?	*identify processing volumes.*
SCL105B	What specific features are needed by the system to help it be scalable?	*identify functions.*
SCL106B	What else should I be asking about scalability "processes"?	*uncover additional requirements.*

6.3 SCL

6.4 VERIFIABILITY (VER)

USER CONCERN:	How easy is it to show that the system performs its functions?
RELATED CATEGORIES:	Implementability, Installability, Testability

6.4.1 Verifiability Definition

Verifiability is the extent to which tests, analysis, and demonstrations are needed to prove that the software system will function as intended.

6.4.2 Verifiability Discussion

Whether buying or building, the software system must be checked to see if it meets the requirements and delivers the functionality expected by the users. *Verification and Validation* (V & V) is a name given to the process of checking the software. *Validation* is checking that you're building the right product, while *verification* is checking that you're building the product right. That is, validation is concerned with making sure the software meets the user expectations, and verification is concerned with making sure the software meets its specified functional and nonfunctional requirements.

There are two complementary approaches used with the verification and validation process to check the software system:

6.4 VER

(1) **Software inspections, also known as peer reviews, are performed to check the system specifications**. Several development deliverables are reviewed such as the requirements document, design models and diagrams, and program source code. Inspections are considered to be static techniques as you don't need to run the software.

(2) **Software testing involves running a version of the software with test data or components.** Testing is a dynamic technique of verification and validation. The outputs of the testing are examined to check if the software is performing as required.

Software inspections are a valuable technique, one that should not be overlooked or minimized during the implementation process. Several studies have demonstrated that inspections are far more effective than testing for error or defect discovery. Many reports show findings of 60 percent error detection through inspections and some as much as 90 percent. There are three major advantages of software inspections over software testing:

♦ INCOMPLETE VERSIONS OF THE SYSTEM CAN BE INSPECTED WITH LITTLE OR NO ADDITIONAL COST. On the other hand, testing an incomplete system requires special processes in order to test the part that is available. These processes and specialized test data add to the system development costs.

♦ AS A STATIC TECHNIQUE, INSPECTIONS CAN DISCOVER MANY ERRORS IN A SYSTEM and don't have to be concerned with interactions between errors. Conversely, during testing, errors can camouflage or hide other errors. Once an error is discovered it is difficult to know if other output anomalies are due to new error or a side effect of the previous discovered error.

♦ INSPECTIONS CAN BE USED FOR PURPOSES BROADER THAN ERROR DETECTION. For instance, the software representation can be reviewed for compliance to standards. Program source code can be reviewed for inappropriate algorithms and poor programming structure that could make the system difficult to maintain, update, and reuse.

6.4 VER

Wallace and Ippolito describe a number of software verification and validation techniques, which are summarized in Table 6-2. The table does not represent an all-inclusive list of techniques.

Table 6-2 Software Verification and Validation Techniques [Wallace, 1996]

TECHNIQUE	Requirements Verification	System Test (Requirements Validation)	Technique Description
Algorithm analysis	◆		Examines the logic and accuracy of the software requirements by translating algorithms into some language or structured format. The analysis involves re-deriving equations or evaluating the suitability of specific numerical techniques.
Back-to-back testing		◆	Detects test failures by comparing the output of two or more programs implemented to the same specification. The same input data are applied to two or more program versions and their outputs are compared to detect anomalies.
Boundary value analysis		◆	Detects and removes errors occurring at parameter limits or boundaries. The input domain of the program is divided into a number of input classes. The tests should cover the boundaries and extremes of the classes.
Consistency analysis	◆		Compares the requirements of any existing software with the new software requirements to ensure consistency.
Control flow analysis	◆		Transforms text describing software requirements into graphic flows where they can be examined for correctness. Control flow analysis is used to show the hierarchy of main routines and their sub-functions and checks that the proposed control flow is free of problems.
Coverage analysis		◆	Measures how much of the structure of a unit or system has been exercised by a given set of tests.
Database analysis	◆		Ensures that the database structure and access methods are compatible with the logical design. It is performed on programs with significant data storage to ensure that common data and variable regions are used consistently between all calling routines, that data integrity is enforced and that no data or variable can be accidentally overwritten by overflowing data tables, and that data typing and use are consistent throughout the program.
Dataflow analysis	◆		Dataflow analysis is important for designing the high-level architecture of applications. It can check for variables that are read before they are written, written more than once without being read, and written but never used.

6.4 VER

Table 6-2 Software Verification and Validation Techniques [Wallace, 1996] (continued)

TECHNIQUE	Requirements Verification	System Test (Requirements Validation)	Technique Description
Decision tables	◆		Provide a clear and coherent analysis of complex logical combinations and relationships. This method uses two-dimensional tables to concisely describe logical relationships between Boolean program variables.
Error seeding		◆	Determines whether a set of test cases is adequate by inserting ("seeding") known error types into the program and executing it with the test cases. If only some of the seeded errors are found, the test case set is not adequate.
Event tree analysis	◆		Event tree analysis uses a bottom-up approach to model the effects of an event that may have serious repercussions. The initiation event is the root of the event tree. Two lines are drawn from the root, depicting the positive and negative consequences of the event. This is done for each subsequent consequence until all consequences are considered.
Finite state machines	◆		Check for incomplete and inconsistent software requirements by modeling the software in terms of its states, inputs, and actions.
Functional testing		◆	Executes part or all of the system to validate that the user requirement is satisfied.
Inspections	◆		Inspections are evaluation techniques whereby the software requirements, software design, or code is examined by a person or group other than the author to detect faults, violations of development standards, and other problems.
Interface analysis	◆	◆	Interface analysis is a static analysis technique. It is used to demonstrate that the interfaces of sub-programs do not contain any errors that lead to failures in a particular application of the software.
Interface testing		◆	Interface testing is a dynamic analysis technique. It is similar to interface analysis, except test cases are built with data that test all interfaces.
Mutation analysis		◆	Determines the thoroughness with which a program has been tested, and in the process detects errors. This procedure involves producing a large set of versions or "mutations" of the original program, each derived by altering a single element of the program. Each mutant is then tested with a given collection of test data sets.

6.4 VER

Table 6-2 Software Verification and Validation Techniques [Wallace, 1996] (continued)

TECHNIQUE	Requirements Verification	System Test (Requirements Validation)	Technique Description
Performance testing		◆	Measures how well the software system executes according to its required response times, CPU usage, and other quantified features in operations.
Prototyping	◆		Prototyping helps to examine the probable results of implementing software requirements. Examination of a prototype may help to identify incomplete or incorrect software requirements and may also reveal if any software requirements will not result in desired system behavior.
Regression analysis and testing	◆	◆	Regression analysis and testing is used to re-evaluate software requirements and software design issues whenever any significant code change is made. It involves retesting to verify that the modified software still meets its specified requirements.
Requirements parsing	◆		Involves examination to ensure that each software requirement is defined unambiguously by a complete set of attributes (for example, initiator of an action, source of the action, the action, the object of the action, constraints).
Reviews	◆	◆	Reviews are meetings at which the software requirements, software design, code, or other products are presented to the user, sponsor, or other interested parties for comment and approval, often as a prerequisite for concluding a given activity of the software development process.
Simulation	◆		Simulation is used to evaluate the interactions of large, complex systems with many hardware, user, and other interfacing software units. Simulation uses an executable model to examine the behavior of the software.
Software failures mode, effects and critical analysis (SFMECA)	◆		Reveals weak or missing software requirements by using inductive reasoning to determine the effect on the system of a unit (includes software instructions) failing in a particular failure mode. A matrix is developed for each unit depicting the effect on the system of each unit's failure in each failure mode.
Software fault tree analysis	◆		Identifies and analyzes software safety requirements. It is used to determine possible causes of known hazards. Its purpose is to demonstrate that the software will not cause a system to reach an unsafe state, and to discover what environmental conditions would allow the system to reach an unsafe state.

6.4 VER

Table 6-2 Software Verification and Validation Techniques [Wallace, 1996] (continued)

TECHNIQUE	Requirements Verification	System Test (Requirements Validation)	Technique Description
Stress testing		◆	Tests the response of the system to extreme conditions to identify vulnerable points within the software, and to show that the system can withstand normal workloads.
Test certification		◆	Test certification ensures that reported test results are the actual finding of the tests. Test-related tools, media, and documentation are certified to ensure maintainability and repeatability of tests. This technique is also used to show that the delivered software product is identical to the software product that was subjected to V & V.
Walkthroughs	◆	◆	Walkthroughs are similar to inspections, but less formal. A walkthrough is an evaluation technique in which a designer or programmer leads one or more other members of the development team through a segment of software design or code, while the other members ask questions and make comments about technique and style, and identify possible errors, violations of development standards, and other problems.

Furthermore, there are a number of words that might be flagged as unverifiable when trying to write requirements. Several examples of these potentially unverifiable words, along with suggested substitutes, are listed in Table 6-3. Additional problematic words are found in the examples of re-written requirement statements provided in Table 6-4 on page 272. In the manner used in these examples, the term *verifiable* is synonymous with *testable*. Here the term is used to describe an attribute of the requirement. A requirement is *verifiable* (testable) if a test can be devised to demonstrate correct implementation.

Table 6-3 Certain Words Flag Unverifiable Requirements [Hooks, 2001]

Unverifiable Words	Possible Substitutes
Flexible	• Bending threshold or spring constant • Features that will cover anticipated changes from operational concepts
Easy or user-friendly	• A maximum number of steps to perform an operation • An educational standard reference • A list of features found on similar popular products • Menus or prompts to guide user
Accommodate	• Precise definition of accommodation from operational concepts
Ad hoc	• List of features that support all uses anticipated in operational concepts
Safe	• List of features that prevent harm from operator error anticipated in operational concepts • References to specific safety standards
Sufficient or adequate	• Quantities or other dimensions
Useable	• Exact features needed
When required or if required	• Exact circumstances • Triggering events from operational concepts
Fast or quickly	• Minimum acceptable speed
Portable	• Dimensions and weight • Description of desired carrying means • Operating systems that the software must run on
Light-weight	• Maximum acceptable weight
Small	• Maximum acceptable dimensions
Large	• Minimum acceptable dimensions
Easily, clearly, or other "-ly" words	• Quantities appropriate for the verb that the "-ly" word modifies (for example, replace "fit easily" with "fit in X by Y by Z space")
Maximize, minimize, optimize, or other "-ize" words	• Limits, greater than or equal to, less than or equal to

6.4 VER

Table 6-4 Rewrites for Unverifiable Requirements [Hooks, 2001]

Unverifiable	Verifiable
ABC shall support ad hoc queries.	• ABC shall retrieve up to five user-specified data items per user query. • ABC shall retrieve those records meeting the criteria in any legal Standard Query Language user query.
The ZZ database shall be flexible.	• The ZZ database shall have eight user-definable fields per record.
The sorting arm shall be flexible.	• The sorting arm shall elastically deform under loads of 0-75 pounds.
PQR shall clearly display safety warnings.	• PQR shall display safety warnings in yellow letters [1" +/- 0.05" high] and [0.5" +/- 0.05" wide].
The power supply shall be portable.	• The power supply shall weigh 25 pounds or less. • The power supply shall be less than or equal to 20 inches in each dimension. • The power supply shall have a carrying handle of the dimensions in drawing 12 of reference 4 (Human Factors Standards).
The case shall accommodate contingency maintenance tools.	• The case shall have maintenance tool storage to hold all tools in drawing A.
The TMS shall handle deposits quickly.	• The TMS shall scan and record customer account number and amount from a single deposit slip in 2 seconds or less.
XYZ shall be user-friendly.	• XYZ shall have controls labeled with their purpose in letters 0.3" +/- 0.03". • XYZ shall have controls positioned in the order (from left to right) of their use. • XYZ shall display menus of control options. • XYZ shall display prompts to remind the user of the next step. • XYZ shall use the display convention of product PQR. • XYZ shall have emergency stop controls colored red.
MNOP shall be safe.	• MNOP shall stop operation if a person comes within 10 feet of any moving component. • MNOP shall stop heaters if the vat temperature exceeds 100 degrees Celsius. • MNOP shall meet UL 544 Section 3.4 standards for temperatures on external surfaces.

6.4 VER

When eliciting verifiability requirements, consider the following aspects:

- VERIFICATION AND VALIDATION (V & V) techniques that might be used during development and/or implementation of the software system (refer to Table 6-2).

- POSSIBLE INSPECTION CHECKS BY FAULT CLASS [Sommerville, 2007].

  ◊ Data faults.

    - Are all program variables initialized before their values are used?
    - Have all constants been named?
    - Should the upper bound of arrays be equal to the size of the array or size -1?
    - If character strings are used, is a delimiter explicitly assigned?
    - Is there any possibility of buffer overflow?

  ◊ Control faults.

    - For each conditional statement, is the condition correct?
    - Is each loop certain to terminate?
    - Are compound statements correctly bracketed?
    - In case statements, are all possible cases accounted for?
    - If a break is required after each case in case statements, has it been included?

  ◊ Interface faults.

    - Do all function and method calls have the correct number of parameters?
    - Do formal and actual parameter types match?
    - Are the parameters in the right order?
    - If components access shared memory, do they have the same model of the shared memory structure?

6.4 VER

◊ Storage management faults.
- If a linked structure is modified, have all links been correctly reassigned?
- If dynamic storage is used, has space been allocated correctly?
- Is space explicitly de-allocated after it is no longer required?

◊ Exception management faults.
- Have all possible error conditions been taken into account?

◊ Input/Output faults.
- Are all input variables used?
- Are all output variables assigned a value before they are output?
- Can unexpected inputs cause corruption?

♦ INSTALLABILITY OF THE SYSTEM COMPONENT.

◊ **Installation instructions.** What documentation is needed to tell the installer what to do? Who is responsible for documenting these instructions?

◊ **Authorization to install.** Who has authority to migrate the software into production? What special elements are needed to appropriate access during installation?

◊ **Upgrading.** This is specifically concerned with installing an upgrade when a previous version of the software is already in production.

◊ **Troubleshooting.** Provide help resources to the installer if problems arise. The resources should help the installer identify the problem and fix it in at least 80% of the instances encountered.

◊ **Security.** What might need to be done to minimize the risk of security attacks or breaches? For example, might the installer need to have access restrictions related to sensitive data?

◊ **Training.** What special training must be provided to the installation personnel?

6.4 VER

◊ **Uninstallation procedures and instructions**. The degree to which software is uninstalled depends largely on what the software is used for. Is it necessary to remove all versions? Does converted data need to be purged?

6.4.3 Verifiability Requirement Examples

a) No member of a test panel of 500 children (aged 8) shall incur an injury while playing with the product. The product must comply with product safety regulations as defined by (specify).

b) The maximum number of test cases to cover testing of any particular source code module shall be 20.

c) The Customer Information System shall be implemented using Release 5 of Library 4B.

d) The system and supporting infrastructure for the automatic shut-down sequence must be validated to the highest reasonable commercial reliability standards.

e) The design of the Payroll System shall include software that tests the operating system and the communication links, memory devices, and peripheral devices.

f) It shall be possible for the All-in-One Printer software to be installed by a typical customer who has no special expertise. The installation process shall be convenient and involve the entry of little information by the user.

g) When a new version of the payroll system is released, it shall be possible to upgrade to it from any previous version.

h) Software testing will require the use of a test database with data extracted from the production database. This test database will be deleted after successful implementation of the software system.

i) At the time of conversion the customer demographic information shall have a 99.5% match rate after data scrubbing.

j) All developers on the project shall have identical development environment configurations, and all testers shall have identical quality assurance environment configurations.

6.4 VER

6.4.4 Verifiability Suggested Questions

DATA (WHAT?)

ID	Verifiability Suggested Questions	Ask this to:
VER1s	What defined validation exists for each data element?	*clarify validations.*
VER2s	How are the calculations validated?	*clarify validations.*
VER3s	What test data must be recorded and how fast must the system output this data?	*identify activities.*
VER4s	What test beds of data exist?	*identify available resources.*
VER5s	What data elements are unique?	*identify data attributes.*
VER6s	What bounds, limits, and ranges of data elements are known?	*identify data attributes.*
VER7s	What data elements have a one-time use?	*identify data attributes.*
VER8s	What data elements can be reused?	*identify data characteristics.*
VER9s	What data or special reports are required by the regulatory agencies?	*identify sources of compliance.*
VER10r	What test data are needed to simulate all user classes?	*identify access security needs.*
VER11r	What classifications of defects are suitable for this system?	*identify classifications.*
VER12r	What simulated data streams will be needed to test the system?	*identify combinations of actions.*
VER13r	What is the source of the calculations used in the system?	*identify definitive sources for validation.*
VER14r	How are the factors used in the calculation traced to their origins?	*identify factors.*
VER15r	What purchased hardware/software can be obtained to start the population of information?	*identify needed resources.*
VER16r	What licenses are required with the purchase of hardware/software?	*identify needed resources.*
VER17r	What defects are documented from the design and development team?	*identify resources.*
VER18r	What information does each team member need to build and test the system?	*identify test information requirements.*
VER19r	What defined data patterns, formats, and presentation styles are there?	*identify types of data.*
VER20r	How valid is the test bed of data?	*identify verification data.*
VER21b	What else should I be asking about verifiability "data"?	*uncover additional requirements.*

6.4 VER

ROLES (WHO?)

ID	Verifiability Suggested Questions	Ask this to:
VER22s	Who are the best testers?	*identify additional stakeholders.*
VER23s	Who loves to beat the system?	*identify additional stakeholders.*
VER24s	Who can supply validation models?	*identify additional stakeholders.*
VER25s	Who will validate help information?	*identify additional stakeholders.*
VER26s	What customer involvement will be needed to test the system?	*identify additional stakeholders.*
VER27s	What user involvement will be needed to test the system?	*identify additional stakeholders.*
VER28s	Who would like to see the project/system fail?	*identify role perspectives.*
VER29s	Who will do user acceptance testing?	*identify role responsibilities.*
VER30s	What agency has jurisdiction over this product line?	*identify role responsibilities.*
VER31s	Who will be signing off the system for promotion into production?	*identify role responsibilities.*
VER32s	Who must perform the test, perform the analysis or demonstration, or inspect the system?	*identify role responsibilities.*
VER33s	What extra reviews from outside experts or inspectors and liability insurance will be required before the product meets standards?	*identify sources of validation.*
VER34s	What liability concerns does the legal department have?	*identify sources of validation.*
VER35s	What liability concerns does the insurance provider have?	*identify sources of validation.*
VER36s	What customer acceptance testing will be necessary?	*identify sources of validation.*
VER37R	What is the known skill level of the development team and their ability to unit test?	*assess lessons learned.*
VER38R	Who gets what hardware?	*determine verification resources.*
VER39R	Who gets what software?	*determine verification resources.*
VER40R	What access is required at start-up?	*identify access security needs.*
VER41R	Who will validate that necessary training occurred?	*identify additional stakeholders.*

6.4 VER

ROLES (WHO?) (continued)

ID	Verifiability Suggested Questions	Ask this to:
VER42R	Whom will users contact for system support?	identify additional stakeholders.
VER43R	Who will validate that the system works at an acceptable level to be implemented?	identify additional stakeholders.
VER44R	Who will create a testing traceability model?	identify role responsibilities.
VER45R	Who is responsible for the Quality Assurance (QA) test plan?	identify role responsibilities.
VER46B	What stakeholders and team members need special access during development?	identify access security needs.
VER47B	What stakeholders and team members need special access during testing?	identify access security needs.
VER48B	What stakeholders and team members need special access to promote to production?	identify access security needs.
VER49B	Who should participate in reviews?	identify additional stakeholders.
VER50B	What else should I be asking about verifiability "roles"?	uncover additional requirements.

6.4 VER

PURPOSE (WHY?)

ID	Verifiability Suggested Questions	Ask this to:
VER51s	What are currently common points of failure with the systems and the users?	*assess conditions.*
VER52s	How important is "cost/time to repair" as an evaluation criteria for going to production with known defects?	*identify criterion.*
VER53s	How important is probability as an evaluation criteria for going to production with known defects?	*identify criterion.*
VER54s	How important is the degree of impact as an evaluation criteria for going to production with known defects?	*identify criterion.*
VER55s	How important is risk as an evaluation criteria for going to production with known defects?	*identify criterion.*
VER56s	With regard to requirements quality criteria, how are the requirements going to be validated?	*identify criterion.*
VER57s	With regard to requirements quality criteria, how are the requirements going to be verified?	*identify criterion.*
VER58s	With regard to requirements quality criteria, how are the design components going to be tested?	*identify criterion.*
VER59s	Where are the particularly complex elements in this system?	*identify criterion.*
VER60s	What is the acceptance criterion for decision regarding promotion to production?	*identify criterion.*
VER61s	What requirements are there for the origination of every factor?	*identify definitive sources.*
VER62s	What requirements will have to be developed in parallel for testing?	*identify dependencies.*
VER63s	What industry standards and any other standards mandated by regulatory agencies apply?	*identify governing/regulatory controls.*
VER64s	What levels of defect are acceptable?	*identify metrics.*
VER65s	What level of confidence in the system is required to promote into production status?	*identify scales of measure.*
VER66s	What verification requirements will the government, regulatory agencies, and/or insurance carriers place on the product?	*identify sources of validation.*

6.4 VER

PURPOSE (WHY?) (continued)

ID	Verifiability Suggested Questions	Ask this to:
VER67S	What industry product standards apply to product certification?	*identify sources of validation.*
VER68S	What tests must be done to satisfy marketing claims?	*identify sources of validation.*
VER69S	What tests will validate that the product meets contractual agreements?	*identify sources of validation.*
VER70S	What requirements may be difficult to verify and increase risk?	*identify types of events.*
VER71S	What additional verification costs must be considered?	*identify verifications.*
VER72R	What is the history of defects from the quality assurance (QA) team?	*assess lessons learned.*
VER73R	What is the history of defects from the development team?	*assess lessons learned.*
VER74R	What business policies apply to the developers and testers of the system?	*clarify business rules with internal and external development staff.*
VER75R	What specific design constraints on size and complexity of components should be considered to facilitate testing?	*identify specific constraints.*
VER76B	What is the cost of testing versus the cost of defect?	*identify possible trade-offs.*
VER77B	What else should I be asking about verifiability "purpose"?	*uncover additional requirements.*

6.4 VER

TIMING (WHEN?)

ID	Verifiability Suggested Questions	Ask this to:
VER78s	What customers/users need to be available during design?	*identify needed resources.*
VER79s	What customers/users need to be available during coding and development?	*identify needed resources.*
VER80s	What customers/users need to be available for testing in the quality assurance (QA) environment?	*identify needed resources.*
VER81s	What customers/users need to be available during promotion to production?	*identify needed resources.*
VER82s	What customers/users need to be available during system roll-out?	*identify needed resources.*
VER83s	What additional time is required to verify the system?	*identify time constraints.*
VER84r	What equipment needs to be purchased for roll-out?	*identify needed resources.*
VER85r	What data will need to be populated at start-up?	*identify roll-out information requirements.*
VER86r	How will user manuals be available and distributed?	*identify roll-out information requirements.*
VER87r	When is equipment for roll-out needed?	*identify timing of resource delivery.*
VER88r	When will development begin?	*identify timing of resource delivery.*
VER89r	What functions of the system must be verified during design?	*identify types and timing of verification.*
VER90r	What functions of the system must be verified during coding and development?	*identify types and timing of verification.*
VER91r	What functions of the system must be verified prior to production implementation?	*identify types and timing of verification.*
VER92r	What functions of the system must be verified after roll-out to production?	*identify types and timing of verification.*
VER93r	What types of combinations of activity are expected to happen concurrently?	*identify types of events.*
VER94r	What various times must the system be tested?	*identify types of events.*
VER95r	When will system testing occur?	*identify types of events.*
VER96b	What else should I be asking about verifiability "timing"?	*uncover additional requirements.*

6.4 VER

LOGISTICS (WHERE?)

ID	Verifiability Suggested Questions	Ask this to:
VER97S	What extreme environment simulations should be considered?	*identify environment conditions.*
VER98S	What regulatory agencies and standards apply to each business location?	*identify localized controls.*
VER99S	Where will system development be done?	*identify locations.*
VER100S	Where will quality assurance (QA) testing be done?	*identify locations.*
VER101S	In which business locations will the system be implemented?	*identify locations.*
VER102R	What different power, cooling or heating, software or hardware support will the system require during development than it will require in operation?	*identify environmental conditions.*
VER103R	Where is equipment for roll-out needed?	*identify location of resource delivery.*
VER104R	What prototypes must be developed?	*identify prototypes.*
VER105R	What various places must be included during system testing?	*identify types of events.*
VER106R	Where will system testing occur?	*identify types of events.*
VER107R	What features must be testable in combination?	*identify types of feature relationships.*
VER108R	What features must be testable in isolation from the rest of the system?	*identify types of features.*
VER109R	What calculations are used in multiple locations?	*identify usage.*
VER110B	What special facilities or equipment will be needed to test the system?	*identify resources.*
VER111B	What additional testing resources (software, hardware, and/or people) are needed?	*identify resources.*
VER112B	What else should I be asking about verifiability "logistics"?	*uncover additional requirements.*

6.4 VER

PROCESS (HOW?)

ID	Verifiability Suggested Questions	Ask this to:
VER113s	What test cases will be written at the requirements level?	*identify approaches.*
VER114s	What features of the system can expect the most frequent changes or enhancements?	*identify features.*
VER115s	What proof of quality, beyond functional requirements testing, is required to make promotion decisions?	*identify sources of validation.*
VER116s	What conditions outside the normal usage must be tested?	*identify types of conditions.*
VER117s	What are the most critical functions to test?	*prioritize functions.*
VER118R	In what processes have similar or predecessor systems run into error conditions?	*assess lessons learned.*
VER119R	Due to complexity or criticality, what elements of the system need to be isolated?	*classify features.*
VER120R	What are the highest risk areas to test?	*identify exposure.*
VER121R	How will the system be rolled out?	*identify implementation processes.*
VER122R	What internal and external interfaces must be tested in addition to the system?	*identify integration.*
VER123R	How will users be trained?	*identify needed resources.*
VER124R	What purchased hardware/software can be obtained to perform specific events?	*identify needed resources.*
VER125R	What test support equipment or software will be needed?	*identify resources.*
VER126R	What need is there for a defect tracking tool?	*identify resources.*
VER127R	What test scripts have been used in the past?	*identify sources of reference.*
VER128R	How will defects/faults be classified?	*identify tactics.*
VER129R	What are the classification levels of defects/faults?	*identify tactics.*
VER130R	What simulators need to be developed for testing?	*identify testing processes.*
VER131R	What special testing tools will the Quality Assurance (QA) team need?	*identify tools.*
VER132R	How will the requirements for this system be verified?	*identify verifications.*
VER133R	What could be used from the development and testing environments for verifying the production system?	*leverage efforts.*
VER134B	What else should I be asking about verifiability "processes"?	*uncover additional requirements.*

6.4 VER

6.5 SUGGESTED READING

Competitive Engineering: A Handbook For Systems Engineering, Requirements Engineering, and Software Engineering Using Planguage, Tom Gilb, [Gilb, 2005]. Chapter 5 presents definitions for quality attributes, including *flexibility*, which decomposes into connectability and tailorability.

Customer-Centered Products, by Ivy Hooks and Kristin Farry, [Hooks, 2001]. Chapter 10 presents an explanation of *verification*.

Software Engineering, 8th Edition, by Ian Sommerville, [Sommerville, 2007]. Part 5 focuses on techniques for *software verification and validation*.

Software Requirement Patterns, by Stephen Withall, [Withall, 2007]. Chapter 10 of this book presents *flexibility* as its own domain category consisting of six requirement patterns: un-parochialness, multiness, multi-lingual, *scalability, extendability*, and installability.

Software Requirements: Styles and Techniques, by Soren Lauesen, [Lauesen, 2002]. Section 6.10 discusses *maintenance* activities such as repairing defects, extending the product, informing and training users, while Section 6.11 presents *maintainability* requirement examples.

System Requirements Analysis, Jeffrey O. Grady, [Grady, 2006]. Although Grady's book focuses on system requirements instead of business requirements, Section 3.7, "Specialty Engineering Requirements Analysis," includes a discussion on reliability and *maintainability* engineering. Grady defines the activities that make up the *Requirements Verification Management* process in Section 6.6.

7 TRANSITION REQUIREMENTS

HOW EASY IS IT TO ADAPT TO CHANGES IN THE TECHNICAL ENVIRONMENT?

Transition requirements describe the ability of the software system to adapt to its surrounding environment. Users who come in contact with the software system by managing the upkeep of the system are generally most concerned with transition requirements. That is, users view *quality* as a system that:

♦   Can be moved efficiently to other operating environments.

♦   Connects easily with other systems.

♦   Lends itself to reuse.

The transition group of nonfunctional categories encompasses the concerns of users that are managing a production system. Transition requirements answer user concerns for the following software qualities:

♦ INTEROPERABILITY. How easy is it to interface with another system?

♦ PORTABILITY. How easy is it to transport?

♦ REUSABILITY. How easy is it to convert for use in another system?

In the same sequence as listed above, this chapter presents the following for each transition category: definition, brief discussion, examples of requirements, and suggested elicitation questions. The introduction to Part Two explains the anatomy of a category and provides guidance for how to use the suggested questions.

7.1 INTEROPERABILITY (IOP)

USER CONCERN: How easy is it to interface with another system?
RELATED CATEGORIES: Compatibility, Connectivity, Operational

7.1.1 Interoperability Definition

Interoperability is the extent to which the software system is able to couple or facilitate the interface with other systems.

7.1.2 Interoperability Discussion

In a broad definition, interoperability is a property referring to the ability of diverse systems and organizations to work together (inter-operate). In software engineering terminology, "interoperability" refers to the capability of a system to work with other systems without special effort from the user. It involves the capability of various technical units to transfer data in a manner such that the user needs little or no knowledge of the specific workings of the technical units.

Interoperability is the ability for multiple software components to interact regardless of their implementation programming language or hardware platform. Interoperability is a term used to describe the ability of different source programs to exchange data via common exchange formats, to read and write the same file formats (a particular way to encode information for storage by a computer—for example, JPEG, GIF), and to use the same protocols (a standard that controls or enables the connection, communication, and data transfer between two computing endpoints, for example, TCP/IP).

7.1 IOP

Interoperability requirements describe the ease with which the system collaborates with partner applications and external operations. Interoperability requirements also identify the ability to add or remove interfaces without disrupting the core system.

When eliciting interoperability requirements, consider the following aspects:

- SOFTWARE TESTING. Software produced to a common standard depends on clarity of the standards. However, there may be discrepancies in their implementation that system or unit testing may not uncover. This requires that systems formally be tested in a production scenario to ensure they actually will inter-operate as expected. Interoperable system testing is different from conformance-based testing as conformance to a standard does not necessarily cause interoperability with another system, which is also tested for conformance.

- PRODUCT ENGINEERING. This means implementing a common standard as defined by the industry with the specific intention of achieving interoperability with other software implementations that also follow the same standard.

- INDUSTRY PARTNERSHIP. Industry partnerships, either domestic or international, sponsor standard workgroups with the purpose to define a common standard that may be used to allow software systems to intercommunicate for a defined purpose. At times an industry will sub-profile an existing standard produced by another organization to reduce options and thus making interoperability more achievable for implementations.

- COMMON TECHNOLOGY. The use of a common technology, such as Internet Protocol (IP), may speed up and reduce complexity of interoperability by reducing variability between components from different sets of separately developed software products, and thus allowing them to intercommunicate more readily.

- STANDARD IMPLEMENTATION. Software interoperability requires a common agreement that is normally arrived at via an industrial, national, or international standard.

7.1.3 Interoperability Requirement Examples

a) The system must be able to interface with any HTML (HyperText Markup Language) browser.

b) The baselined version 2 of the spreadsheet must be able to access information from the previous baselined version 1.

c) The Automated Teller Machine (ATM) must interface with the Automated Clearing House (ACH) in order to complete withdrawal transactions.

d) The product shall not use picture icons that could be considered offensive in any country where the product is marketed.

e) The common language used in the incoming mail department shall be English to increase communication effectiveness and reduce processing errors.

f) Any change or upgrade to the interface between the Order Entry System and the Inventory Warehouse system shall be installed simultaneously by both systems.

g) Local communications for each SmartMeter system can be used within the premises to link to local devices through utilization of standard protocols. There will be no reliance or operational mandate upon a Supplier to organize a site visit in order to install and/or maintain operation of any local device out of the SmartMeter system.

h) Physical communications will be guaranteed as interoperable through the use of an agreed minimum national service standard (to be defined) for prioritized exchanges of data. Any such service standards would be expressed in the time taken to complete the data exchange, for example, 15 minutes, 2 hours, 1 day. It will not be prescriptive about the number of retries required or delivery performance—all exchanges of data will complete.

i) All SmartMeter systems will provide a standard interface that can be used by meter operators for installation and maintenance purposes without disturbing any meter seals and reinstating any tamper detection covers.

j) To be interoperable with the SmartMeter energy system, any local device must support the chosen local communications, data interface, protocol and security solutions.

7.1 IOP

7.1.4 Interoperability Suggested Questions

DATA (WHAT?)

ID	Interoperability Suggested Questions	Ask this to:
IOP1s	Why are the data important to the business?	*clarify business needs.*
IOP2s	What data are expected to be customizable by the customer?	*clarify business needs.*
IOP3s	Describe the purpose of the data used.	*clarify business needs.*
IOP4s	How would other departments or people describe the data?	*clarify business needs.*
IOP5s	What information is missing from reports currently produced?	*identify additional data needed.*
IOP6s	What need is there to record what was sent and received on the interface?	*identify data types.*
IOP7s	Where can documentation for industry standards for this interface be found?	*identify external factors.*
IOP8s	What kinds of data exchange are envisioned (query, update, create)?	*identify usage types.*
IOP9R	What need is there to record acknowledgment of receipt from the other system?	*identify communication types.*
IOP10R	What documentation exists for the interface?	*identify documentation.*
IOP11R	What need is there to detect missing or duplicated traffic?	*identify monitoring techniques.*
IOP12B	What information must be exchanged with other systems?	*identify information sources and targets.*
IOP13B	What else should I be asking about interoperability "data"?	*uncover additional requirements.*

7.1 IOP

ROLES (WHO?)

ID	Interoperability Suggested Questions	Ask this to:
IOP14S	Who should not be using this system?	*clarify users.*
IOP15S	How does one user role type differ from another?	*clarify users.*
IOP16S	Does each person, department, or system that interfaces with the system under development receive and/or provide information?	*clarify why the system is used.*
IOP17S	How many of each role type are expected to interact with the system in the first month of operation? First year?	*estimate size of user community.*
IOP18S	What are the standards and abilities of the external supplier?	*evaluate suppliers.*
IOP19S	How does this external supplier rate on the vendor scorecard?	*evaluate vendors.*
IOP20S	Who should be involved in supplying requirements regarding business policies, rules, and procedures?	*identify additional stakeholders.*
IOP21S	How will customers find the information they want?	*identify customer needs.*
IOP22S	What customers expect the latest device to be available?	*identify customer types.*
IOP23S	What customers are early adapters of new technology?	*identify customer types.*
IOP24S	What are the roles and responsibilities of each "who" identified?	*identify responsibilities.*
IOP25S	What role will the business partners play in the development of this system?	*identify responsibilities.*
IOP26S	What external suppliers use the interface?	*identify types of interfaces.*
IOP27S	What kind of customers will want to use this system?	*identify users.*
IOP28S	What internal departments will interface with the system under development or installation?	*identify users.*
IOP29S	What external departments will interface with the system under development or installation?	*identify users.*
IOP30S	What new roles will be needed?	*identify users.*
IOP31S	How important is each "who" that has been identified?	*prioritize responsibilities.*
IOP32R	Who owns the interface?	*identify accountability.*
IOP33R	What other interfaces exist with this external supplier?	*identify relationships.*

7.1 IOP

ROLES (WHO?) (continued)

ID	Interoperability Suggested Questions	Ask this to:
IOP34R	Who has expertise in the technology?	*identify resources.*
IOP35R	Who will build the interface adapter?	*identify responsibilities.*
IOP36R	Who must be alerted when the interface fails?	*identify responsibilities.*
IOP37R	Who is responsible for the interface?	*identify responsibilities.*
IOP38R	Who maintains the interface documentation?	*identify responsibilities.*
IOP39R	Who (role) coordinates the interfaces?	*identify responsibilities.*
IOP40R	Who (role) approves the addition/removal of interfaces?	*identify responsibilities.*
IOP41R	Who will be responsible for the integration of the interfaces?	*identify responsibilities.*
IOP42R	Who has access to the required technology?	*identify sources of knowledge.*
IOP43B	What else should I be asking about interoperability "roles"?	*uncover additional requirements.*

PURPOSE (WHY?)

ID	Interoperability Suggested Questions	Ask this to:
IOP44S	Why is the system needed?	*clarify business purpose.*
IOP45S	What is the impact of not having the interface?	*evaluate usage strategies.*
IOP46S	What agreements (contracts, obligations) have been put in place?	*identify agreements.*
IOP47S	What agreements (contracts, obligations) must be secured?	*identify agreements.*
IOP48S	What state, national, and international laws affect the processes performed by the system under development?	*identify business rules.*
IOP49S	What corporate policies will affect the system?	*identify business rules.*
IOP50S	What additional limits exist that should be imposed on customers?	*identify business rules.*
IOP51S	What additional limits exist that should be imposed on business partners?	*identify business rules.*

7.1 IOP

PURPOSE (WHY?) (continued)

ID	Interoperability Suggested Questions	Ask this to:
IOP52s	What policies must change to meet new business objectives?	*identify business rules.*
IOP53s	How quickly do new devices reach the market?	*identify market rates.*
IOP54s	What other applications would interface for exchange of data?	*identify partner applications.*
IOP55s	What corporate policies of business partners conflict with the system?	*identify policy risks.*
IOP56s	What is the effect on business if an imposed policy was not followed?	*identify policy risks.*
IOP57s	What legal policies must be enforced to protect the company?	*identify policy risks.*
IOP58s	For each policy, what would be the impact on the business if the rule is not enforced?	*identify policy risks.*
IOP59s	What data are important to the business?	*identify scope of the effort.*
IOP60s	What data are important to the business partners?	*identify scope of the effort.*
IOP61s	What information is the customer interested in?	*identify scope of the effort.*
IOP62s	What types of future interfaces are anticipated?	*identify types of changes.*
IOP63s	What is the purpose for the interface?	*identify usages.*
IOP64s	What protections are needed from the external vendor? (For example, warranty, bonding)	*identify vendor agreements.*
IOP65s	What would be the effect on the business if this event were not handled by the system?	*prioritize events.*
IOP66s	How important is each data group to the success of this system?	*prioritize requirements.*
IOP67s	How important is each policy to the success of the system?	*prioritize requirements.*
IOP68s	What rules must be enforced to maintain profitability?	*prioritize requirements.*
IOP69s	How important is each event to the system under development?	*prioritize requirements.*
IOP70s	How important is each location to the system?	*prioritize requirements.*
IOP71s	How are conflicts with the standards reconciled?	*prioritize standards.*
IOP72R	What are restrictions on the format or medium that must be used for input or output?	*identify formats and media.*

7.1 IOP

PURPOSE (WHY?) (continued)

ID	Interoperability Suggested Questions	Ask this to:
IOP73R	What specifications are needed for the interface adapter?	*identify implementation constraints.*
IOP74R	What controls are needed over change?	*identify limitations.*
IOP75R	What interfaces require special access control?	*identify limitations.*
IOP76R	What specific technology must be used?	*identify technical constraints.*
IOP77R	What specific technology should not be used?	*identify technical constraints.*
IOP78B	What industry standard protocols must be applied to this application?	*identify constraints.*
IOP79B	What version(s) of industry standards must be followed?	*identify constraints.*
IOP80B	What need is there to switch the interface on and off?	*identify controls.*
IOP81B	What additional usages exist for this interface?	*identify options.*
IOP82B	What is the trade-off with efficiency, reliability, and integrity?	*identify possible trade-offs.*
IOP83B	If there are multiple interface alternatives, which alternative is the preferred priority for use?	*identify priorities.*
IOP84B	What standards for interfaces does the company require?	*identify standards.*
IOP85B	What industry standards exist for the interface?	*identify standards.*
IOP86B	What is a widely-accepted standard for this interface?	*identify standards.*
IOP87B	Describe the purpose of the interface.	*identify strategies.*
IOP88B	What inputs are coming from systems outside the proposed system?	*identify various inputs.*
IOP89B	What outputs are sent to systems outside the proposed system?	*identify various outputs.*
IOP90B	What else should I be asking about interoperability "purpose"?	*uncover additional requirements.*

7.1 IOP

TIMING (WHEN?)

ID	Interoperability Suggested Questions	Ask this to:
IOP91s	When are periods of time that information will be accessed more than others?	*clarify usage.*
IOP92s	During what peak times will the system be used for any of the role types?	*clarify usage.*
IOP93s	What business conditions would trigger an action by the system?	*identify events.*
IOP94s	What happens at the start of a normal work day?	*identify time-triggered events.*
IOP95s	What happens at the end of a normal work day?	*identify time-triggered events.*
IOP96s	What events occur weekly?	*identify time-triggered events.*
IOP97s	What events occur monthly?	*identify time-triggered events.*
IOP98s	What events occur quarterly?	*identify time-triggered events.*
IOP99s	What events occur annually?	*identify time-triggered events.*
IOP100s	What other standard periods drive activities?	*identify time-triggered events.*
IOP101s	When are the peak times that each event occurs, if any?	*identify time-triggered events.*
IOP102s	What business events are cyclical?	*identify time-triggered events.*
IOP103s	How much new information is expected the first month through the first year that the new system is operating?	*identify volume metrics.*
IOP104s	What is the minimum number of occurrences of each event?	*identify volume metrics.*
IOP105s	What is the maximum number of occurrences of each event?	*identify volume metrics.*
IOP106s	What is the average number of occurrences of each event?	*identify volume metrics.*
IOP107R	How often is the interface upgraded?	*identify change controls.*
IOP108R	What timing expectations exist when using the interface?	*identify implementation constraints.*
IOP109R	What timing constraints must be considered while using interfaces?	*identify implementation constraints.*
IOP110R	How well and how quickly must the interface recover from a failure?	*identify implementation tactics.*
IOP111R	When is the interface upgraded?	*identify timing.*
IOP112R	When is the information exchanged?	*identify timings.*
IOP113B	What else should I be asking about interoperability "timing"?	*uncover additional requirements.*

7.1 IOP

LOGISTICS (WHERE?)

ID	Interoperability Suggested Questions	Ask this to:
IOP114S	What volume of information is currently provided from each location?	*clarify usage.*
IOP115S	What volume of information is currently received from each location?	*clarify usage.*
IOP116S	Where do the business partners operate?	*identify business locations of business partners.*
IOP117S	Where are customers located?	*identify business locations of clients.*
IOP118S	Where does the business operate?	*identify business locations.*
IOP119S	What are the plans for additional locations?	*identify business locations.*
IOP120R	Where will software be changed or added?	*identify location resources.*
IOP121R	Where will hardware be changed or added?	*identify location resources.*
IOP122R	Where will the system be developed?	*identify location resources.*
IOP123B	What else should I be asking about interoperability "logistics"?	*uncover additional requirements.*

PROCESS (HOW?)

ID	Interoperability Suggested Questions	Ask this to:
IOP124S	How quickly must the application adopt the new devices?	*identify adoption rates.*
IOP125S	What events must the business support?	*identify essential processing.*
IOP126S	What internal systems will interface with the system under development or installation?	*identify interfaces.*
IOP127S	What external systems will interface with the system under development or installation?	*identify interfaces.*
IOP128S	What are other systems this specific system must connect with?	*identify interfaces.*
IOP129S	What forms of access will the customers use?	*identify technology issues.*
IOP130S	What forms of access will the business partners require?	*identify technology issues.*

7.1 IOP

PROCESS (HOW?) (continued)

ID	Interoperability Suggested Questions	Ask this to:
IOP131R	What are alternatives when the interface fails?	*identify business continuation tactics.*
IOP132R	What happens when the interface changes?	*identify configuration controls.*
IOP133R	What configuration parameters are required?	*identify configurations.*
IOP134R	What commercial software will be part of the interface?	*identify configurations.*
IOP135R	What ways are necessary to support users adding their own devices?	*identify deployment strategies.*
IOP136R	What problems can we anticipate with upgrading users to new technology?	*identify deployment strategies.*
IOP137R	When adding new devices will the communications protocol be standard?	*identify devices.*
IOP138R	What alternate routes (multiple interfaces) exist between the systems?	*identify implementation options.*
IOP139R	What influence on interface design can we exercise?	*identify implementation strategies.*
IOP140R	How will the interface be stress-tested?	*identify implementation verification tactics.*
IOP141R	What load level has been tested on the interface?	*identify implementations.*
IOP142R	How many generations of interfaces must be supported?	*identify implementations.*
IOP143R	How is the interface upgraded?	*identify implementations.*
IOP144R	How many versions of the communications protocol are in use?	*identify installations.*
IOP145R	How widely used is the interface?	*identify installations.*
IOP146B	What options are available for the interface?	*identify variations.*
IOP147B	Where is the interface incomplete for our intended use?	*identify variations/deviations.*
IOP148B	What are possible alternatives for the interface?	*identify various types of interfaces.*
IOP149B	What else should I be asking about interoperability "processes"?	*uncover additional requirements.*

7.1 IOP

7.2 PORTABILITY (POR)

> USER CONCERN: How easy is it to transport the system?
> RELATED CATEGORIES: Compatibility, Connectivity, Migratability, Transferability

7.2.1 Portability Definition

Portability is the ease with which a software system can be transferred from its current hardware or software environment to another environment.

7.2.2 Portability Discussion

Portability requirements describe the ability to migrate software from one operating system (OS) to another. The most common operating system platform is the Microsoft Windows® family of products such as Vista®. True multi-user, multi-task software can be easily ported to other systems if it is designed properly. The software should run well on a multitude of platforms, including Windows®, Linux®, Unix®, and even IBM mainframes. There would not be different versions of the software written for each operating system platform, but rather one set of source and object code and one set of data files. The same software program that runs on a Windows XP® machine should function on the latest Macintosh®, with no need for the user to re-learn the software.

As technology advances and software environments get more complicated, one must take into account all associated components that combine to make the whole system. Identifying all the right components is critical to portability. Components to consider include the following:

◆ SIZE OF WHAT IS BEING TRANSPORTED.

◆ ORIGINAL AND THE TARGET ENVIRONMENTS (compatibility).

- MEANS OF TRANSPORT (such as a manual or automated conversion).

- RESOURCES NEEDED TO PERFORM THE TRANSPORT, and the attributes of the new system compared to the old (side-effects).

Developing a system that is portable requires that you first identify everywhere that the system might be installed. For example, determine if the system is intended for a single site, different sites or departments, different organizations, different industries, or different regions and countries. Second, identify all variations from one installation to another.

When eliciting portability requirements, consider the following aspects:

- DATA PORTABILITY. Will data files be transferable and run as is on all platforms?

- PROGRAM PORTABILITY. Will the code run exactly the same on all platforms?

- END-USER PORTABILITY. Will the program have the same look and feel across platforms? Will the commands and keystrokes be identical? This flexibility must be designed in from the outset.

- DEVELOPER/DOCUMENTATION PORTABILITY. Will a developer or user be able to use a standard set of skills to understand the program?

7.2 POR

7.2.3 Portability Requirement Examples

a) All timestamps recorded by the transaction processing system shall be in UTC (Universal Time Coordinated) when placed into permanent storage.

b) The time zone shall be obvious to the user whenever a time element is displayed.

c) The product is targeted for sale next year in the European market.

d) The product is designed to run in business offices, but the intent is to have a version which will run in manufacturing assembly plants.

e) The system shall be developed for Microsoft Vista® and Macintosh® operating system platforms.

f) The HomeAccounting software may be ported to any personal computer or workstation environment supporting at least 16-bit color on a 15-inch display monitor, achieving a SPECfp95 benchmark rating of at least 5.0, and having a data storage capacity of at least 8 MB.

7.2.4 Portability Suggested Questions

DATA (WHAT?)

ID	Portability Suggested Questions	Ask this to:
POR1S	What portability requirements must be communicated to suppliers?	*identify data needs.*
POR2S	What portability requirements must be communicated to customers/users?	*identify data needs.*
POR3R	Where should portability requirements be stored for accessibility?	*identify data storage requirements.*
POR4B	What portability requirements from other systems or projects can be reused?	*identify existing information.*
POR5B	What data files must be portable?	*identify data needs.*
POR6B	What else should I be asking about portability "data"?	*uncover additional requirements.*

ROLES (WHO?)

ID	Portability Suggested Questions	Ask this to:
POR7S	How adaptable to technology changes are the customers?	*identify customer acceptance.*
POR8S	What customers are expected to be early adopters of new technology?	*identify customer types.*
POR9R	Who will be porting the system to different environments or locations?	*identify responsibilities.*
POR10R	Who is accountable for the portability requirements?	*identify responsibilities.*
POR11R	Who might identify the portability requirements?	*identify responsibilities.*
POR12R	Who is knowledgeable in the portability requirements of the technology being used?	*identify potential stakeholders.*
POR13B	What else should I be asking about portability "roles"?	*uncover additional requirements.*

7.2 POR

PURPOSE (WHY?)

ID	Portability Suggested Questions	Ask this to:
POR14s	How important is portability?	*gauge importance.*
POR15s	What is the possibility of moving to a new platform?	*identify alternatives.*
POR16s	What will be different when moving to a new environment?	*identify combinations.*
POR17s	How do competitors release their products?	*identify competition strategies.*
POR18s	What copyright, patent, and trademark requirements need to be addressed internationally?	*identify corporate assets.*
POR19s	What intentions are there to remain an industry leader?	*identify industry potential.*
POR20s	What local governmental regulations need to be addressed?	*identify local controls.*
POR21r	What are the required operating environments?	*clarify environments.*
POR22r	What operating environment is considered the base environment?	*establish a base environment.*
POR23r	What is the transportability of the software? Hardware?	*identify capabilities.*
POR24r	When moving to a new platform which components are included?	*identify component severability.*
POR25r	What other applications will co-exist in the operating environment?	*identify comprehensive configuration.*
POR26r	How is configuration management coordinated between environments: development, test, and deployment?	*identify configuration combinations.*
POR27r	What types of database platforms are expected to be supported?	*identify configurations.*
POR28r	How mature is the industry this system supports?	*identify knowledge sources.*
POR29r	What constraints exist in the target component configuration?	*identify limitations.*
POR30r	What are the criteria for selecting new hardware configurations?	*identify selection criteria.*
POR31r	What are the criteria for selecting new software and firmware configurations?	*identify selection criteria.*
POR32r	What standard display formats for all data attribute types must be used?	*identify standards.*
POR33r	What date management and terminology will be used consistently by the system?	*identify universal attributes.*

7.2 POR

PURPOSE (WHY?) (continued)

ID	Portability Suggested Questions	Ask this to:
POR34R	What are the numeric data attributes that must be enforced consistently?	*identify universal attributes.*
POR35R	What data, time, date and time, attributes must be enforced consistently?	*identify universal attributes.*
POR36R	What new device types can be anticipated for future implementation?	*identify various devices.*
POR37R	What plans are being made to move to new environments?	*identify vision.*
POR38B	What is the growth potential for the industry?	*identify future demand.*
POR39B	How will this environment change with new systems?	*identify impacts due to change.*
POR40B	How will this implementation be an industry leader?	*identify industry positions.*
POR41B	What are possible trade-offs between portability and reusability?	*identify possible trade-offs.*
POR42B	What are possible trade-offs between portability and reliability?	*identify possible trade-offs.*
POR43B	What are expectations for new or emerging implementations in the industry?	*identify rates of change.*
POR44B	How soon will technology changes be available?	*identify rates of change.*
POR45B	How rapidly are new devices expected to be introduced?	*identify rates of change.*
POR46B	When an opportunity arises to move to a new environment, how quickly must the business be available?	*identify response rate.*
POR47B	What else should I be asking about portability "purpose"?	*uncover additional requirements.*

TIMING (WHEN?)

ID	Portability Suggested Questions	Ask this to:
POR48S	What is the established time zone standard?	*clarify standards.*
POR49S	How quickly do competitors move to new technology?	*identify competition tactics.*
POR50B	What else should I be asking about portability "timing"?	*uncover additional requirements.*

7.2 POR

LOGISTICS (WHERE?)

ID	Portability Suggested Questions	Ask this to:
POR51S	What taxes and customs must be managed when adding new countries?	*identify differences by country.*
POR52S	What languages may be added in the future?	*identify potential languages.*
POR53S	What language is the base language?	*identify the base.*
POR54S	Who can approve language translation?	*identify translation activities.*
POR55S	How will language translation be managed?	*identify translation activities.*
POR56S	What languages do customers/users speak?	*identify various languages.*
POR57S	What import/export taxes could apply in other countries?	*identify various taxes and fees.*
POR58R	What is the capability to partially disassemble the software/hardware for physically moving?	*identify constraints.*
POR59R	What equipment will need special documentation to cross the borders?	*identify customs constraints.*
POR60R	What is the likelihood that the software/hardware or product will survive shipping hazards?	*identify fragility.*
POR61R	What configuration constraints might exist in certain countries?	*identify political constraints.*
POR62R	How will international support be addressed?	*identify support needs.*
POR63R	What is the compatibility of the software/hardware with standard moving equipment and vehicles such as trucks and forklifts?	*identify various resources.*
POR64B	What else should I be asking about portability "logistics"?	*uncover additional requirements.*

7.2 POR

PROCESS (HOW?)

ID	Portability Suggested Questions	Ask this to:
POR65R	How stable/mature is the development environment?	*identify centers of knowledge.*
POR66R	How are enhancement releases managed through multiple configuration environments?	*identify configuration combinations and priorities.*
POR67R	What interfaces are required? (legacy systems, certain platforms)	*identify minimum configurations.*
POR68R	When upgrades are made to the systems, what is the release sequence by configuration environment?	*identify release schedule priorities.*
POR69R	When deploying devices, what configurations must be considered?	*identify various combinations.*
POR70R	What combinations of components will be used?	*identify various combinations.*
POR71R	What changes in technology are available and may be possible to take advantage of in the future?	*identify various components.*
POR72R	What various combinations of system by environment are there?	*identify various configurations.*
POR73R	What could be the expected changes to development environments? (For example, compilers, languages, versions)	*identify various configurations.*
POR74R	What component configurations are expected?	*identify various configurations.*
POR75R	What network configurations are expected?	*identify various configurations.*
POR76R	What implementation strategies should be used to develop portable software?	*identify various configurations.*
POR77R	What system/applications are dependent upon other system/applications or components?	*identify various dependencies.*
POR78R	What system/applications or components are dependent upon the organization's system/application?	*identify various dependencies.*
POR79R	With what other system/applications or components must the organization's system/application co-exist?	*identify various dependencies.*
POR80R	On what operating environments will this system be deployed?	*identify various environments.*
POR81R	What are the expected operating environments?	*identify various environments.*
POR82R	How many database platforms are anticipated to be used on installations?	*identify various environments.*

7.2 POR

PROCESS (HOW?) (continued)

ID	Portability Suggested Questions	Ask this to:
POR83R	If the product will be shipped, what considerations must be given to protecting the product during shipping? For example, packing it in cushioned containers, covering it with temporary coatings, or requiring handlers to use removable lifting attachments.	*identify various handling techniques.*
POR84R	What possible constraints exist in potential component configurations?	*identify various limitations.*
POR85R	Which components are most likely to move to a new platform?	*identify various types of components.*
POR86B	What else should I be asking about portability "processes"?	*uncover additional requirements.*

7.2 POR

7.3 REUSABILITY (REU)

> USER CONCERN: How easy is it to convert for use in another system?
>
> RELATED CATEGORIES: Commonality, Leveragability, Modularity

7.3.1 Reusability Definition

Reusability is the extent to which a portion of the software system can be converted for use in another system.

7.3.2 Reusability Discussion

There are two views that typically come to mind when using the term "reusability." One view of reusability refers to the reuse of requirements documentation from previous projects. The other is the reusability of software functions. This second view is used as the primary intent of reusability described in this book, and we'll come back to it after a brief discussion on reusing requirements.

Let's begin with the merits of reusing requirements. In short, requirements reuse saves money and time. According to the experience of Sommerville and Sawyer [Sommerville, 1977], up to 80 percent of the requirements may be more or less the same for similar systems, while other authors indicate as much as 85 percent of the requirements come from existing similar application areas. Even if accurate predictions are difficult to make, significant gains are likely when reusing the requirements across several systems. One could safely expect some reuse of design, code, and test components, thus further reducing development time and cost.

Furthermore, requirements reuse reduces risks. If you are reusing requirements that have already been implemented (verified and validated) in other systems, you might reduce the risks of introducing requirements that are difficult to implement or that interact in undesirable ways with existing requirements.

7.3 REU

In the process of requirements elicitation, requirements may be either reused directly or indirectly. Direct reuse occurs when requirements from one system are implemented as requirements for some other system with minimal changes. Whereas, indirect reuse occurs when existing requirements are used in the elicitation process to prompt end-users for their specific requirements for a current project effort.

Let's turn our attention to the primary definition of reusability. Software reuse is the reapplication of knowledge about one system to another similar system in order to reduce the effort to develop and maintain the other system. Therefore, reusability requirements identify functions that already exist and may be partially or fully utilized in developing the system at hand. Reusing the functionality saves development time and costs as analysis and validation have already been demonstrated in the existing system. Reuse can improve reliability and reduce software management risks.

Some narrow views of software reuse include "reuse is the reapplication of source code," or "reuse is the use of subroutines, modules, or object libraries." By focusing narrowly on the reapplication of code components, the most highly reusable components tend to be rather small. This is because source code languages have a high degree of specificity. It takes a lot of work to piece together several small components to build a large system. Thus, the cost to build a large system is generally greater than the savings brought about by reuse.

Reusability advocates Ted Biggerstaff and Alan Perlis [Perlis, 1989] have helped to broaden the view of reusability by pointing out that domain standards are essential for the overall coordination of software components. This is similar to standards established for manufacturers of hardware components so that they can plug their components together.

For those looking to create libraries of reusable software, Biggerstaff and Perlis recommend that the library be based on a standard for the domain specific types of the data produced and consumed by the software components in that library. This is only to be accomplished by designing a library of components that have a common architectural guideline that reflects both the nature of the problem domain, as well as the computational complexities of the organization.

Since the emergence of workable standards and their acceptance by the software industry, it is now easier to develop reusable and portable application systems. Development according to standards can minimize the costs of implementing a system on different types of computers. Standards that have been accepted include:

♦ Programming language standards, such as COBAL and SQL.

♦ Operating system standards, such as Microsoft XP®, Macintosh®, and UNIX®.

♦ Networking standards, such as TCP/IP protocols.

♦ Graphical User Interface (GUI) window standards, such as Microsoft Windows®.

In summary, the reuse of software source code is a reasonable first step toward reusability. The reuse of design has a greater potential payoff, but will require significant breakthroughs to realize its magnitude potential in a broad automated way.

When eliciting reusability requirements, consider the following aspects:

♦ FEASIBILITY OF SOFTWARE REUSE.

◊ **Size and complexity**. Generally, as the size and complexity of the software increases, the feasibility for reuse usually decreases. Small modules and components are more easily designed, tested, and maintained.

◊ **Life-cycle phase**. As a component of the system approaches implementation, the less likely it is to be reusable. It is generally easier to reuse a requirement document, for example, than to reuse source code. There are many assumptions that go along with the code such as parameter passing conventions and operating system utilities. Also, reusable code implies that all traceable documentation preceding the code is also reusable and reliable.

7.3 REU

◊ **Range of applications**. The range of applications in which the software is intended to be reused can affect its feasibility for reuse. If a component is used within a narrow range of application where the terminology and assumptions are well understood, the component doesn't need rigorous definition. On the other hand, when the range of application is broad, the component must be rigorously defined since the terminology and assumptions would be more varied and less well-known.

◊ **Organizational distance**. This refers to the number of organizational layers that separates the person who reuses a component from the person who initially developed the component. "Within the same department in a company," and "between departments within the same company," are examples of organizational distance. If the distance is short, the component is more easily reused since the information needed to reuse the component is likely to be accessible and available. If the distance is long, the information if often more difficult to obtain.

◊ **Variability**. If the component has a high degree of consistent interpretation, then feasibility of reuse will be high. For example, if the component deals with basic math calculations such as addition and subtraction, there is little potential for misinterpretation. Conversely, if the component deals with many variables for calculating interest amounts in multiple currencies, then the chances for consistent interpretation are lower.

♦ POSSIBLE AREAS FOR REUSE.

◊ Language (reusable by people, computers).

◊ Environment (reusable tools).

◊ Methodology (reusable concepts).

◊ Technology (education, measurement, and integration).

◊ Information (restructuring existing knowledge to make it more accessible to humans).

7.3 REU

The Quest for Software Requirements

- Development standards.
  - ◊ Programming languages.
  - ◊ Operating systems.
  - ◊ Networks.
  - ◊ Graphical User Interfaces.

- Portability trade-offs.

7.3.3 Reusability Requirement Examples

a) The payment subsystem design is based on the payment module from the ALPHA product line. The ePAYZ system should not be modified unless absolutely necessary.

b) Development of functionality to support the Electronic Funds Transfer (EFT) payment option shall be modularized such that it can be reused by other departments of the organization.

c) Web applications shall be developed to adhere to HyperText Markup Language (HTML) guidelines and standards.

d) All software that runs on a client device shall be written in a prevalent programming language such that the software can be run on a personal computer without having to download a supporting environment.

e) The hard-copy materials in the Library of Congress shall be converted to an electronic form such that the existing knowledge can be flexibly presented in different formats for use in different contexts. (Note that this involves more than just putting the materials into computer repositories and accessing the knowledge through information retrieval systems. Accessibility must also comply with copyright laws.)

7.3 REU

7.3.4 Reusability Suggested Questions

DATA (WHAT?)

ID	Reusability Suggested Questions	Ask this to:
REU1S	What documents from other projects could be useful?	*identify sources of information.*
REU2S	What current presentation standards exist?	*identify standards.*
REU3B	What else should I be asking about reusability "data"?	*uncover additional requirements.*

ROLES (WHO?)

ID	Reusability Suggested Questions	Ask this to:
REU4S	Who may have an issue with providing reusability?	*identify concerns.*
REU5S	Who may have knowledge of similar projects or similar requirements?	*identify resources.*
REU6S	Who else has done a similar project in the past?	*identify sources of information.*
REU7S	Who is onboard with reusability?	*identify supporters.*
REU8S	What other projects in the organization are compatible, or that cover substantially the same domains or work areas?	*identify various projects.*
REU9S	What other products involve the same users and thus have similar usability requirements?	*identify various user bases.*
REU10S	What other types of uses of the components are expected?	*identify various user types.*
REU11B	What else should I be asking about reusability "roles"?	*uncover additional requirements.*

7.3 REU

The Quest for Software Requirements

PURPOSE (WHY?)

ID	Reusability Suggested Questions	Ask this to:
REU12s	What assumptions from other projects apply?	*identify alternatives.*
REU13s	What constraints have already been defined for another project?	*identify alternatives.*
REU14s	What are the advantages of developing software with reusable components?	*identify business objectives.*
REU15s	What expectations are there to expand the system and be able to reuse elements?	*identify expansion opportunities.*
REU16s	How much funding is available for reusability in the project?	*identify limits.*
REU17s	Which of these components is company policy?	*identify mandated components.*
REU18s	What other projects have been launched that are similar?	*identify synergies.*
REU19s	What other uses for similar applications apply?	*identify various alternatives.*
REU20s	What specific elements will be used in other applications?	*identify various applications.*
REU21s	What is the growth potential for similar applications?	*identify various options.*
REU22s	What standards have been defined and implemented in previous projects?	*identify various sources of information.*
REU23R	What are problems associated with developing software with reusable components?	*identify business risks.*
REU24R	What industry standard elements can function in isolation?	*identify separable elements.*
REU25B	What are relevant facts from recent projects?	*identify lessons learned.*
REU26B	What are possible trade-offs between reusability and portability?	*identify possible trade-offs.*
REU27B	Where has the company been successful with past reusability efforts?	*identify successes.*
REU28B	What is the scope of projects for adjacent systems?	*identify various extensions.*
REU29B	What components are so standard they have usability elsewhere?	*identify various options.*
REU30B	Which of these components are fundamental to the application domain and thus will be implemented in future projects or have been implanted in previous projects?	*identify various options.*
REU31B	What else should I be asking about reusability "purpose"?	*uncover additional requirements.*

7.3 REU

TIMING (WHEN?)

ID	Reusability Suggested Questions	Ask this to:
REU32S	What triggering events are the same as in other business processes?	*identify similar events.*
REU33S	What event triggers could be used in new ways as a result of this project?	*identify similar events.*
REU34S	What business processes have the same timing of use?	*identify similar processes.*
REU35S	What future business processes could have the same timing of use?	*identify similar processes.*
REU36B	What else should I be asking about reusability "timing"?	*uncover additional requirements.*

LOGISTICS (WHERE?)

ID	Reusability Suggested Questions	Ask this to:
REU37S	What processes are in use in the same locations as the processes from this project?	*identify similar processes.*
REU38S	What future processes may be deployed in the same locations?	*identify similar processes.*
REU39B	What else should I be asking about reusability "logistics"?	*uncover additional requirements.*

7.3 REU

PROCESS (HOW?)

ID	Reusability Suggested Questions	Ask this to:
REU40s	What functionality is considered pilot from this project?	*classify features.*
REU41s	How will pilot functionality be monitored?	*identify metrics.*
REU42s	How will pilot functionality be expanded?	*identify potential implementations.*
REU43s	What capabilities can be adopted and modified for this project?	*identify similar capabilities.*
REU44s	What capabilities can be adapted to other processes as a result of this project?	*identify similar capabilities.*
REU45s	What similar functionality exists?	*identify similar functionality.*
REU46s	How will pilot functionality be implemented?	*prioritize functionality.*
REU47R	What implementation strategies should be used to develop reusable software?	*identify improvement areas.*
REU48R	How must software processes evolve to incorporate reuse?	*identify reusable processes.*
REU49R	How can software components be generalized so that they are usable across a range of systems?	*identify reuse opportunities.*
REU50R	How do application generators support the reuse of domain concepts?	*identify reuse opportunities.*
REU51R	How can entire application systems be reused by making them available on a range of machines?	*identify reuse opportunities.*
REU52B	What else should I be asking about reusability "processes"?	*uncover additional requirements.*

7.3 REU

7.4 SUGGESTED READING

Mastering the Requirements Process, by Suzanne Robertson and James Robertson, [Robertson, 1999]. Chapter 12 provides a lengthy discussion on *reusing* requirements.

Requirements Engineering: A Good Practice Guide, by Ian Sommerville and Pete Sawyer, [Sommerville, 1977]. Requirements elicitation guideline 4.13 discusses *reuse* requirements, including suggested steps for eliciting direct and indirect reuse requirements.

Software Engineering, 8th Edition, by Ian Sommerville, [Sommerville, 2007]. Chapter 18 describes the benefits and challenges in developing software for *reusability*.

Software Quality Engineering: A Total Technical and Management Approach, by Michael Deutsch and Ronald Willis, [Deutsch, 1988]. Chapter 3 describes the classification of nonfunctional requirements, which includes definitions for *interoperability, portability, reusability* and others.

Software Quality Metrics Enhancements, Volume 1, by James McCall and Mike Matsumoto, [McCall, 1980]. This research report presents a software quality framework consisting of quality factors, criterion, and metrics. Section 1 provides definitions for several software quality factors such as *interoperability, portability*, and *reusability*.

Software Requirements, 2nd Edition, by Karl Wiegers, [Wiegers, 2003]. Chapter 12 defines several software quality attributes, such as *interoperability, portability*, and *reusability*.

Software Requirements: Objects, Functions, & States, by Alan M. Davis, [Davis, 1993]. Davis discusses *portability*, reliability, efficiency, and human engineering (usability) in Chapter 5, "Specifying Nonbehavioral Requirements."

System Requirements Engineering, by Pericles Loucopoulos and Vassilios Karakostas, [Loucopoulos, 1995]. Techniques for *reuse* of requirements are presented in Chapter 3, section 7.

Software Reusability, Volume 1: Concepts and Models, edited by Alan Perlis and Ted Biggerstaff, [Perlis, 1989]. This is a collection of works by various authors about software *reusability*.

REFERENCES

[**Alexander, 2002**] Alexander, Ian F. and Richard Stevens, 2002. *Writing Better Requirements*. Addison-Wesley. ISBN 0-321-13163-0.

[**Boehm, 1976**] Boehm, Barry W., J. Randall Brown, and Myron Lipow, 1976. "Quantitative Evaluation of Software Quality," International Conference on Software Engineering ICSE, *Proceedings of the 2nd ICSE*.

[**Boehm, 1988**] Boehm, Barry W., 1988. "A Spiral Model of Software Development and Enhancement," *IEEE Computer*, volume 21, No. 5, pp. 61–72.

[**BRG, 2000**] Business Rules Group, July 2000. *Defining Business Rules: What Are They Really? (3rd Edition)*. Available online from http://www.BusinessRulesGroup.org.

[**Charette, 1990**] Charette, Robert, 1990. *Applications Strategies for Risk Analysis*. McGraw-Hill. ISBN 0-07-010888-9.

[**Chrissis, 2007**] Chrissis, Mary Beth, Mike Konrad, and Sandy Shrum, 2007. *CMMI, 2nd Edition: Guidelines for Process Integration and Product Improvement*. Addison-Wesley. ISBN 0-321-27967-0.

[**Chung, 2000**] Chung, Lawrence, Brian A. Nixon, Eric Yu, and John Mylopoulos, 2000. *Non-Functional Requirements In Software Engineering*. Kluwer Academic Publishers. ISBN 0-7923-8666-3.

[**Davis, 1993**] Davis, Alan M., 1993. *Software Requirements: Objects, Functions, and States*. Prentice Hall. ISBN 0-13-805763-X.

[Deutsch, 1988] Deutsch, Michael S. and Ronald R. Willis, 1988. *Software Quality Engineering: A Total Technical and Management Approach*. Prentice Hall. ISBN 0-13-823204-0.

[Dorfman, 2000] Dorman, Merlin and Richard H. Thayer, editors. Institute of Electrical and Electronic Engineers, Inc. (IEEE), 2000. *Software Engineering*. John Wiley & Sons. ISBN 0-8186-7609-4.

[Ellison, 2002] Ellison, Robert, et al., 2002. *Foundations of Survivable Systems Engineering. Crosstalk: The Journal of Defense Software Engineering*. http://www.stsc.hill.af.mil/crosstalk/2002/07/ellison.html.

[Ferdinandi, 2002] Ferdinandi, Patricia L., 2002. *A Requirements Pattern: Succeeding in the Internet Economy*. Addison-Wesley. ISBN 0-201-73826-0.

[Gause, 1989] Gause, Donald C. and Gerald M. Weinberg, 1989. *Exploring Requirements: Quality Before Design*. Dorset House Publishing. ISBN 0-932633-13-7.

[Gilb, 1988] Gilb, Tom, 1988. *Principles of Software Engineering Management*. Addison-Wesley. ISBN 0-201-19246-2.

[Gilb, 2005] Gilb, Tom, 2005. *Competitive Engineering: A Handbook For Systems Engineering, Requirements Engineering, and Software Engineering Using Planguage*. Butterworth-Heinemann. ISBN 0-750-66507-6.

[Gottesdiener, 2002] Gottesdiener, Ellen, 2002. *Requirements By Collaboration: Workshops for Defining Needs*. Addison-Wesley. ISBN 0-201-78606-0.

[Grady, 2006] Grady, Jeffrey, 2006. *System Requirements Analysis*. Academic Press. ISBN 0-12-088514-5.

[Hay, 2003] Hay, David C., 2003. *Requirements Analysis: From Business Views to Architecture*. Prentice Hall PTR. ISBN 0-13-028228-6.

[Hooks, 2001] Hooks, Ivy F. and Kristin A. Farry, 2001. *Customer-Centered Products: Creating Successful Products Through Smart Requirements Management*. Amacom. ISBN 0-8144-0568-1.

[Hull, 2005] Hull, Elizabeth, Ken Jackson, and Jeremy Dick, 2005. *Requirements Engineering, 2nd Edition*. Springer. ISBN 1-85233-879-2.

[IBM, 2009] Rational Software Corporation, 2002. *Rational Unified Process*. Available online from http://www.ibm.com/software/rational/.

[IEEE, 1990] Institute of Electrical and Electronics Engineers (IEEE). IEEE Std 610.12-1990: "IEEE Standard Glossary of Software Engineering Terminology." IEEE Computer Society Press.

[IEEE, 1998] Institute of Electrical and Electronics Engineers (IEEE). IEEE Std 1233-1998: "IEEE Guide for Developing System Requirements Specifications." IEEE Computer Society Press.

[IIBA, 2009] International Institute of Business Analysis, 2009. *A Guide to the Business Analysis Body of Knowledge (BABOK®), release 2.0*. Available online from http://www.theiiba.org.

[ISO, 1991] ISO/IEC 9126, International Organization for Standardization (ISO) and International Electrotechnical Commission (IEC), 1991. *Software Engineering—Product Quality*. Available online from http://www.iso.org.

[Keller, 1990] Keller, Steven E., Laurence G. Kahn, and Roger B. Panara, 1990. "Specifying Software Quality Requirements with Metrics," reprinted in *System and Software Requirements Engineering*. IEEE Computer Society Press. ISBN 0-8186-8921-8.

[Kotonya, 1998] Kotonya, Gerald and Ian Sommerville, 1998. *Requirements Engineering: Processes and Techniques*. John Wiley & Sons. ISBN 0-471-97208-8.

[Kruchten, 1999] Kruchten, Philippe, 1999. *The Rational Unified Process: An Introduction*. Addison-Wesley. ISBN 0-201-60459-0.

[Lauesen, 2002] Lauesen, Soren, 2002. *Software Requirements: Styles and Techniques*. Addison-Wesley. ISBN 0-201-74570-4.

[Leffingwell, 2003] Leffingwell, Dean and Don Widrig, 2003. *Managing Software Requirements, 2nd Edition: A Use Case Approach*. Addison-Wesley. ISBN 0-321-12247-X.

[Loucopoulos, 1995] Loucopoulos, Pericles and Vassilios Karakostas, 1995. *System Requirements Engineering*. McGraw-Hill Book Company. ISBN 0-07-707843-8.

[Lyu, 1996] Lyu, Michael R., 1996. *Handbook of Software Reliability Engineering*. McGraw-Hill. ISBN 0-07-039400-8.

[McCall, 1980] McCall, James and Mike Matsumoto, 1980. "Software Quality Metrics Enhancements, Volume 1, Final Technical Report," Rome Air Development Center (RADC), General Electric Co.

[Musa, 2004] Musa, John D., 2004. *Software Reliability Engineering: More Reliable Software Faster and Cheaper, 2nd Edition*, Arthurhouse. ISBN 1-418-49388-0.

[Perlis, 1989] Perlis, Alan J. and Ted J. Biggerstaff, editors, 1989. *Software Reusability*, Volume 1: Concepts and Models. ACM Press and Addison-Wesley. ISBN 0-201-08017-6.

[Pfleeger, 2003] Pfleeger, Charles P. and Shari Lawrence Pfleeger, 2003. *Security in Computing, 3rd Edition*. Prentice Hall. ISBN 0-13-035548-8.

[Pullum, 2001] Pullum, Laura L., 2001. *Software Fault Tolerance Techniques and Implementation*. Artech House. ISBN 1-58053-137-7.

[Robertson, 1999] Robertson, Suzanne and James Robertson, 1999. *Mastering the Requirements Process*. Addison-Wesley. ISBN 0-201-36046-2.

[Robertson, 2006] Robertson, Suzanne and James Robertson, 2006. *Mastering the Requirements Process, 2nd Edition*. Addison-Wesley. ISBN 0-321-41949-9.

[Royce, 1970] Royce, Winston W., 1970. "Managing the Development of Large Software Systems: Concepts and Techniques," in *WESCON Technical Papers, volume 14*. Reprinted in *Proceedings of the Ninth International Conference on Software Engineering*, 1987, pp. 328-338.

[Sommerville, 1977] Sommerville, Ian and Pete Sawyer, 1977. *Requirements Engineering: A Good Practice Guide*. John Wiley & Sons. ISBN 0-471-97444-7.

[Sommerville, 1992] Sommerville, Ian, 1992. *Software Engineering, 4th Edition*. Addison-Wesley. ISBN 0-201-56529-3.

[Sommerville, 2007] Sommerville, Ian, 2007. *Software Engineering, 8th Edition*. Addison-Wesley. ISBN 0-321-31379-8.

[Standish, 1995] The Standish Group International, Inc., 1995. *The CHAOS Report.* Standish Group International.

[Thayer, 1990] Thayer, Richard H. and Merlin Dorfman, editors. Institute of Electrical and Electronic Engineers, Inc., 1990. *System and Software Requirements Engineering*. IEEE Computer Society Press. ISBN 0-8186-8921-8.

[Thayer, 2000] Thayer, Richard H. and Merlin Dorfman, editors. Institute of Electrical and Electronic Engineers, Inc., 2000. *Software Requirements Engineering, 2nd Edition*. IEEE Computer Society Press. ISBN 0-8186-7738-4.

[Tian, 2005] Tian, Jeff, 2005. *Software Quality Engineering*. IEEE Computer Society Press. ISBN 0-471-71345-7.

[Wallace, 1996] Wallace, Dolores R. and Laura M. Ippolito, 1996. "Verifying and Validating Software Requirements Specifications," reprinted in *Software Requirements Engineering, 2nd Edition*. IEEE Computer Society Press. ISBN 0-8186-7738-4.

[Wiegers, 2003] Wiegers, Karl E., 2003. *Software Requirements, 2nd Edition*. Microsoft Press. ISBN 0-7356-1879-8.

[Withall, 2007] Withall, Stephen, 2007. *Software Requirement Patterns*. Microsoft Press. ISBN 0-7356-2398-8.

[Zachman, 1987] Zackman, John, 1987. "A Framework for Information Systems Architecture," *IBM Systems Journal, 26:3* (IBM Publication G321-5298). Available online from http://www.almaden.ibm.com/research/.

[Zackman, 2009] Zackman, John A., 2009. *The Zachman Enterprise Framework 2*™. Available online from http://www.zachmaninternational.com/.

Roxanne E. Miller is a self-proclaimed "Requirements Super Freak." She has been involved in the Information Technology (IT) industry since 1984. She has been consulting on requirements process improvement and business analysis practices for over 15 years. Roxanne earned a bachelor's degree in Management Information Systems (MIS) at the University of Wisconsin–Eau Claire, Eau Claire, Wisconsin, USA. Prior to founding Requirements Quest® in 2001, Roxanne worked as a consultant, primarily in the banking and insurance industries in the roles of Programmer/Analyst, Business Analyst, and Requirements Management Process Owner and Implementation Leader.

As a result of her expertise, passion, and energizing presentation style, Roxanne is a frequent speaker at business analysis industry conferences. Furthermore, she is a "back-by-popular-demand" presenter for non-profit organizations, such as the Project Management Institute (PMI), the Software Process Improvement Network (SPIN), and Wisconsin Information Systems Quality Assurance (WISQA). Roxanne also serves on a panel of requirements experts for Search Software Quality, an online site that offers help in developing, deploying, and managing software quality. For more information, visit http://www.SearchSoftwareQuality.com.

Roxanne is an active member and advocate of the International Institute of Business Analysis (IIBA®), and is a Certified Business Analysis Professional™ (CBAP®) recipient. She serves as President of the IIBA® Greater Madison Chapter, Wisconsin, USA. Additionally, Roxanne helped Wisconsin IIBA® chapters unite and launch an annual event, Wisconsin Business Analyst Development Day (WI BADD), which is devoted to education, development, and networking opportunities for business analysis professionals. To learn more about how IIBA® can benefit you and your organization, visit http://www.theiiba.org.

I met Roxanne as a result of glowing recommendations from several of my team members who had attended one of her requirements seminars. Roxanne is the person I confer with when I have questions pertaining to requirements development and solution design. She truly is a certified requirements guru, who provides focused, valued, and engaged training experiences. Roxanne is very responsive, helpful in many ways, and well connected in the Wisconsin BA community. She is instrumental in fostering networking opportunities for people who are genuinely interested in moving the business analysis profession forward.
—Carl Henzel

I've worked closely with Roxanne in her role as President of the IIBA Madison Chapter, and participated in one of her requirements workshops. I have been uniformly impressed with the knowledge base, communication skills and professionalism that she brings to the table. I've recommended her services to a number of colleagues without hesitation.
—John Argentiero, Senior Business Analyst

There are a lot of people who enjoy their work. There are very few who have the passion and success in their career that Roxanne has. We have collaborated on many projects. On each one, she creates a unique, enjoyable environment and "can do" motivation in the team. Roxanne is highly credible and works diligently to transfer her expertise to help her clients accomplish their goals effectively. I would recommend Roxanne for any requirements-related initiative of any size.
—Jim Dawkins

ABOUT REQUIREMENTS QUEST

Requirements Quest is an industry leader in requirements management and business analysis consultancy. Requirements Quest is renowned for its Requirements Quest Process™, a superior, repeatable approach to requirements elicitation, analysis, representation, and validation, which is deployed on client consulting engagements. Requirements Quest's core competency is Requirements Management Process Improvement, as well as Business Analysis Skills Development and Coaching. As a solution-driven consulting company, Requirements Quest is devoted to working with organizations to improve their requirements development and management processes, and committed to developing the skills of business analysis practitioners.

Requirements Quest is a corporate sponsor of the International Institute of Business Analysis (IIBA®), and founder of the Greater Madison Chapter, Wisconsin, USA. Furthermore, Requirements Quest is an active sponsor of IIBA® chapters, as well as project management and business analysis educational events. Requirements Quest is a chartered Endorsed Education Provider of IIBA®, and has enhanced the skills of thousands of practitioners in business analysis and requirements management techniques. Requirements Quest's unique training provides a role-based approach to implementing requirements practices. Quality requirements and successful software projects are not the sole responsibility of the business analyst role; rather, quality requirements are the result of collaboration from multiple stakeholders.

The Requirements Quest logo ("the hand") symbolizes the importance of user involvement, both internal and external, as a critical factor for project success. The goal of a successful Requirements Management Process is to get a consistent interpretation of the requirements from all the stakeholders. Requirements Quest applies a proven repeatable, five-stage Requirements Management Process that significantly elevates the involvement of the right stakeholders, and fosters a collaborative team approach with increased commitment to the requirements.

The five stages of the process are symbolized by the five fingers on "the hand." The first four fingers represent the iterative activities of requirements development: Elicitation, Analysis, Representation, and Validation. Upon successful refinement, detailing, and approval, the requirements are baselined in the Change Control stage (represented by the thumb) where requests for change are monitored to maintain scope.

Requirements Quest's highly-credible consultants are IIBA® Certified Business Analysis Professionals™ (CBAP®). They bring years of practical experience and knowledge into your organization, and work diligently to transfer that knowledge and promote the development of your own internal requirements expertise.

Requirements Quest's goal is **bringing your business into focus**® so you can achieve effective and efficient business results. To learn more about Requirements Quest's consulting services, or to contact Roxanne Miller, please visit http://www.RequirementsQuest.com.

Roxanne and Requirements Quest takes an approach to business analysis that makes understanding intuitive and results efficient. She is a leading expert in coaching and developing business analysis resources and business requirements practices. Her tutelage, insight, and facilitative skills allow everyone around her to become more effective. People that implement her approach have an impact on their organizations and deliver better results.
—Mark Swiderski, President, Praxilient, Inc.

Roxanne's passion and depth of knowledge about business analysis is inspiring. Her presentations are full of energy, enthusiasm and fun! We have incorporated many of the tools and techniques delivered in Requirements Quest's training seminars to our Project Process with immediate improvement and success. Business Analysts, and other project stakeholders alike, reap a variety of methods that can be used to navigate through the challenges faced on a daily basis.
—Clare Jones, Director, Wipfli, LLP

Roxanne is a leader in the business analysis and requirements engineering industry. She has coached and mentored countless numbers of BAs and people in other software development roles, on the importance of documenting requirements before developing the solution to a business problem. Through her founding of Requirements Quest and the Greater Madison IIBA Chapter, Roxanne has been a mentor to me and a role model for many others. I, along with the entire BA community in Wisconsin, owe Roxanne a debt of gratitude for her contributions.
—David DeBruine, Owner, DeBruine & Associates, LLC